D1453913

All Those Strangers

All Those Strangers

THE ART AND LIVES OF JAMES BALDWIN

Douglas Field

OXFORD

UNIVERSITY PRESS

OXFORD
UNIVERSITY PRESS

Oxford University Press is a department of the University of Oxford.
It furthers the University's objective of excellence in research, scholarship,
and education by publishing worldwide.

Oxford   New York
Auckland Cape Town Dar es Salaam Hong Kong Karachi
Kuala Lumpur Madrid Melbourne Mexico City Nairobi
New Delhi Shanghai Taipei Toronto

With offices in
Argentina Austria Brazil Chile Czech Republic France Greece
Guatemala Hungary Italy Japan Poland Portugal Singapore
South Korea Switzerland Thailand Turkey Ukraine Vietnam

Oxford is a registered trade mark of Oxford University Press
in the UK and certain other countries.

Published in the United States of America by
Oxford University Press
198 Madison Avenue, New York, NY 10016

© Oxford University Press 2015

All rights reserved. No part of this publication may be reproduced,
stored in a retrieval system, or transmitted, in any form or by any means,
without the prior permission in writing of Oxford University Press,
or as expressly permitted by law, by license, or under terms agreed with the
appropriate reproduction rights organization. Inquiries concerning reproduction
outside the scope of the above should be sent to the Rights Department,
Oxford University Press, at the address above.

You must not circulate this work in any other form
and you must impose this same condition on any acquirer.

Library of Congress Cataloging-in-Publication Data
Field, Douglas, 1974–
All those strangers : the art and lives of James Baldwin / Douglas Field.
p.   cm.
Includes bibliographical references and index.
ISBN 978–0–19–938415–0 (cloth) — ISBN 978–0–19–938416–7 (updf) —
ISBN 978–0–19–938417–4 (epub) 1. Baldwin, James, 1924–1987—Political and social views.
2. Politics and literature—United States—History—20th century. I. Title.
PS3552.A45Z653 2015
818'.5409—dc23
2014037215

1 3 5 7 9 8 6 4 2

Printed in the United States of America on acid free paper

For Sonny, a budding poet and disturber of the peace

{ CONTENTS }

{ ACKNOWLEDGMENTS }

I am grateful to a number of institutions for funding this project. In particular, the Arts and Humanities Research Council in the United Kingdom for a Research Leave Award, which included funding for a research trip to the Schomburg Center for Research in Black Culture in New York City. This funding and sabbatical was generously matched by my own institution at the time, Staffordshire University, which also contributed towards several research trips. Thank you to the Lilly Library at Indiana University for awarding me an Everett Helm Fellowship to view the archive of Harold Norse, along with some of James Baldwin's letters. Thank you also to the British Academy for an Overseas Conference Award, which enabled me to present a paper on Baldwin at the American Studies Association Conference in 2008. The British Academy also awarded me a Small Research Grant, which funded three research trips to the United States. Thank you to the British Association for American Studies, which funded a research trip to the Tamiment and Robert F. Wagner Labor Archives in New York City, where I tried to pin down Baldwin's early red credentials, and to the School of Arts, Languages and Cultures at the University of Manchester for funding the last stages of the project.

The first part of chapter 1 is a revised and updated version of "James Baldwin's Life on the Left: A Portrait of the Artist as a Young New York Intellectual." Copyright © 2011 by The Johns Hopkins University Press. This article was first published in *English Literary History* 78, no. 4 (2011): 833–62. Reprinted with permission by Johns Hopkins University Press. The first part of chapter 4 builds on an essay titled "'One Is Mysteriously Shipwrecked Forever, in the Great New World': James Baldwin from New York to Paris" in *Paris, Capital of the Black Atlantic*, edited by Jeremy Braddock and Jonathan P. Eburne, reproduced with permission from Johns Hopkins University Press, 2013. The second half of chapter 4 is an altered and expanded version, which was first published as "What Is Africa to Baldwin? Cultural Illegitimacy and the Step-fatherland" in *James Baldwin: America and Beyond*, edited by Cora Kaplan and Bill Schwarz, reproduced with the permission of the University of Michigan Press.

There are a number of individuals who contributed to this project and I have felt particularly lucky to be part of a thriving community of scholars working on James Baldwin. Thank you in particular to Jonathan Dollimore who pushed me to think about Baldwin's complexity. Thank you also to Cora Kaplan, Quentin Miller, Magdalena Zaborowska, Robert Reid-Pharr, Michele

Elam, Bill Schwarz, Brian Norman, Rich Blint, Lynn Orilla Scott, Harvey Teres, and Alan Wald, all of whom had input. I am extremely grateful to the anonymous readers of this manuscript who offered incisive and thoughtful suggestions. Thank you to Brendan O'Neill at Oxford University Press, and to the Press for a grant that enabled me to include images in the book. I am also indebted to friends of Baldwin who graciously answered my questions. These include Caryl Phillips, David Leeming, Harold Norse, Themistocles Hoetis (George Solomos), and Lucien Happersberger. Sedat Pakay deserves a special mention for generously allowing me to use his beautiful photographs in this book. James Campbell has embodied the Baldwin spirit with his collegiality and sharp insight, which he has shared with me over the years. Finally, thank you also to my family for putting up with my obsessions, and in particular Wilf, Sonny, and Ellie for making me smile.

All Those Strangers

Introduction

> . . . all those strangers called Jimmy Baldwin. . . . There's the older
> brother with all the egotism and rigidity that implies. . . . Then there's
> the self-pitying little boy. . . . There's a man. There's a woman, too.
> There are lots of people here.
>
> —EVE AUCHINCLOSS AND NANCY LYNCH, "DISTURBER OF THE PEACE:
> JAMES BALDWIN—AN INTERVIEW"

> Do I contradict myself? Very well then I contradict myself,
> (I am large, I contain multitudes.)
>
> —WALT WHITMAN, "SONG OF MYSELF"

I want to begin by speculating, not on Baldwin's reputation as seen by literary
critics, but to consider him from another country outside the boundaries of
academia. It is, of course, difficult to gauge how readers respond to a writer
and the very notion immediately introduces a tumbling set of questions:
What kind of reader? From which country? From which racial, economic, or
cultural background? I would like, though, to leave my questions dangling in
their rhetorical wilderness and suggest, quite simply, that there is something
remarkable about Baldwin's life and work—something more than charisma—
that continues to draw readers from inside and outside of the academy. Readers of Baldwin often have more affection for his life and work than those
reading the works of Richard Wright or Ralph Ellison, two writers with whom
he is frequently grouped. On a simple level, given the choice, most people
would rather spend an evening carousing with Baldwin than a more formal
and cerebral evening with Wright or Ellison. As I have traveled, researching
this book, I have been struck by the varied responses to Baldwin in the United
Kingdom, Europe, and the United States. Teachers tend to sigh with envy at
the thought of working on Baldwin; many include at least an essay or novel of

his in their American literature courses, often wishing they could do more. Students are often drawn to his penetrating but comprehensible prose, and those lucky enough to read for pleasure (or instruction) often marvel at his searing and impassioned writing. Baldwin, for many readers, is the voice of the civil rights movement, the angry and eloquent voice of *The Fire Next Time* (1963), a writer who came of age in step with the dawn of televisual culture. Frequently cited as an inspiration to queer writers and readers both black and white, Baldwin is correctly lauded for being one of the first "out" African American authors. His work, which grapples with a number of difficult twentieth-century concerns, including those of race, sexuality, religion, and displacement, may indeed, as the Irish writer Colm Tóibín puts it, "fit whatever category each reader requires."[1]

Taking heed of the author's own description of himself as "all those strangers called Jimmy Baldwin," this book looks not at a fixed notion or reading of James Baldwin, but instead at the shifting and developing James Baldwins from the 1940s to the 1980s. In so doing, it avoids reducing the author and his work to one or other critical idea; it aims to exceed rote, institutionalized parameters by reading Baldwin's work in relation to several key contexts. Its structure, therefore, is not chronological or sequential, but selective and exploratory and the book makes no claim to be a conventional biography, though it necessarily covers cultural context and important events in Baldwin's life, along with his work.

While I engage with a range of Baldwin's well-known and neglected works, I have honed in on certain aspects of his more troubling texts, in particular *Giovanni's Room* (1956), a novel that is not generally held up as representative of the author's work. As we will see, Baldwin's second novel is not only a groundbreaking account of male homosexuality but also an acute reflection on racial anxieties during the Cold War. When viewed through more recent theories of transnationalism and the Black Atlantic, *Giovanni's Room* emerges as a prescient meditation on home, exile, and nationality, rather than a work that sits uncomfortably on African American literature syllabi because there are ostensibly no black characters. For the purposes of this book, the illegitimate status of Baldwin's second novel—one penned by an African American, but not overtly about black Americans—serves to highlight the ways in which racial authenticity is frequently canonized to the detriment of texts, like *Giovanni's Room*, which do not ostensibly demonstrate this quality. While the novel is held up as a pioneering work of homosexual literature, Baldwin disavowed this interpretation, claiming it was about love. Ultimately, the precarious status of the novel reflects and refracts Baldwin's own position as an author in the ways that he repeatedly thwarts critical expectations.

This book also focuses on Baldwin's fiction and nonfiction to show how his work responds to and shapes important changes in American culture from the 1950s to the 1980s. As one critic astutely points out in relation to Baldwin's essays—to which I would add his fiction—it was arguably the case that "the political climate changed, not necessarily Baldwin's essays."[2] The purpose of the present book is threefold. First, it hopes to shed light on some under-researched areas in Baldwin's life and work, such as his life on the Left, his FBI files, and his relationships to Africa, and the civil rights and Black Arts Movements. Second, it contributes toward a broader understanding of some key twentieth-century themes, including the Cold War, African American literary history, religion, spirituality, and transnationalism. Finally, it shows that Baldwin's ideas and writing—like those of most writers—were often in flux. It is, therefore, crucial to distinguish between his early reviews of other writers' work in the *New Leader* and *Commentary* in the 1940s and his more experienced writing after the mid-1960s. It is only by paying attention to Baldwin's developing rather than fixed views, his ideological shuffles and even his outright contradictions, that his large body of writing begins to cohere.

Here, it might be useful to illustrate the book's main concerns by looking at some of the controversies and paradoxes surrounding Baldwin's third novel, *Another Country* (1962), a work that shaped his literary reputation but one commonly seen as his last accomplished novel. In his recollections of its writing, Baldwin recalls both how the novel "almost *killed*" him and "made him feel as if he were giving birth following a long-term pregnancy."[3] *Another Country* represents something of a crossroads, not only in Baldwin's career but also in the political and sexual landscape of mid-twentieth-century United States. The novel was a searing indictment of liberal midcentury New York City, written by a man who had left the United States nearly fifteen years before. As Magdalena Zaborowska, author of *James Baldwin's Turkish Decade*, has suggested, though a quintessentially New York novel, *Another Country* "articulated a turning point in Baldwin's views on race and sexuality in a transnational context."[4] For Baldwin, America is increasingly the "other country," a place that he needed to leave in order to write about it.

Spending several weeks on the *New York Times'* bestseller list, *Another Country* catapulted Baldwin into the league of major writers. Despite the novel's commercial success, however, critics were divided, with the New York literati in particular dismissing the novel outright. In many accounts of Baldwin's literary odyssey, *Another Country* is a turning point where the tight modernist control of his first novel (and to a certain extent of *Giovanni's Room*) became unanchored, ending with the commonly perceived narrative bagginess and self-indulgence of his remaining three novels. Although Baldwin recollected that his third novel "saved his life as a writer," the damning critical assessments suggest that the author, like the character of the tormented saxophonist in *Another Country*, "had received the blow from which he never would recover."[5] Augusta Strong, reviewing it in *Freedomways*, a leading African American political and cultural journal of the 1960s, concluded that *Another Country* was "a novel that those who have admired his earlier work must find bafflingly inexpert and disappointing."[6] Even as sales soared, Irving Howe declared with authoritative gravitas that "Baldwin's future as a novelist is decidedly uncertain."[7]

The disparity between the critical reception and the sales suggest the ways that Baldwin's work, even from the early 1960s, unsettled literary critics who struggled to place him—and then berated him for it. For the Jamaican-born civil rights activist Michael Thelwell, Baldwin's third novel was met "with some of the most fatuous, inept, and at times downright dishonest criticism" that he had seen, a view shared by Norman Podhoretz, the former editor of *Commentary*, who noted that readers "were repelled by the militancy and the cruelty of its vision of life."[8] Podhoretz, who was writing as a liberal before he re-emerged as a neoconservative, claimed that Baldwin, in fact, achieves "a totally new, totally revolutionary conception of the universe."[9] According to Thelwell, *Another Country* deeply unsettled its white reviewers because "no previous novel by a Negro has ever appropriated this function [writing about white consciousness] so completely, probingly, and relentlessly."[10] Thelwell concludes that "the [white] reviewers were just not prepared to have their class prerogative of defining and interpreting the dynamics of their own social experience assumed by this black man from Harlem."[11]

For Thelwell and Podhoretz, Baldwin's third novel was revolutionary in the way that it looked anew at the racial and political landscape of the United States and this innovative approach was something that preoccupied the author. In "As Much Truth as One Can Bear," an article published in the *New York Times Books Review* the same year as *Another Country*, Baldwin rejected the white male literary canon of American letters (singling out Faulkner, Eliot, and Hemingway), urging young writers to break away. "[T]he air of this time and place is so heavy with rhetoric, so thick with soothing lies," Baldwin wrote, "that one must really do great violence to language, one must somehow disrupt the comforting beat, in order to be heard."[12] In a *Transatlantic Review* interview with John Hall, Baldwin pointed out that "[a] lot of people in that book [*Another Country*] had never appeared in fiction before," adding that there were "no antecedents" for his protagonist, Rufus Scott, a musician whose downfall drives the novel.[13]

Baldwin's novel was revolutionary in another way, suggested by the short story writer Eugenia W. Collier's conclusion that it provides "as the cliché says, something for everyone—in this instance, something offensive for everyone."[14] Many reviewers, including the FBI director, J. Edgar Hoover, were simply appalled at the graphic descriptions of sex—and particularly interracial sex. Augusta Strong wrote that *Another Country* "begins and ends in an animal comprehension of sex," a curiously vague comment that fails to pick up on the emotional force of Baldwin's descriptions of sexual encounters. Stanley Hyman, then-critic for the left-leaning journal the *New Leader*, even suggested that Baldwin had made the sex scenes graphic to help sell the book,

concluding with the "hope that the hundreds of thousands who read it as por-
nography will profit from the Negro bitterness and fury to which they are
incidentally exposed."[15] In one of the most damning and well-known indict-
ments of the novel, the Black Panther leader Eldridge Cleaver described the
novel's protagonist, Rufus Scott, as "a pathetic wretch . . . who let a white bisexual homosexual fuck him in the ass . . . [and] was the epitome of a black
eunuch who has completely submitted to the white man."[16]

Baldwin's emphasis on sex, and in particular his depiction of Eric, the novel's "white Southern bisexual" character, might instead be seen as a radical
rewriting (or re-Wrighting) of earlier themes in African American literature.
Eric, the reader learns, owns a copy of Richard Wright's 1940 novel *Native
Son*, and his first homoerotic encounter occurs with an African American
servant who tends the furnace. In contrast to *Another Country*, where the furnace is associated with desire, in Wright's novel, it is the place where Bigger
tries to dispose of Mary Dalton's body. By transforming the furnace from a
site of heterosexuality and violence into a site of homosexual love, Baldwin
offers an alternative vision to Wright's novel, suggesting, as he wrote in relation to *Native Son*, that there is "a great space where sex ought to be; and what
usually fills this space is violence."[17]

Although Baldwin claimed that his aim in *Another Country* was "to
show how a difference in skin color between two lovers could corrupt everything, even the most sincere and intimate feelings," most critics ob-
jected to his coupling of love and racial politics.[18] The *New York Times*
complained in its 1962 review that "[l]ove does not lead to community, pro-
creation, productive collaboration, character change, or even personal security."[19] Echoing Goodman, the poet Amiri Baraka (then known as LeRoi
Jones) stated that the phrase "'[p]eople should love each other,' . . . has very
little meaning to the world at large."[20] Lest such criticism be attributed to
the fervor of an inflamed political era, later critics have also puzzled over
Baldwin's faith in the power of love. At the end of the 1990s, one critic
wrote: "By 1962 . . . in the face of increased black activism and demands for
civil rights, it would have seemed disingenuous for Baldwin to claim that
individual love could conquer racial discord."[21] Baldwin's despairing accounts of relationships between black and white—Rufus and Vivaldo,
Rufus and Leona, and Rufus and Ida—suggest, on the contrary, that love,
as he made explicit in his next novel *Tell Me How Long the Train's Been
Gone* (1968) was "not enough" to deal with racism.

The above criticism, though, does point to the surprising, even troubling
absence of a political framework in *Another Country*. Cleaver castigated Baldwin for abdicating his social responsibility, writing that Baldwin's third novel
was "void of a political, economic, or even a social reference," a view shared
by the *New York Times*, who complained that there was no discussion of political action or any solution to the problems raised.[22] Baldwin based Rufus on

his friend, Eugene Worth, who committed suicide, like Rufus, by hurling himself off the George Washington Bridge. Worth encouraged Baldwin to become a member of the Young People's Socialist League, briefly lighting his leftist political torch. And yet if Eugene was the model or inspiration for Rufus, then why is there no mention of the political Left?[23]

The reasons for the disparate critical views of *Another Country* are in part illuminated by a closer look at the historical and political time frame of the novel, as well as Baldwin's developing political views. Some would argue that white liberalism had reached its peak in the 1960s, which, by implication, might explain many white reviewers' discomfort with Baldwin's relentless attack on their ideological position, a connection that Michael Thelwell explicitly makes.[24] By the late 1960s, Baldwin's declaration from a decade earlier that "[n]o one in the world . . . knows Americans better, or, odd as this may sound, loves them more than the American Negro," enraged black militants, even though Baldwin had amended his message of love in his 1963 essay, *The Fire Next Time*, to include consciousness raising.[25] By 1972, Baldwin had fueled his prose with borrowed rhetoric from the Black Power movement.

A more straightforward explanation to the confusion and unenthusiastic critical reaction generated by *Another Country* may in fact be attributed to the argument that the novel—conceived, written, and set in the 1950s— belongs to the political and social sways of that decade, which bore witness to the birth of the civil rights movement.[26] As one critic points out, "[t]he climate of the late fifties in which Baldwin's novel was set offered little possibility for social revolution, leaving Rufus with only the self-destructive path of individual rebellion."[27] Baldwin's novel can be read less as a timely social comment on emerging civil rights tensions that came to the fore in the 1960s, but more as a reply to prominent critics such as Lionel Trilling, who insisted in the late 1940s that racial matters were subordinate to class as a focus for the novelist.[28]

Yet, despite such potentially clarifying claims, *Another Country* remains a puzzling and enigmatic work. If, as Baldwin stated, Rufus is "the black corpse floating in the national psyche," why is the black community largely absent from the novel? And why is the only developed African American male character, Rufus Scott, killed off in the first fifth of the novel? Why, then, is "the figure for Baldwin's self-representation—the gay black man—so determinedly written out of the work that, he insisted, he "*had* to write?"[29] If white liberalism can offer no answer to "the racial nightmare," what suggestions does Baldwin give?[30] How is the reader to reconcile Baldwin's views that there is an impasse between black and white, that they can never understand one another, with Ida's insistence, as an African American woman, that "you've got to *know*, you've got to know what's happening?"[31] Is Baldwin toeing a liberal humanistic line—that the suffering of any person is really universal—or he is suggesting instead that there are irreconcilable differences between black and white?

The contradictions and paradoxes surrounding *Another Country* suggest the ways in which Baldwin was frequently called upon not only to "bear witness," as he termed it, but to represent and stand for one or other movement. Although his work may indeed, as Tóibín suggests, fit whatever category each reader requires, by the late 1960s, Baldwin was only too aware of the perception that he was "an aging, lonely, sexually dubious, politically outrageous, unspeakably erratic freak."[32] As Baldwin repeatedly stated in interviews, he was not a spokesman for the civil rights movement. At the same time, Baldwin lived in turbulent political times and was only too aware that an artist, as he put it, "has always been a disturber of the peace."[33] As *Another Country*'s reception illustrates, Baldwin's work is frequently contradictory and often inflammatory; he is a writer who confounds and therefore remains both reflective of his turbulent age and relevant well beyond it.

Baldwin lived long enough to acknowledge that his work left him open to "a vast amount of misunderstanding."[34] Born James Jones in Harlem in the year 1924, Baldwin took his first steps as the Harlem Renaissance gathered momentum and grew up during the Depression, dying sixty-three years later in the south of France midway through Ronald Reagan's second term in office. An inveterate traveler who lived in the United States, France, and Turkey, Baldwin's work traversed disciplines and scaled genres, uncontained, it seems, like the writer himself, by conventional boundaries and categories. Baldwin's writing demands a new kind of critical reading: not only one in step with the political, cultural, and literary developments that his work inhabits but also one that recognizes the harmony of paradox and contradiction—to "recreate," as Baldwin wrote early in his career, "out of the disorder of life that order which is art."[35]

In Baldwin's work the writer refuses to stay still: dancing in and out of frame—or in and out of focus—as scholars point their critical lens, searching for "the flash of cinematic revelation."[36] For others, the writer "seems . . . to always slip the yoke of his various identities, some self-imposed, others not."[37] There is, of course, a danger of celebrating or even fetishizing ambiguity in Baldwin's work, not least because of the writer's repeated references to his life and work as indescribable or irreducible. Frequently, Baldwin describes his life and work in aphoristic riddles, writing, for example, that he conceived of his "life as a journey toward something I do not understand."[38] I want to make it clear, however, that the paradoxical moments in Baldwin's work are also shot through with coherence; that his call to individual experience and morality demands belief in "one's own moral center." Baldwin's writing sustains a number of distinguishing characteristics, as well as paradoxes and riddles, often riffing on familiar themes. In his first collection of essays, *Notes of a Native Son* (1955), Baldwin declared that "[a]ll theories are suspect," adding that "one must find, therefore, one's own moral center and move through the world hoping that this center will guide one aright."[39]

For Baldwin, who later wrote that it was "impossible to indoctrinate" him, theories were inadequate because they failed to capture the complexity of life.[40] Baldwin's repeated repudiation of theories, labels, and identity categories presents a major challenge to literary critics and cultural historians who strive to place his work within a critical narrative.[41] As the introduction to a 2011 volume on Baldwin makes clear, "[f]or too long one Baldwin has been pitted against another Baldwin, producing a series of polarities that has skewed our understanding: his art against his politics; his fiction against his nonfiction; his early writings against his late writings; American Baldwin against European Baldwin; black Baldwin against queer Baldwin."[42] Criticism has tended to focus on Baldwin as either black or gay, essayist or novelist, religious writer or fierce critic of the church in ways that often say as much about the contemporary critical climate as they do about Baldwin.[43]

Despite recent strides in the study of Baldwin's work, it resembles, as Quentin Miller puts it, "a half-finished jigsaw puzzle rather than a complete portrait."[44] One particular example is Baldwin's shifting relationship to religion and the church, which has divided literary critics, who claim variously that the author was secular or preoccupied with religion. A close examination of Baldwin's views on religion and spirituality—and in particular his Pentecostal past—reveals his developing views on religion rather than a mere set of surprising conundrums. To borrow from Whitman, Baldwin contained multitudes that often seem to contradict one another. If, as Baldwin wrote early in his career, America is a "country devoted to the death of the paradox," then it seems, too, that literary criticism has a tendency to skirt round, rather than confront the contradictions in the writer's work.[45] A similar denial of paradox lies in much of the early criticism that examines Baldwin as a black queer writer. These approaches mirror the ways the author was repeatedly sidelined by black activists on account of his sexuality and there have been some remarkable and sometimes unexpected silences about his sexuality. That said, some recent scholarship has dismantled earlier, more simplistic criticism that tended to view Baldwin's sexual and racial identities as somehow mutually exclusive—or at least unconnected.[46] And yet the elephant in the room of less sophisticated readings of Baldwin as a queer writer is his repeated disavowals of the terms "gay" and "homosexual," as well as his unflattering, at times offensive, descriptions of "effeminate" homosexuals. As a fierce critic of identity categories, it is unlikely that Baldwin himself would have taken to the term "black queer."[47]

Although Baldwin's second novel, *Giovanni's Room*, is frequently taught as a pioneering text of homosexual American literature, little criticism points to its more uncomfortable portrayals of male homosexuality, in particular, its portrait of a transvestite character, a figure who blurs the distinctions between masculine and feminine, salvation and damnation:

> It looked like a mummy or a zombie—this was the first, overwhelming impression—of something walking after it had been put to death. . . . It carried a glass, it walked on its toes, the flat hips moved with a horrifying lasciviousness. . . . The shirt, open coquettishly to the navel, revealed a hairless chest and a silver crucifix . . . and made one feel that the mummy might, at any moment, disappear in flame.[48]

In Baldwin's description of the transvestite, the figure is terrifying because s/he cannot be located. Here, as elsewhere, Baldwin's writing troubles the critical romance of "fluid" identity: liminality or undecidability for the writer is rarely celebrated. The transvestite is a paradox: neither wholly female nor male, a figure who for David, the novel's protagonist, is both mesmerizing and repulsive. As Baldwin's writing reminds us, association with one identity category or other, such as black or homosexual, does not preclude a spectrum of reactions, attitudes, and seemingly contradictory responses.[49] To suggest otherwise is to limit the complexity that Baldwin's writing embraces—even, and indeed especially—when it makes for uncomfortable reading.[50]

Baldwin's discussions of masculinity are another case in point. Although he provided welcome relief from the aggressively heterosexual black masculinity championed by the likes of Eldridge Cleaver in the 1960s, Baldwin's views on black manhood were not static. In fact, as David Ikard has noted in his study of gender and African American culture, Baldwin seems at times caught in the crossfire between Cleaver and critics who question the author's treatment of women: "Whereas Cleaver condemns Baldwin for misrepresenting black men, [Trudier] Harris [in *Black Women in the Fiction of James Baldwin*] attacks him precisely for his uncritical view of black womanhood," particularly in the way that his female characters depend on men to assert their female identity.[51] Ikard is right to call attention to Baldwin's precarious position. In a conversation with the poet Nikki Giovanni, published in 1973 as *A Dialogue*, Baldwin's responses underscore his complicated position as an elder statesman, illustrated by his numerous references to "your generation" in conversation with the younger poet. At times, Baldwin seems to reproduce the very masculinist rhetoric he was once famous for critiquing: "Your manhood is being slowly destroyed hour by hour, day by day," Baldwin tells the poet, addressing Giovanni as "sweetheart."[52] As the conversation becomes charged, Baldwin seems challenged by Giovanni's position as a radical insider, seemingly set off balance by her youth and sex, as evinced by his need to "pull rank," telling her that "[y]ou have to understand the man's point of view":[53]

> Look, if we're living in the same house and you're my wife or my woman, I have to be responsible for that house. If I'm not allowed to be responsible for that house, I'm no longer in my own eyes—it doesn't make any difference what you may think of me—in my own eyes I'm not a man.[54]

Baldwin's outmoded views on patriarchy and manhood do not sit well with Giovanni, who tells the older writer that "I can get my own damn steak."[55] Similarly, as Lawrie Balfour has observed in a public dialogue with the feminist author and activist Audre Lorde, "the subtlety of Baldwin's understanding of how men and women mirror each other is lost in his reiteration that the great harm of American racism is that it takes from black men the capacity to support and protect their women and children."[56] Of particular interest to my project is the way in which Baldwin invokes a heterosexual and conservative view of male-female relationships and responsibility in order to make a more general point about the difficulties of black manhood.[57] My aim is not to set up Baldwin as a straw man, but to illustrate that his own positions—political, sexual, gendered—were precarious and complicated, particularly by the early 1970s.

As interest in Baldwin grows, illustrated by a spate of publications and high-profile conferences, his work and reputation are becoming established; his bold and groundbreaking essays on sexuality in particular are being recognized and disseminated.[58] While Baldwin should rightly be recognized as a pioneering voice on the subjects of race and sexuality, there is a danger that his more complicated and troubling views will be airbrushed out by critics as he is canonized. Or, as the critic George Shulman terms it, there is a tendency for critics to "sanitize" readings of the writer.[59] My aim is not to diminish Baldwin's importance as a black queer writer, or to diminish the importance of black queer theory but rather to encourage an ongoing examination of his complexity, particularly when it unsettles more comfortable interpretations that sometimes stifle rather than stimulate insightful criticism. In this book I consistently refer to Baldwin as queer, rather than as "homosexual" or "bisexual," two labels that he frequently called into question. He "viewed homosexuality as a practice or disposition of desire, not as an identity defining the existence of an individual's cultural belonging."[60] For Baldwin, it was reductive and even dangerous to align people's private sexual practices with a public ideology, a theme in his work that may—or may not—belie his own discomfort at the increasing visibility of homosexual culture in the United States. By using the term "queer," my aim is to signal that Baldwin's writing disrupts and calls into question the rigid categories that he found so stifling, rather than suggesting his sexual orientation or preference.[61] In other words,

I use the term "queer" in relation to Baldwin as a radical dis-position through which a deep examination of his work may take place.[62]

As I suggested earlier—and continue to argue throughout the book—one of the difficulties in conceptualizing and analyzing Baldwin is that he moved around so much: geographically, ideologically, and generically. What is more, Baldwin's writing comes out of four turbulent and radically changing post-war decades, during which time he published some of the most startling, incendiary, and pioneering work of any twentieth-century American writer. Baldwin's later work, in particular, needs to be read not simply as evidence of his decline "but instead as one aspect of his attempt to come to terms with the changing social, political, and ideological realities of the universe he was trying to map."[63]

In these pages, I have resisted the temptation to apply theories onto Baldwin's work, or to reduce his writing to one or other critical approach. Rather I explore the author's life and work against the radically transformative politics of his time. During the course of his career, a number of different Jimmy Baldwins emerge, which are reflected in Sedat Pakay's intimate shots of the author as uncle, friend, comrade, and public figure. As we will see, we encounter Baldwin the Trotskyite and acerbic book reviewer; Baldwin the deviant rabble rouser (as he was depicted in FBI files); Baldwin the civil rights activist and impassioned public speaker; Baldwin the passé novelist and homosexual sidelined by Black Nationalists; Baldwin the expatriate; and the Baldwin struggling to work out his conflicted relationship to Africa. By being attentive to "all those strangers" I hope to offer a nuanced portrait of Baldwin, who, in his final interview, spoke of his refusal "to make myself fit in" and "to wash myself clean for the American literary academy."[64]

{ Chapter 1 }

Baldwin's Life on the Left:
From New York Intellectual to Disturber of the Peace

I also realized that to try to be a writer (which involves . . . disturbing
the peace) was political, whether one liked it or not; because if one is
doing anything at all, one is trying to change the consciousness of
other people.

—JAMES BALDWIN, *THE BLACK SCHOLAR INTERVIEWS JAMES BALDWIN*

In the introduction to *The Price of the Ticket: Collected Nonfiction, 1948–1985*,
James Baldwin looked back to his beginnings as a writer in New York during
the 1940s. It was, Baldwin recollected, "unexpectedly difficult to remember, in
detail, how I got started," adding, however, that "I will never, for example,
forget Saul Levitas, the editor of the *New Leader*, who gave me my first book
review assignment . . . nor Mary Greene . . . but I do not remember exactly
how I met them."[1]

Baldwin's first review was, in fact, published in the *Nation* in 1947. A confi-
dent and caustic overview of the Russian writer Maxim Gorky's collection of
short stories, it was followed by sixteen book reviews between 1947 and 1949 for
the *Nation*, *Commentary*, and the *New Leader*.[2] By 1949 Baldwin had established himself as a promising new writer in Paris, where his notorious essay
"Everybody's Protest Novel" announced the arrival of a highly gifted essayist
and not just a precocious and acerbic book reviewer. Despite cutting his teeth
on a group of magazines associated most closely with the "New York Intellectuals" (including later articles for *Partisan Review*), Baldwin repeatedly played
down his early political associations while at the same time offering tantalizing
hints at the importance of several anti-Stalinist editors on his early career. Saul
"Sol" Levitas of the *New Leader*, Randall Jarrell of the *Nation*, Elliot Cohen and
Robert Warshow of *Commentary*, and Philip Rahv of *Partisan Review*, Baldwin
acknowledged, "were all very important to my life. It is not too much to say that
they helped to save my life."[3] And yet Baldwin is curiously reticent

about his connections to the political scene of the 1940s. "My life on the Left is of absolutely no interest," Baldwin wrote in the introduction to *Price*. "It did not last long. It was useful in that I learned that it may be impossible to indoctrinate me."[4]

Baldwin's reluctance or inability to recall his early years as a writer on the Left is in keeping with other accounts of his youth where he frequently forgets or misremembers dates and details.[5] And yet Baldwin's claim that his "life on the Left" is of no interest echoes the accounts of numerous former left-wing intellectuals of the period who have exercised (or exorcised) what Alan Wald calls "political amnesia" in relation to their radical past.[6] As Lawrence Jackson has pointed out, Ralph Ellison, for example, "censored his public career to omit the years between 1937 and 1947—the indignant leftist years," in what he describes as an "acrobatics of rhetoric" to distance himself from involvement with communist publications such as *New Masses*.[7] Although Baldwin, unlike Sidney Hook or Elliot Cohen, did not move in that now familiar political trajectory of radical anti-Stalinism to neo-Conservatism, a substantial account of his leftist past has never been performed by critics or biographers.[8]

The relative lack of interest in Baldwin's leftist intellectual past has no doubt been influenced by the author who not only let it be known that it was impossible to indoctrinate him but who also reveled in the role of outsider and maverick. Of the numerous reviews that Baldwin wrote in the *Nation*, the *New Leader*, *Commentary* (and later *Partisan Review*), only one—a review of Ross Lockridge's *Raintree County* (1948)—is collected in *Price*. Although Baldwin later claimed that he wrote "Everybody's Protest Novel" as "a summation of all the years I was reviewing those 'be kind to niggers' and 'be kind to Jews' books," few of his reviews in fact focused explicitly on race.[9] While it may be true that he was offered a number of books on "the Negro problem," his recollection that "the color of my skin made me automatically an expert" is not reflected in the works of American literature and culture that the young Baldwin reviewed.[10] For Mary McCarthy, Baldwin stood out because he "had read *everything*," adding "[n]or was his reading colored by his color—this was an unusual trait. He had what is called taste—quick, Olympian recognitions that were free of prejudice."[11]

Despite his cautious recollection of his leftist past, Baldwin singles out the importance of Eugene Worth, a young African American whom he "loved with all . . . [his] heart."[12] Although Worth is most often remembered as the inspiration for Rufus in *Another Country* (Worth committed suicide in 1946), Baldwin makes it clear that his friend ignited his political life.[13] Worth, Baldwin recalled, "was a Socialist—a member of the Young People's Socialist League (YPSL) and urged me to join, and I did. I, then, outdistanced him by becoming a Trotskyite—so that I was in the interesting position (at the age of nineteen) of being an anti-Stalinist when America and Russia were allies."[14] Recollecting his early teenage years in *No Name in the Street* (1972), Baldwin recalled that he "had been a convinced fellow traveler." "I marched in one May Day Parade," Baldwin recalled, "carrying banners, shouting, *East Side, West Side, all around the town, We want the landlords to tear the slums down!*"[15] Baldwin's involvement with the YPSL is not surprising, especially given the emphasis that the Party's periodical, *Challenge*, placed on civil rights. The first issue (1943) demanded equality for African Americans and subsequent articles continued to lobby for the desegregation of the army and an end to Jim Crow segregation.[16]

Baldwin's recollection of his YPSL membership at the age of nineteen (in 1943), however, has yet to be corroborated. It is not clear whether the YPSL Baldwin mentions was the Socialist Party or Shachtmanite; whether Baldwin was a member of the Trotskyite association known as YPSL/4ths or the Shachtmanite Youth (which used the name Socialist Youth League).[17] In a 1989 article, "Meetings with James Baldwin," the labor leader and writer Stan Weir recalls working with Baldwin at The Calypso restaurant during the Second World War and the author's later support of the West Boat longshoremen in the late 1960s. During his recollections of the eighteen-year-old Baldwin, Weir makes it clear that the aspiring writer considered joining the Workers Party (which later became the Independent Socialist League). "He already knew," Weir recalls, "that it was the product of a split with orthodox Trotskyism and Trotsky."[18] According to Weir, Baldwin had no complaints about how he had been treated by the Shachtmanites but would not join on account of his sexuality. Weir contends that the young writer responded to his invitation as follows:

> I know that your group does not expel those who join and then are "discovered" after the fact. But like you, they attempt to ignore this human difference. That it is a matter which cannot be discussed means that the discussion of every subject leads always to that closed door.[19]

Baldwin's concerns that his homosexuality would close the door to his full participation in political life were no doubt well founded (although, as Gary Edward Holcomb has shown in his study of Claude McKay, being African American, Marxist, and queer was a possible—if not easy—grouping of identities).[20]

Despite the biographical gaps in Baldwin's leftist past, his avowed anti-Stalinism and support of Trotsky fit into the wider history of his involvement with New York Intellectual publications—particularly his associations with writers of the *New Leader*—who were known as "Trotskyites."[21] I do not intend to claim that Baldwin was a committed anti-Stalinist or ardent Trotsky supporter throughout his career, which would be hard to do, given his disavowal of organizations and ideologies. At the same time, there is scant critical work on Baldwin's associations with the New York Intellectuals, and his early writings in key radical publications do much to illuminate the wider connections between leftist (largely Jewish) radical writers and the role of African American intellectuals in the 1940s. As James Campbell observes, it was "surprising to find a young Negro with no formal education beyond the age of seventeen contributing regularly to the nation's top intellectual magazines."[22] In the chapter that follows, I trace Baldwin's early reviews in key New York Intellectual publications up to and including "Everybody's Protest Novel" and "Preservation of Innocence" in 1949; pieces written before he was lured by the financial rewards of more prominent and popular publications such as the *New Yorker*. Baldwin's reviews, far from corroborating his claim that he wrote solely on race, in fact reveal, as Geraldine Murphy has pointed out, that his early publications engage with "the political and literary shortcomings of proletarian and Popular Front literature."[23] Baldwin's reviews from the late 1940s suggest that his life on the Left was in fact of great interest; his participation in New York leftist circles at the very least invites us to read his early work in the context of the intellectual circles within which he moved. To do so is to shed light on a political aesthetic that has been either disavowed or left out of biographical and, significantly, autobiographical portraits, where Baldwin is frequently described as a political lone wolf.[24] For example, even as he proclaims in "Autobiographical Notes" that "all theories are suspect," his emphasis on the individual—"one's own moral center"—itself connects him to the avant-garde Left, which as Roderick Ferguson has noted, focused "primarily on the individual and the freedoms of the individual."[25]

Baldwin's introduction to the left-wing artistic scene of the early 1940s coincided with his move from Harlem to Greenwich Village around 1943–44. Born in 1924, Baldwin was too young to have been involved in the numerous cultural and political activities sponsored and promoted by the Communist Party in the 1930s—such as the Negro People's Theatre or the John Reed Club. Through his friendship with the African American artist Beauford Delaney, Baldwin worked at The Calypso, a small restaurant on MacDougal Street, a favored hangout for artists, musicians, actors, and political radicals.[26] As Baldwin waited tables during the evenings, he would encounter Marxist and Trotskyite intellectuals, including Claude McKay, Alain Locke, and C. L. R. James. Although the move to Greenwich Village certainly accelerated Baldwin's entrance into the leftist cultural and political arena, he had mixed with a variety of young intellectuals (both black and white) during his years at DeWitt Clinton High School, an impressive school in the Bronx whose alumni included the lyricist of "Strange Fruit," Abel Meeropol; the artist Romare Bearden; the author Richard Condon; and Max Shachtman, one of the leaders of the American Trotskyist movement. After leaving DeWitt Clinton, Baldwin kept in touch with Brad Burch, a former school friend who launched a short-lived literary magazine in 1945 called *This Generation*—to which Baldwin contributed several articles, and, with Sol Stein, another former class mate, who played a significant role in transforming Baldwin's essays into his first collection, *Notes of a Native Son*.[27]

Baldwin's Trotskyite leanings—however short-lived—need to be seen in the wider context of shifting left-wing allegiances in relation to pre- and post-war ideological currents. By 1934, huge numbers of intellectuals in New York had severed their ties to the Communist Party. That same year, *Partisan Review* was launched with the editorial statement that "[t]he defense of the Soviet Union is one of our principal tasks."[28] As news of the Moscow trials where millions of workers, intellectuals, and party members were imprisoned or executed filtered to the United States between 1936 and 1938, New York Intellectuals increasingly abandoned the Party, unable to reconcile its ideology with widespread accounts of injustice and cruelty.

However, the New York Intellectuals' repudiation of Stalinism was not a renunciation of communism and many intellectuals strove to keep alive and revive revolutionary Marxism. *Partisan Review*, for example, which began as "the literary arm of the Communist Party in the United States" closed at the end of 1936 and was relaunched in 1937 independently of the Communist Party.[29] In keeping with a number of New York Intellectuals of the mid- to late 1930s, the editors of *Partisan Review*, William Phillips and Philip Rahv, vehemently opposed Stalinism but were drawn to the political and aesthetic views of the exiled Leon Trotsky. Although the magazine was never officially connected to the Trotskyite movement, Phillips and Rahv approached the Russian in exile, publishing two long letters from Trotsky, "Art and Politics" and "Manifesto: Towards a Free Revolutionary Art," in 1938.

Trotsky's appeal was so widespread in metropolitan cultured circles of the mid- to late 1930s that the group that became known as the "New York Intellectuals" were originally referred to as "the Trotskyist intellectuals."[30] Baldwin's association with the Trotskyist movement, then, was far from unusual for an aspiring writer of the late 1930s and early 1940s. For many intellectuals (including the philosopher Sidney Hook and the editor of *Commentary*, Elliot Cohen), Trotsky's views on art and politics offered a viable leftist alternative to the betrayal of Stalinist ideology. As Wald points out:

> It is not surprising that Trotsky, who incarnated internationalism and cosmopolitanism, the Jew who had shattered the manacles of religious identity and who strove to merge himself with the forces of the world revolution in every country and culture, should for a period become their [the New York Intellectuals'] rallying point.[31]

Trotsky's nonreligious Jewishness appealed to the main players of the New York Intellectuals, many of whom were secular Jews who wore their religion lightly. And yet, Trotsky's appeal to the New York Intellectuals went beyond the question of Jewishness or simply of politics.

For many intellectuals at the time, Trotsky was unique in the ways that he coupled impressive revolutionary credentials and a keen critical eye for artistic production. Even well-respected and progressive critics such as Granville Hicks and V. L. Parrington "insisted that the best authors expose the abuses of capitalism."[32] Trotsky, on the other hand, had demonstrated his flair as a literary critic in his 1924 classic *Literature and Revolution* and clearly saw the limitations of blindly eliding ideology with aesthetics.[33] As Wald has noted, Trotsky "had no patience with critics who claimed that a certain political ideology might automatically enhance an aesthetic work or guarantee a more profound and sensitive exploration of life through the imagination."[34]

Uniquely, perhaps, for a prominent left-wing figure, Trotsky rarely championed works of art solely because they vilified capitalism or reified the proletariat. In fact, Trotsky forcefully distanced himself from the *Proletkult* (the Organization for Proletariat Culture), which championed new writing by working-class writers. In *Literature and Revolution*, Trotsky makes it clear that style—not just social and political content—is important: "It is not true," he writes, "that we regard only that art as new and revolutionary that speaks of the worker, and it is nonsense to say that we demand that the poets should describe inevitably a factory chimney, or the uprising against capital!"[35] In fact, for Trotsky, the working class needed to build on prerevolutionary formal and stylistic accomplishments as they "cannot begin the construction of a new culture without absorbing and assimilating the elements of the old cultures." In addition, Trotsky foregrounded artistic production as a unique form of skilled labor, writing that "[e]very peasant is a peasant, but not everyone can express himself."[36]

Trotsky's sophisticated grasp of politics and literature clearly inspired a number of New York Intellectuals—most notably Phillips and Rahv at *Partisan Review*—who insisted that criticism must be socially engaged but also attuned to the aesthetics of the text. In this way, Baldwin's reviews, and in particular "Everybody's Protest Novel," are in keeping with *Partisan Review*'s (and Trotsky's) keen dislike of ideologically driven art and criticism. Baldwin's criticism of Harriet Beecher Stowe as a pamphleteer—rather than an artist—is clearly reminiscent of *Partisan Review*'s editorial leanings.[37]

For William Phillips, Trotsky was "the only major Marxist leader who had written authentic literary criticism" and it is indeed hard to imagine enjoying reading Stalin on poetics.[38] Importantly, Trotsky's views on modernism influenced—or at least coincided with—the early championing of modernist writing by *Partisan Review*, a further connection between Baldwin and the New York Intellectual scene. Baldwin's early work in particular stresses the importance of modernist writing—most notably the work of Henry James, whom Baldwin referred to as "the greatest of our novelists" as late as 1962.[39] Baldwin's indebtedness to modernism at first seems to connect him back to his literary forefathers of the Harlem Renaissance. Yet, Baldwin's interest in modernism has little to do with the experimental writing of Jean Toomer or the angular Cubism of Aaron Douglas. Although critics such as Houston Baker and James de Jongh have demonstrated the importance of race and modernism in the Harlem Renaissance, Baldwin rarely mentions this period at all—and certainly eschews discussing the writers' and artists' formal contributions to modernism.[40]

For Baldwin, coming of age in the 1940s, it was unclear which literary forebears he should turn to. Both white and black critics noted the "astonishing number of . . . manuscripts," on "what we call the Negro problem" (Edwin Seaver), echoed by J. Saunders Redding's exaggerated claim in the mid- to late 1940s that "[i]f it's about colored people, it'll get published."[41] Such comments feed into more serious questions about the function and limitations of literature to affect social change. As Helen Parker observed in 1947, "the issue of racial discrimination should logically have been atomized now, what with the sheer weight of literary tracts against it."[42] Writing two years later in "Everybody's Protest Novel," Baldwin suggested that white Americans experienced a sense of complacent virtue when they picked up a work of protest fiction, an experience that led to self-congratulation rather than direct political action. It is within this political and literary quagmire that Baldwin emerged, citing the Master, rather than Richard Wright, as his literary and political hero.

Baldwin's emphasis on Henry James is a striking and constant feature in interviews and writings on his development as a writer. For Baldwin, two of Henry James's novels, *The Portrait of a Lady* (1881) and *The Princess Casamassima* (1886) helped him to "break out of the ghetto," a remark that echoes his comment that writing his first novel was "a fairly deliberate attempt to break out of what I always think of as the 'cage' of Negro writing."[43] Baldwin also recalled that reading James helped him with formal difficulties that had plagued him while writing *Go Tell It on the Mountain*. In a 1984 *Paris Review* interview Baldwin recollected how

> [t]here were things I couldn't deal with technically at first. . . . This is where reading Henry James helped me, with his whole idea about the center of consciousness and using a single intelligence to tell the story. He gave me the idea to make the novel happen on John's birthday.[44]

Baldwin's indebtedness to James continued in recognizable ways certainly until the publication of *Another Country* (1962), whereas Robert Corber has persuasively argued, Baldwin "adopts a Jamesian narrative strategy, relying on what James . . . called 'successive reflectors' or multiple centers of intelligence, through which he filters the novel's action."[45] On the one hand, as Corber rightly points out, Baldwin's strategy of employing Jamesian narrative techniques left him open to charges that he wanted "to deny his debt to his African-American antecedents." Such a view was alluded to in Ralph Ellison's

1952 dismissal of "the tight well-made Jamesian novel" which, "for all its artistic perfection" was "too concerned with 'good taste' and stable areas."[46]

However, Baldwin's reasons for employing Jamesian narrative techniques are clearly not straightforward and Cyraina Johnson-Roullier is surely right to suggest that Baldwin's fascination with James "opens up what might be considered a new cultural path within the framework of African-American literature," particularly in the ways in which Baldwin rewrote the idea of protest.[47] At the same time, Baldwin's interest in James fits squarely with a 1930s and 1940s championing of the earlier writer—particularly in his *Partisan Review* pieces. This, in turn, raises important questions about the New York Intellectuals' (including Baldwin's) relationship to modernism.[48] In contrast to Ellison's conclusion that a Jamesian narrative was unable to capture the complexity of postwar American life, critics such as F. O. Matthiesen and Philip Rahv maintained that James's work "succeeded in depicting 'the finer discriminations' of the self within the 'envelop of circumstances' in which they are contained."[49]

Rahv, Trilling, and F. W. Dupee, in particular, championed Henry James as a key modernist writer.[50] But the very question of why leftist writers (including Baldwin) would want to champion modernist authors is not straightforward, although it is quite possible that Baldwin was drawn to James's muted explorations of homoeroticism in addition to his narrative ingenuity.[51] For the editors of *Partisan Review*, as Harvey Teres has documented, the "justification of modernist literature was largely based on the kind of argument Trotsky made in the 'Manifesto': modernism is subversive because it exposes and invariably resists the social and psychological ills brought about by capitalism."[52] For a number of New York Intellectuals (most notably Clement Greenberg and Dwight Macdonald), mass culture was viewed with suspicion, seen as little more than propaganda for Stalin's Popular Front campaigns.[53] And yet, this "radical appropriation of modernism" as Teres terms it, is not clear-cut, a point picked up by Trotskyite critics such as Malcolm Cowley who criticized *Partisan Review* for "retreating into a 'red ivory tower.'"[54] For Rahv, in particular, "[m]odern literature . . . essentially involves a dispute with the modern world."[55] In other words, by refusing to publish works that could be easily understood (and sold), modernist authors withdrew from the marketplace, placing emphasis on cultural capital rather than capitalism. Despite such claims, the New York Intellectuals' championing of difficult modernist works and distrust of mass culture inevitably smacked of elitism and cultural snobbery. As Alan Wald has argued, "it is difficult to locate a sustained and consistent theoretical statement about the origins and political significance of modernism that justifies their dogged valorization of the genre above all others."[56] Despite *Partisan Review*'s continued efforts to endorse, support, and valorize modernism, their justifications "never seriously answered the question of whether modernism is an authentic antibourgeois tendency or, in fact, a decadent phase in bourgeois culture."[57] One might argue, instead, that an aesthetic affiliation with modernist writing was yoked to a leftist political affiliation, despite some logical inconsistencies between these two affiliations.

The African American and the Jewish Intellectual

According to Nathan Abrams in his cultural history of *Commentary* magazine, Baldwin was "the black equivalent of a New York Jewish intellectual," a description echoed by Harvey Teres who writes that "Baldwin was in some ways the black analogue of the New York Jew." Such neat encapsulations do not explain the reasons why a young African American was publishing in magazines predominantly about Jewish topics and edited, for the most part, by Jewish intellectuals.[58]

What is more, as a number of critics have noted, Baldwin's later career has been dogged by uncomfortable criticism of his at times ill-advised comments on black-Jewish relations. As Herb Boyd has noted in his biography of Baldwin and Harlem, the author's attacks on Jewish landlords as early as 1948 in "The Harlem Ghetto" "was the source of relentless charges that Baldwin was anti-Semitic."[59] In an article titled "What Do Negroes Expect of Jews?" published in the *Amsterdam News* in 1960, the (unnamed) author discusses *Fortune* magazine's critique of Baldwin's "savage comment on both Gentiles and Jews."[60] Later in his career, Baldwin had to defend several charges that he was anti-Semitic, not least after the publication of his provocative essay "Negroes Are Anti-Semitic Because They're Anti-White" in 1967 and an article published the same year in *Freedomways* called "Anti-Semitism and Black Power." In his 1970 essay for the *New York Review of Books*, "An Open Letter to My Sister, Angela Davis," Baldwin described the activist, author and academic as a "Jewish housewife in the boxcar headed for Dachau," which precipitated an acrimonious public debate with Shlomo Katz, editor of *Midstream*.[61] In open letters to Baldwin published in *Midstream*, Katz took Baldwin to task for comparing Davis's experience to that of Holocaust victims, lambasting the African American writer's comparison. As John Murray Cuddihy points out, the exchange was not only a battle for "victim status," but illustrative of larger black-Jewish tussles for cultural priority, of which Baldwin was keenly aware.[62]

Boyd rightly points out that Baldwin held close friendships with Jewish writers and editors (including Emile Capouya, Sol Stein, and Richard Avedon). Moreover, Baldwin himself recalled in *The Fire Next Time* (1963) that his "best friend in high school was a Jew."[63] Such biographical information, however, adds little to an understanding of how Baldwin's early writing fits into wider questions about black-Jewish relations, which by the early to mid-1960s had become increasingly strained. Although the anti-Semitic content in some statements from the civil rights and Black Power movements is often remarked upon, the racism of some contemporary Jewish intellectuals remains underexplored. How and why, for example, fifteen years after Baldwin's first publications in *Commentary*, did Norman Podhoretz recount his profound distrust of African Americans in "My Negro Problem—and Ours" (1963)?

Much has been written about the importance of the New York Intellectuals' Jewish identities. As Ruth R. Wisse has pointed out, up until the 1930s, New York Jewish intellectual life was largely confined to publications in Yiddish newspapers. As she notes in an acerbic and penetrating article, "The New York intellectuals were the first 'immigrant' group to be fully absorbed into American literary culture, enlarging the idea of America as it encompassed them."[64] Crucially, although many of the key contributors and editors of journals such as *Partisan Review*, the *New Leader*, and *Commentary* were Jewish, most, as Wisse documents, "did not feel compelled to renounce their Jewishness—or, what may be more to the point, to affirm it strongly."[65] This point is an important one, as even magazines such as *Commentary*, which was sponsored by the American Jewish Committee (AJC), gave its founding editor, Elliot Cohen, editorial independence.[66] Cohen would joke about how the "main difference between *Partisan Review* and *Commentary* is that we admit to being a Jewish magazine and they don't" and yet Cohen also refused to publish articles on Jewish culture unless they were well crafted and met his exacting editorial standards.[67]

Under Cohen's editorship, *Commentary* "interpreted race hatred and prejudice very widely to include blacks as well as Jews."[68] Not only did Cohen publish Baldwin's early short stories (the only fiction published in *Commentary* at the time that did not deal with the Jewish experience), but he also steered the journal toward civil rights issues. Cohen's decision, then, to publish Baldwin's essay "The Harlem Ghetto" is not surprising—although the force of the essay shocked a number of readers. Baldwin's article, which focuses on Harlem, turns to a discussion of sermons by Harlem preachers who rail against Jews for "having refused the light" but also points out that many African Americans identify themselves "almost wholly with the Jew."[69] Baldwin's article then moves from journalistic observation to anecdote. "Jews in Harlem are small tradesmen, rent collectors, real estate agents and pawnbrokers," Baldwin writes. In other words, "they are therefore identified with oppression and are hated for it."[70] (The association of Jews and wealth particularly affronted Norman Podhoretz, who was at pains to point out the counternarrative in "My Negro Problem—and Ours"). Baldwin concludes by stating that "[t]he Negro, facing a Jew, hates, at bottom, not his Jewishness but the color of his skin." However, Baldwin's article is peppered with personal asides, such as "I remember meeting no Negro in the years of my growing up, in my family or out of it, who would really ever trust a Jew."[71]

Baldwin's inflammatory article needs to be seen in the context of wider postwar black–Jewish relations, what Ethan Goffman has called an "intricate archaeology of hatred and identification."[72] This uneasy relationship is illustrated by two 1942 articles, both published in *Negro Quarterly*: L. D. Reddick's essay, "Anti-Semitism among Negroes," and Louis Harap's "Anti-Negroism among Jews."[73] In a brief article for *Politics* in 1945 Harold Orlansky writes of how "[a]nti-Semitism among Negroes and its converse, anti-Negro feeling among Jews, are two of the sadder manifestations of the times."[74] Foreshadowing Baldwin's comment that "Jews in Harlem are small tradesmen, rent collectors, real estate agents and pawnbrokers," Orlansky writes that, "[c]oncerning the cause of this anti-Semitism, much has been made of the Jew's contact with the Negro on an exploitative or competitive level as landlord, shopkeeper, pawnshop operator, employer, doctor, lawyer or social worker."[75]

Writing two years before Baldwin (and again in *Commentary*) the African American sociologist Kenneth B. Clark anticipated many of Baldwin's themes. "Antagonism toward 'the Jewish landlord' is so common," Clark notes, "as to have become almost an integral aspect of the folk culture of the northern urban Negro."[76] Clark's piece, published as "Candor about Negro–Jewish Relations: A Social Scientist Charts a Complex Social Problem," though it touched on many of Baldwin's themes in "The Harlem Ghetto," was presented as research, not anecdote. In contrast to Baldwin's wild claims about distrust between African Americans and Jews, Clark's article references statistics, citing, for example, how

> [a]n investigation of inter-group attitudes in one of the larger, more isolated communities that make up metropolitan New York, found that nearly 60 per cent of Jews held some unfavorable stereotyped reaction toward Negroes and 70 per cent of Negroes had some unfavorable stereotyped reaction towards Jews.[77]

Even Clark's measured article, however, loses its objective cool when faced with claims that the black and Jewish struggle is one and the same. Baldwin, too, would continue to argue that Jews were disadvantaged—but at least they were white, a point that he reiterated clumsily at times. For Baldwin, as for other African American social commentators, race increasingly took precedence over class as the key problem of the American Left.

RACE, REVIEWS, AND THE LEFT

By the time Baldwin had published his first novel, *Go Tell It on the Mountain* in 1953, a number of African American writers were openly critical of the Communist Party. In 1950, Richard Wright, along with André Gide and others, had openly expressed his disillusionment with communism in *The God That Failed* followed by Ralph Ellison's famously scathing description of Communist Party activity in *Invisible Man* (1952). Around the time Baldwin's first novel was published, the American Communist Party had ceased being a dynamic force in black American radical and cultural politics. Paul Robeson's newspaper *Freedom* faded away in the mid-1950s and the African American communist Claudia Jones was deported in 1955, along with C. L. R. James.

Twenty years earlier, as Christopher Phelps has shown in the reissuing of Max Shachtman's 1933 *Communism and the Negro*, the Trotskyist Left held a number of progressive, if not irreproachable, views on racial oppression. Published a year before the inaugural edition of *Partisan Review* (although not widely circulated), *Communism and the New Negro* anticipates the better-known writing of the Trinidadian Trotskyist intellectual C. L. R. James whose articles—particularly *The Revolutionary Answer to the Negro Problem in the United States* (1948)—established him as the leading authority on "Negro issues" for the American revolutionary socialist movement, which by the late 1930s included around thirty black members.[78] Shachtman's views, which dovetailed and diverged from those of Trotsky and James, were prescient and forward thinking at a time when most white Americans were indifferent to struggles for racial equality.[79] Shachtman's *Communism and the New Negro* dismisses "[s]hoddy theories of scientific charlatans . . . established to prove the inherent racial superiority of the white man over the black man"; he makes it clear that American workers can only "make any real progress towards freedom" with "the support of the vast reservoir of strength and militancy constituted by the twelve million black people."[80] Attuned to the ways in which class and race have interlocked in American history, Shachtman points out how the American Left also has "no distinctions of race," while at the same time asserting that his own vision for racial freedom was distinctly anti-Stalinist.[81] (Unlike the Communist Party, Shachtman and other Trotskyites refuted the notion that African Americans desired a separate "Black Belt," the geographical grouping of self-reliant black states put forward by Stalinist theorists including J. S. Allen.)[82] For Shachtman, "the caste status of the American Negro does not place him in the category of a nation," reminding his readers of how Lenin had distinguished between the Irish (nation) and Jews (nation-less).[83]

Shachtman's views on racial oppression have been eclipsed by those of C. L. R. James, not only because the latter had Trotsky's official support but because James was much more familiar with the cultural achievements and nuances of black literature and art. Shachtman, despite his commendable efforts at dismantling the reasons for lynching and the economic exploitation of share croppers, falters on the question of African American culture. "Has the Negro population a common culture distinct from that of the rest of the country?" Shachtman asks.[84] "Only by the most impossible stretch of the imagination," is Shachtman's response, adding that "[g]enerally speaking, the culture of the Negro is the culture of the section of the country where he resides."[85] Shachtman's well-intentioned but uninformed views suggest the gaps in left-wing politics of the 1930s, as well as how ripe the time was for a channeling of political thought, culture, and a championing of civil rights—something that *Partisan Review*, founded a year after Shachtman's publication, promised to deliver.

In 1934, the editorial statement of *Partisan Review* signaled its intent to "participate in the struggle of the workers and sincere intellectuals against imperialist war, fascism, national and racial oppression," and yet despite the pledge to participate in the struggle against racism, no article on race appeared in the journal until 1940. Moreover, the new editorial statement in 1937 made no mention of racial oppression. Aside from a few brief book reviews of works by African American authors (including Langston Hughes and Richard Wright), *Partisan Review*'s contributions to the struggles of racial oppression were few and far between.

After fifteen or so years, *Partisan Review* began to publish essays by African American writers, including pieces by Ellison and LeRoi Jones's (Amiri Baraka's) essay, "The Beat Generation," in 1958. The 1930s and 1940s, however, was a period of ghostly silence for black American left-wing radicals who wished to publish with Rahv and Phillips. Not even C. L. R. James, who had spent time with Trotsky, graced the pages of *Partisan Review*. The first significant postwar article in *Partisan Review* by an African American was, in fact, Baldwin's "Everybody's Protest Novel."[86] In William Phillip's history of the magazine, "there are no entries in the index under civil rights, Montgomery, Martin Luther King, black power, or race. Wright, Ellison and Baldwin are the only African-American writers listed."[87]

It should be noted, too, that *Partisan Review* only republished "Everybody's Protest Novel" after it had achieved notoriety in France. However, *Partisan Review* was by no means the only New York Intellectual magazine that was slow to publish works by and about black American life. Teres rightly concludes that "in the end the New York Intellectuals remained relative strangers to African-American life."[88] He adds that "their own success as intellectuals encouraged them to superimpose an ethnic, assimilationist model on an American dilemma fraught with racial and class (not to mention gendered) contradictions."[89] Baldwin is a case in point: although several of his early reviews were on books by or about African American themes, it was not until his 1948 article "The Harlem Ghetto" for *Commentary* that the writer explored the conditions of racial oppression. Despite occasional articles on race in the 1940s (notably early articles on the desegregation of the armed forces in the short-lived *Politics*), few New York Intellectual magazines discussed race until the late 1950s and early 1960s when a cluster of high-profile books and articles appeared—including Nathan Glazer's *Beyond the Melting Pot* (1959) and his article "Negroes and Jews: The New Challenge to Pluralism," in the December 1964 edition of *Commentary*. As Alexander Bloom notes, when "the civil rights movement turned to more specific questions of black identity and Afro-American heritage, the position of both James Baldwin and Ralph Ellison in the otherwise white literary world of the New York

Intellectuals grew problematic."[90] For Ellison, in particular, although *Partisan Review* published the prologue of *Invisible Man* in the January–February issue of 1952, the writer is probably best remembered in this milieu for his ongoing spats with Irving Howe as much as being welcomed into New York Intellectual life. Howe's slight of Ellison in "Black Boys and Native Sons" (published in *Dissent*, 1963) precipitated the latter's seminal essay "The World and the Jug" in the *New Leader*. Although Ellison would later accuse *Commentary* of being "apologists for segregation," his duel with Howe only increased respect for Ellison, bolstering his role as an intellectual in his own right.[91] As Arnold Rampersad notes, "[p]robably for the first time in modern American history, a black intellectual had fought a public duel against a white intellectual and won."[92] Baldwin's own split with the New York Intellectuals, though less dramatic, is illustrated by the publication of *The Fire Next Time*, which Norman Podhoretz had originally commissioned for *Commentary*. When Podhoretz berated Baldwin for selling his piece to the *New Yorker*, Baldwin told the *Commentary* editor that he should write his own article about race. Podhoretz was only too willing to oblige, and his piece became the infamous "My Negro Problem—and Ours."

Baldwin's own contributions to a discussion of race in New York Intellectual publications were not as many as he claimed. Baldwin in fact reviewed works on Catholic philosophy (*The Person and the Common Good*), Brooklyn Jewish gangs (*The Amboy Dukes*), Russian literature, and two works about Robert Louis Stevenson. Baldwin's first review to tackle the subject of race was *There Was Once a Slave: The Heroic Story of Frederick Douglass* by Shirley Graham—the future wife of W. E. B. Du Bois—in the *Nation*. As Baldwin notes, Graham won the Julian Messner Award "for having written the best book combating intolerance in America," but he has little to say about the merits of this prize-winning tome.[93] Anticipating his criticism in "Everybody's Protest Novel" of Uncle Tom who "has been robbed of his humanity," Baldwin argues that Graham "has robbed him [Douglass] of dignity and humanity by glossing over any of the abolitionist's imperfections."[94] Douglass, Baldwin asserts, was "frequently misguided, sometimes pompous, gifted and no saint at all." Baldwin further argues that Graham's portrait of Douglass, like Stowe's characterization of Uncle Tom, is little more than the flip side of the "tradition that Negroes are never to be characterized as anything than amoral, laughing clowns."[95]

If Baldwin's first review on African American culture reads as a warm-up for "Everybody's Protest Novel," then his second, a damning review of Chester Himes's *Lonely Crusade* (1947), could only have strained social relations with another future compatriot in Paris. Far from offering any solidarity to another black American writer, Baldwin launches into a languid yet barbed assault on the older writer who uses "what is probably the most uninteresting and awkward prose I have read in recent years."[96] Reading more and more like a poor school report (written by a reviewer not long out of school), Baldwin's review awards Himes "an A for ambition—and a rather awe-stricken gasp for effort," adding that "Himes seems capable of some of the worst writing this side of the Atlantic."[97] Baldwin's review becomes another sketchpad for his more finely tuned assault on Wright and Stowe, concluding that "Uncle Tom is no longer to be trusted . . . [and] Bigger Thomas is becoming irrelevant."[98] In this review, in particular, Baldwin shifts gear from harsh reviewer to sharp-eyed essayist. Despite the plethora of novels about racial oppression, Baldwin asserts that "not one has exhibited any genuine understanding of its historical genesis or contemporary necessity or its psychological toll."[99]

Central to Baldwin's dismissal of contemporary African American fiction is his criticism that writers continue to draw on types (the "minstrel man . . . or the Negro rapist, or the brave, black college student"), which fail to adequately capture American life.[100] While Sterling Brown's 1933 essay, "The Negro Character as Seen by White Authors," pilloried American literature for perpetuating black American stereotypes—"contented slave, wretched freeman, comedian or buffoon, brute, tragic mulatto, 'local color' negro, and 'exotic primitive,'" in 1947 Baldwin was still chastising black American authors along similar grounds.[101] Baldwin's repeated call for psychological complexity is echoed by Ernest Kaiser, the future founding associate editor of *Freedomways*, a journal to which Baldwin would contribute. Critiquing the black Left, Kaiser noted that African American writers failed "to deal with Negro psychology," lambasting writers such as Du Bois and Lloyd Brown "for their inadequate psychological depth when analyzing masses of blacks as the fundamental challenge for the writer and intellectual."[102] Again foreshadowing his argument in "Everybody's Protest Novel," that the dangers are in "overlooking, denying, evading his complexity," Baldwin argues in "History as Nightmare" that in postwar America, "human beings are too complex" to be reduced to symbols and types.[103] In Baldwin's criticism of Himes, the most avid proponent of social-realist literature of the early 1940s, the young reviewer anticipated the demise of protest fiction, which hastened as Wright left for France in 1947. As Lawrence Jackson has noted, with reference to Gunnar Myrdal's 1944 study *An American Dilemma: The Negro Problem and Modern Democracy*, "Americans went from shock at the moral ugliness Myrdal had exposed to a feeling that the protest fiction genre was overworked exaggeration."[104]

In the April 1948 issue of *Commentary*, Baldwin reviewed five books under the heading "The Image of the Negro." Baldwin's truculent essay begins by announcing "the really stupendous inadequacy of the five novels under consideration" and barely lets up its tirade, pausing only to wonder "what, in these days, is a novel?"[105] Baldwin's review, which by now has the hallmarks of his later essays, again pounces on the protest novel, a genre that was inevitable because of "the initial debasement of literary standards."[106] Several important features surface in this piece that anticipate Baldwin's more well-known views in "Everybody's Protest Novel." Ideas that align him with the postwar New York Intellectual landscape are also clearly discernible in this group review.

Baldwin derides the protest novel, comparing it to "a kind of writing becoming nearly as formalized as those delicate vignettes written for the women's magazines," asking "whether . . . its power as a corrective social force is sufficient to override its deficiencies as literature."[107] Baldwin's comment would no doubt have riled John Killens and Richard Wright, two well-known writers of protest fiction associated with tough masculine characters and chiseled prose. Baldwin could have compared protest fiction to any number of formulaic cultural products and his choice suggests that he wanted to take a swipe at what he perceived as the hypermasculinity of the genre. In "Everybody's Protest Novel" Baldwin would compare the sentimentality of *Uncle Tom's Cabin* (1852) to *Native Son* (1940), suggesting that if you peek beneath Wright's tough exterior you can find a little lady from New England.[108] And yet his comment in "The Image of the Negro" is more than a cheeky parting shot: Baldwin dismisses protest fiction, not only as literary froth but also as an example of mass culture.[109] When Baldwin asks "whether . . . its [protest fictions'] power as a corrective social force is sufficient to override its deficiencies as literature" his comments open up key contemporary leftist questions about realism and debates about literary merit versus social worth. "How closely do these novels reflect the social questions which," Baldwin asks, "since—admittedly, they are not, by and large, good novels—are their sole reason for being?" "With what reality are they concerned, how is it probed," Baldwin continues, "what message is being brought to this amorphous public mind?"[110]

Baldwin's central questions dovetail with key arguments that circulated in the 1940s and beyond regarding social realism and the relationship between politics and art. In his early essay, "The Literary Class War" (1932), Rahv distinguished between proletarian literature and what he termed "social or protest fiction," a genre that he saw as "bourgeois," "based on the premises of idealism."[111] Both Phillips and Rahv, like Baldwin, were skeptical about social realism. Picking up this thread toward the end of "The Image of the Negro," Baldwin writes of how "nothing is illuminated. The worthlessness of these novels consists precisely in that they supposedly expose a reality that in actuality they conspire to mask."[112] In contrast to Marxist critics who applauded realism for its ability to depict the social inequality of contemporary life, Phillips and Rahv spoke rather of realism in terms of "a deflection with crooked mirrors."[113] As I outlined earlier, for Trotsky as well as Phillips, Rahv, and Baldwin, works of literature were not to be judged on their political conviction alone. As Baldwin would later write in "Everybody's Protest Novel," "literature and sociology are not one and the same."[114] Baldwin's emphasis on complexity—psychological, historical, narrative, and theological—echoes Phillips and Rahv in their refusal to value work solely on the basis of its social contributions. At the same time, Baldwin's work did not go as far as Rahv's championing of modernist culture, which asserted "that art does not derive its value from its relation to society but that it has value 'in itself.'"[115] For Baldwin, there was simply too much at stake.

Baldwin's last review of this period to discuss race is an essay on seven books, published as "Too Late, Too Late," for *Commentary* in 1949. The grouping of nonfiction books included *The Negro Newspaper*; *Jim Crow America*; *The High Cost of Prejudice*; *The Protestant Church and the Negro*; *Color and Conscience*; *From Slavery to America*; and *The Negro in America*. Again, Baldwin has little positive to say about any of these works. Vishnu Oak's *The Negro Newspaper* is, Baldwin contends, a "hysterical little pamphlet," a further foreshadowing of his criticism of Stowe's pamphleteering.[116] Earl Conrad's argument in *Jim Crow America*—that the racial problems can be reduced to a question of economics and labor—is not discounted by Baldwin, but again, he pulls up the author for not considering the psychological damage on whites and blacks. Conrad, Baldwin writes in what is becoming a familiar refrain, "ignores this complexity and confusion."[117] Baldwin's conclusion is that these books "record the facts, but they cannot probe the immense, ambiguous, uncontrollable effect," a task that he would set himself with his fiction and nonfiction.[118]

Baldwin's reviews prior to the publication of his first short story ("The Death of the Prophet" in *Commentary*, 1950) read, on the one hand, as a warm up to his more incisive and distilled insights published in "Everybody's Protest Novel."[119] At the same time, his pronounced critique of social realism, sentimentality, dependence on types, and the Popular Front firmly anchor Baldwin in the New York Intellectual milieu. In Baldwin's reviews of the later 1940s, as Geraldine Murphy astutely points out, "the debt to anti-Stalinist liberal discourse is obvious in his disdain for left-wing faith in a committed art, for abstractions like 'the common man,' and 'the people,' for sentimentalism and mass culture as well as in his corresponding respect for individuality and psychological complexity, for social contradictions over false unity."[120] Hodding Carter's *Flood Crest* (1947), Baldwin writes, "is yet another addition to the overburdened files of progressive fiction concerning the unhappy South," and James M. Cain "writes fantasies, and fantasies of the most unendurably mawkish and sentimental sort."[121]

Baldwin's views on the Popular Front and ideology are best illustrated in two reviews of the Russian writer, Maxim Gorky. In "Maxim Gorky as Artist," Baldwin's first published piece—a review of the writer's *Best Short Stories* published in the *Nation* in 1947—Baldwin observes that he is "almost always painfully verbose and frequently threatens to degenerate into simple propaganda."[122] Gorky's range is not only "narrow" and "sentimental" but his writing "remains a report." Gorky, Baldwin avers, does not develop characters with psychological awareness, but "a *type*, with his human attributes sensitively felt and well reported but never realized." Gorky's writing, which purports to show the reality of oppression, Baldwin concludes is little more than "the key to the even more dismal failure of present-day realistic novelists."[123]

Baldwin's dismissal of Gorky (and, in particular, his social realism) showed no signs of abating in a second review of the Russian author. In a review of Gorky's *The Mother* (published in the *New Leader*, 1947), considered by many to be a classic work of social realist literature, Baldwin opens by claiming that "in a word, this is Gorky's best-seller," a statement which might have misled readers who bought *Mother* hoping for an easy read.[124] Baldwin further reduces this acclaimed novel, noting that "[w]ith some ideological concessions and the proper makeup *Mother* would make an impressive vehicle, for . . . Bette Davis," adding that "[i]t is rich in struggle, tears, courage and good old-fashioned mother love."[125] Leaving aside Baldwin's admiration for Bette Davis, it is clear that his review sought to reduce *Mother* to a footnote in popular or mass culture, a mode of production heavily criticized by Dwight Macdonald, Clement Greenberg, and other anti-Stalinist intellectuals.

Baldwin levels his strongest criticism at Gorky's barely disguised ideologically driven aims:

> He [Gorky] was the foremost exponent of the maxim that "art is the weapon of the working class." He is also, probably, the major example of the invalidity of such a doctrine. (It is rather like saying that art is the weapon of the American house-wife.) . . . Art, to be sure, has its roots in the lives of human beings . . . I doubt that it is limited to our comrades; since we have discovered that art does not belong to what was once the aristocracy it does not therefore follow that it has become the exclusive property of the common man. . . . Rather—it belongs to all of us.[126]

For Baldwin, Gorky's work characterizes the subordination of art to politics, a feature that rankled with many of the anti-Stalinist Left—and, in particular, Phillips and Rahv. While Baldwin does not discuss race directly, his comment that art does not "become the exclusive property of the common man," suggests how race, rather than class, would dominate the American literary and political scene in the following decades—and it is no coincidence that his most significant early essay would be a piece written about race while in another country.

Baldwin's expatriation to Paris in 1948 had a discernible impact on his writing and political outlook. Welcomed as part of an American expatriate community by the writers and publishers Albert Benveniste and George Solomos (known then as Themistocles Hoetis) Baldwin became, Solomos recalled, "a sensation" in the Parisian café society.[127] Toward the end of 1949, Solomos and Benveniste asked Baldwin to contribute a piece to their newly formed avant-garde magazine, *Zero*. In a recent interview Solomos recalls that he asked

Baldwin to submit an essay several days before the magazine was ready to go to the printers, and the result was "Everybody's Protest Novel." This famous essay was first published in the inaugural issue of *Zero*, and not, as often attributed, in *Partisan Review*.[128] In *Zero*, Baldwin's essay appeared alongside impressive British and American contributions, including poetry by John Goodwin, William Carlos Williams, and Kenneth Patchen and a short story by Christopher Isherwood. Midway through the magazine, Richard Wright's story "The Man Who Killed a Shadow" sits before Baldwin's "Everybody's Protest Novel." Solomos is adamant that Baldwin was unaware that Wright was contributing to *Zero* and yet the title of the older writer's story seems uncomfortably prophetic.

According to the editorial statement, *Zero* "acts as a raw and basic channel for creative assumptions, affiliating itself to all and to no techniques: conscious and unconscious, erudite and untutored, therapeutic and unpragmatic, right, left." If the editorial veered toward the abstract, claiming allegiance only with creativity, the contributions suggested a leftist political aesthetic. Running for seven issues and published in Paris, Tangier, Mexico, and Philadelphia, *Zero* published poetry, art, fiction, and essays by a diverse range of international writers, including Gore Vidal, Max Ernst, and Paul Bowles. *Zero*, the editorial statement continued, "will apply itself to the introduction and continuation of American writings and art coming most especially from Europe and secondly from America in order to form a double channel of presentation." The "double channel of presentation" was no doubt a reference to the cultural ebb and flow between Europe and North America and yet it unwittingly picks up on the way art was used by the US State Department to win over "the hearts and minds" of Europe during the cultural Cold War, where in Arthur Koestler's words, postwar Paris "was the world capital of fellow travelers."[129] Baldwin's early essays were published in magazines that were ideologically opposed to Stalinism. Avant-garde journals such as *Partisan Review* and the *New Leader* sought to efface the legacy of the Popular Front, the Communist International's attempt to recruit liberal intellectuals to the Communist Party. If the Popular Front sought to revolutionize society through propaganda, the goal of avant-garde magazines such as *Partisan Review* was to revolutionize literature. In the case of "Everybody's Protest Novel," Baldwin's views on truth, complexity, and the individual fit squarely with the views of the anti-Stalinist Left. "Everybody's Protest Novel" was republished by *Partisan Review* and then by *Perspectives USA*, an anti-Stalinist magazine started in the 1950s "to woo European intellectuals to the side of freedom."[130] Sol Stein, executive editor of the American Committee for Cultural Freedom—an organization that sought to fight communism with its own propaganda—took great interest in Baldwin's work. *Notes of a Native Son*, which contains "Everybody's Protest Novel," was published in Stein's "Contemporary Affairs Series," alongside famously anticommunist writers, including Sidney Hook and Arthur Koestler.[131]

"Everybody's Protest Novel" and "Preservation of Innocence" were published in the first and second issues of *Zero*. Baldwin's first essay is concerned with race without mentioning homosexuality, in contrast to "Preservation," a bold essay that discusses homosexuality but does not allude to blackness. Baldwin would explore homosexuality, though again with no over mention of race, in *Giovanni's Room*, his only sustained piece of fiction set in Paris aside from the short story, "This Morning, This Evening, So Soon" (1960), first published in *Atlantic Monthly*. "Everybody's Protest Novel" and "Preservation" share more similarities than their respective themes of protest fiction and homosexual literature might suggest. Although neither essay refers directly to the Popular Front, the language in "Everybody's Protest Novel" and "Preservation" is shot through with the rhetoric of the anti-Stalinist Left. Baldwin demands representational complexity in both pieces, whether in protest literature or fictional depictions of sexuality. One of Baldwin's central objections to *Uncle Tom's Cabin* is that it is formulaic: a self-consciously populist novel that Baldwin compares to James M. Cain's *The Postman Always Rings Twice* (1946). For Baldwin, Cain's work epitomizes the worst of formulaic mass culture, a concept that he picks up on in "Preservation." Baldwin pillories Cain, like Stowe, because such writers "are wholly unable to recreate or interpret any of the reality or complexity of human experience." The result, Baldwin concludes, "has now become to reduce all Americans to the compulsive bloodless dimensions of a guy named Joe."[132] Here Baldwin makes a thinly veiled attack on what he sees as the limitations of Popular Front cultural forms that ignore the complexity of the individual.

"Everybody's Protest Novel," though an accomplished and incisive essay, is not without its shortcomings.[133] Baldwin never really explains how Stowe's novel is both a pamphlet and the source of theological terror, nor does he explain how this "very bad novel" became such a bestseller.[134] And yet one of the strengths of "Everybody's Protest Novel," published in France—and surely one of the reasons that it quickly gained a transatlantic readership—is Baldwin's ability to harness contemporary discussions of the Left with issues of race. In this essay, Baldwin is able to combine discussions of Protest fiction with the wider concerns that I have outlined, namely, the individual, mass culture, and ideology. Toward the end of the essay, Baldwin illustrates his understanding of the interconnections between race and class. "Within this cage," Baldwin writes,

> it is romantic, more, meaningless, to speak of a "new" society as the desire of the oppressed, for that shivering dependence on the props of reality which he shares with the *Herrenvolk* makes a truly "new" society impossible to conceive. What is meant by a new society is one in which inequalities will disappear, in which vengeance will be exacted; either there will be no oppressed at all, or the oppressed and the oppressor will change places.[135]

Baldwin dismisses what he sees as the vagaries and romanticism of a "new society" in what reads as a thinly veiled critique of Stalinism. At the same time, his language, though charged with the vocabulary often associated with class, quietly shifts to a discussion of wider, circum-Atlantic power struggles as Baldwin talks of "the African, exile, pagan" who is taken from the auction block to the church and where the "oppressed" and "oppressor" invoke race, not just class. "This tableau," Baldwin follows, "this impossibility, is the heritage of the Negro in America," connecting the empty promises of religion to the concluding remarks that focus on *Native Son*.[136]

Baldwin's two essays in *Zero* marked a turning point in the writer's career; from African American reviewer to transatlantic essayist and commentator, now more concerned with race than class. Viewing the list of Baldwin's subsequent publications prior to *Go Tell It on the Mountain* in 1953, it is clear to see how Baldwin's writing developed: in 1950 *Commentary* published "The Death of the Prophet," a draft of *Go Tell It*, and one of the few stories in the magazine's early years that did not deal with a Jewish theme. In the same year, "The Negro in Paris," for *Reporter* would become "Encounter on the Seine," followed by several now collected pieces, including a second article for *Partisan Review*, "Many Thousands Gone." Not long after Baldwin's first novel was published he was starting to command sizable fees for his articles, and his work appeared in *Harper's*, *Encounter*, *Mademoiselle*, and, by the end of the 1950s, the *New York Times Book Review*.

While Baldwin continued to publish for *Commentary* and *Partisan Review* in the mid- to late 1950s, he had started to distance himself from his New York Intellectual roots. In fact, after publishing a section of *Another Country* in *Partisan Review* (1960), Baldwin never again published with those intellectual magazines. As an emerging transatlantic writer, Baldwin had moved away geographically but also politically. Focusing more on race than anti-Stalinism, Baldwin's work also remained committed to a critique of Hoover and McCarthyism, a point I will discuss at more length later. In contrast to New York Intellectuals who moved from the intellectual Left to the Right of conservative, Baldwin continued to tread a disreputable path in the eyes of the establishment. Unlike the former radical Sydney Hook who became an important player in the American Committee for Cultural Freedom or the large number of New York Intellectuals who failed to unite against Senator Joseph McCarthy, Baldwin would continue to voice his dissent.[137] In 1963, for example, Baldwin contributed to the satirical collection, *A Quarter-Century of Un-Americana: A Tragi-comical Memorabilia of HUAC* [House Un-American Activities Committee]. Unlike many former left-wing intellectuals, Baldwin spoke unequivocally of the HUAC as "one of the most sinister facts of the national life" and he would later dismiss McCarthy as "a coward and a bully" in *No Name in the Street*.[138] If, by the late 1960s, Baldwin felt that younger African American radicals considered him to be "of too much use to the

Establishment to be trusted by blacks," then it is important to remember how his early reviews and essays were forged in the crucible of the Left long before Cleaver and other Black Panthers were selling Mao's Little Red Book to raise funds on university campuses.[139] As Lawrie Balfour has observed, Baldwin was "dismissed by some critics as an assimilationist and by others as a militant unable to acknowledge the progress that took place during his lifetime," and yet "his message is more radical than either critique suggests."[140] Baldwin's early contributions to the harnessing of race with left-wing politics deserve to be reexamined, despite—and indeed because of—the author's unwillingness to embrace his early radical associations.

On the surface, Baldwin's second novel *Giovanni's Room* (1956) added little to discussions of race. Set in Paris without any clearly defined black characters, Baldwin's novel seems at first glance to be far removed from his early interest in leftist politics and its relationship to race. In recent years, *Giovanni's Room* has been rightly celebrated as a pioneering work of homosexual literature; it is seen as "political" insofar as it boldly explored love between two men at a time when few novelists dared to tackle such a theme. And yet the novel is far more political than the subject matter of homosexuality, something I contend has been overlooked as it has entered the canon of pathbreaking homosexual literature. Published at the height of the Cold War, *Giovanni's Room* at least invites us to read this work in the political and cultural context within which it was written. While Baldwin left the milieu of the New York Intellectuals, his first major piece set in Paris is in fact preoccupied with the impact of the Cold War on the American subject and taps into keenly felt and debated arguments about the boundaries between white and black US culture.

Giovanni's Room and the Cold War

I always wonder
what they think the niggers are doing
while they, the pink and alabaster pragmatists,
are containing
Russia

—JAMES BALDWIN, "STAGGERLEE WONDERS"

Baldwin's move to Paris in 1948 offered him greater sexual and racial tolerance, but it did not remove him from the impact of the Cold War.[141] By the early 1950s, there was a proliferation of newspaper headlines in Paris, such as "McCarthyism, Forerunner of Fascism in the USA" and *Le Monde's* "The Mania of the Witch Hunt: Every Day McCarthy Weighs More Heavily on the Lives of Americans," a weight, as James Campbell notes, that also bore down on Americans in Paris.[142] There were rumors that magazines such as *Paris Review* were being funded by the CIA, illustrated by Baldwin's wry remark that he covered the first International Congress of Black Writers and Artists in Paris, 1956, "for *Encounter* (or for the CIA)."[143] In Paris, as the poet Christopher Logue recalls, "everybody thought everybody else was informing on someone or other for somebody," paralleling Baldwin's recollection that, on his return to America, "friends were throwing their friends to the wolves, and justifying their treachery by learned discourses . . . on the treachery of the Comintern."[144]

Baldwin's surveillance in America and France points to a wider connection between the Bureau's monitoring of racial progress and the ways in which early civil rights achievements were connected to subversive political activity. African Americans broke the color-line in the National Football League and major league baseball in 1946 and 1947, respectively. In film, The National Association for the Advancement of Colored People (NAACP) continued to lobby Hollywood, demanding an end to the portrayal of African Americans as two-dimensional stereotypes, while an executive order prevented discrimination in application to federal government posts.[145] Most significantly of all, the army was finally desegregated in 1948, followed six years later by the, at first largely unenforced, legal mandate for desegregation of the education system provided by the Supreme Court in the case of *Brown v. Board of Education of Topeka, Kansas*. Crucially, the connection between racial equality and political subversion was reinforced, not relaxed, in the immediate postwar years.

During the dismantling of racial boundaries in postwar America, two crucial and interconnected points emerge. The first is that underneath Truman's progressive racial policies lurked a private ambivalence toward desegregation. Racial advancement was viewed as a secondary priority to combating communism (unless, of course, the two coincided). After the Supreme Court ruled that segregated public schools were a violation of the Fourteenth Amendment, Eisenhower privately held the ruling as "morally repugnant," giving his assurances to southern congressmen that he would not uphold the court's decision to desegregate schools "with all deliberate speed."[146] The second—and more crucial—point is that the advances of racial progress were seen by many as tantamount to the collapse of the racial order. In this way, the postwar years simultaneously saw a relaxing but also a sharp delineation of racial boundaries.

Nowhere is this reinscription of racial boundaries made more acute than in the *Brown v. Board* ruling of 1954, which gave rise to fears that racial parameters were increasingly permeable. Although many schools would remain segregated for another ten years, the highly publicized 1954 ruling fueled concerns that black America would be assimilated into white America, illustrated by a newly wrought Cold War rhetoric. While Cold War critics have usually attributed the pervasive fear of what Andrew Ross terms "germophobia" to the threat of communism and homosexuality, there were increasing concerns, as James F. Davis has noted, "perhaps paranoid is not too strong a term—about the specter of 'invisible blackness.'"[147] Davis has noted the ways in which "[m]uch of the rhetoric advanced in the 1950s and 1960s against desegregating the public schools and other public facilities featured the assertion that racial integration would destroy the purity of the races."[148] Robert Patterson, a founder of the first White Citizens Council, opposed what he saw as the "dark cloud of integration," objecting to what he described as "the Communist theme of all races and mongrelization," pledging that "we will defeat this communistic disease that is being thrust upon us."[149]

In March 1956, the year that *Giovanni's Room* was published, ninety-six southern congressmen (every congressman from the Old Confederacy's eleven states and every southern senator except three) pledged to overturn the recently desegregated education system, protesting in an open letter to the *New York Times*.[150] Thomas Brady, a well-known southern judge, warned that the desegregation of schools would lead to "the tragedy of miscegenation."[151] Like William Faulkner, who famously predicted that "the Negro race will vanish by intermarriage," adding that "if it came to fighting, I'd fight for Mississippi against the United States even if it meant going out into the streets and shooting Negroes," Brady pledged to die for the principles of racial purity.[152] Although Brady's and Faulkner's views on integration were clearly extreme, it is important to realize that they were by no means isolated. As Leerom Medovoi has posited, even liberal whites could only accept integration in schools "through the piecemeal admission and assimilation of non-whites who could then be brought to cross-identify racially with the primarily white and white-staffed schools."[153] Integration, as Medovoi notes, was perceived as "the collapse of the racial order," fueling concerns that whiteness would be indistinguishable from blackness, rendering permeable racial boundaries that hitherto had been sharply delineated.[154]

The mid-1950s in America witnessed a sharp redrawing of racial boundaries, illustrated most acutely by a resurgence of the Ku Klux Klan after the *Brown v. Board* decision.[155] Crucially, domestic racial concerns over miscegenation were increasingly linked to wider anxieties about the spread of communism, acutely illustrated by Albert Canwell, chair of the Washington State Legislative Fact-Finding Committee on Un-American Activities. "If someone insists that there is discrimination against Negroes in this country," Canwell declared, "there is every reason to believe that person is a Communist."[156] By linking racial progress to the geopolitical threat of communism, integration moved from being a southern to a national concern. As Benjamin Muse noted in his study of integration after 1954, "[f]ear stimulated opposition to desegregation most stubbornly on two counts: fear of Communism, with which the crusade for Negro rights was believed to be somehow related; and a horror of racial amalgamation."[157] The links between communist and African American organizations such as the NAACP were widespread; not only was there a wide belief that the *Brown v. Board* decision was a "communist plot," but, as a 1956 FBI report "revealed," there was a "'tremendous' Communist presence among the State's Negro leadership."[158]

The "horror of racial amalgamation" was illustrated most violently in the South through a resurgence of lynching, most famously in the murder of the fourteen-year-old Emmett Till in 1955 and the lynching of Mack Parker in 1959. In 1957 Ku Klux Klansmen from Birmingham castrated African American war veteran Edward Aaron, calling out the name of the Supreme Court chief justice as they tortured him: "Look here, nigger! You ever heard of a nigger-loving Communist named Earl Warren?"[159] While interracial sex remained the primary cause of anxiety, the fear of integration moved beyond concerns that whites and blacks would mingle, to a more general concern that black American culture would miscegenate or pollute (white) America. Although the influence of African American culture was most evident in the growing popularity of black-influenced rock and roll, debates about assimilation and integration dominated numerous cultural practices, not least in the boundaries of "American" and "African American" literature.

Giovanni's Room: Passing as a Cold War Novel

Some day, Dr. Lancaster was saying, perhaps a Negro writer will write a novel about white people.

—CARL VAN VECHTEN, *NIGGER HEAVEN*

The success of Ralph Ellison's *Invisible Man* in 1952 arguably drew attention away from the precarious state of black American fiction. In the early 1950s, Gwendolyn Brooks and Langston Hughes were the only black American authors who held contracts with high-profile publishers.[160] What is more, there were fiercely disputed arguments about the direction of the African American novel—and, in particular, how to reinvigorate a black literary tradition, a debate to which the young Baldwin was attuned. In 1947, for example, as Baldwin's career was taking off, the professor and critic John S. Lash published several articles on the state of black American fiction, including "What Is 'Negro Literature?'" and "On Negro Literature."[161] According to Lawrence Jackson, "Baldwin's earliest years as a critic tended to reinforce a politics that wanted blacks to live up to a whiteness that it was proposed they could never be without," adding that Baldwin's message was "that though African Americans looked black, they were really white."[162] As I suggest in the final chapter—where I return to *Giovanni's Room*—Jackson's comments are overreaching, glossing over Baldwin's developing political aesthetic, which called into question the category of whiteness, rather than eliding black and white identities. Baldwin's reviews of the late 1940s did not often focus on race, and those that did in fact pointed out that the race question "is merely growing more complex."[163]

Baldwin's second novel, which has historically occupied an uneasy place in the black American canon, fed directly into arguments about the tradition and direction of the African American novel. According to Arthur Davis in a 1956 *Phylon* article, "Integration and Race Literature," the shifts in racial politics had a detrimental effect on black American writing. Davis argued that "[i]t has forced the Negro creative artist to play down his most cherished tradition," what Jackson describes as "the style of writing, elegant or vitriolic, that wailed against racial conditions."[164] In a 1957 essay titled "The Literature of the Negro in the United States," Richard Wright predicted that, as "the Negro merges into the main stream of American life, there might result actually a disappearance of Negro literature as such."[165] As America achieved more social equality, Wright believed that African American literature would become less "racial," resulting in "a merging of Negro expression with American expression."[166] And yet such a merging of black and white fiction was not always straightforward. In the case of Frank Yerby, the best-selling author of historical novels, his decision to populate his fiction with white characters was strategic. As Jackson points out in a persuasive reading of his work, "[t]he conservative wisdom held that black writers could not make a career of writing books with black characters and selling them to white audiences."[167]

Baldwin's decision to write a "white" novel cannot be reduced to pressing arguments regarding integration and assimilation.[168] To do so would be to ignore the complex entanglement of race and sexuality that Baldwin would have faced with the inclusion of black characters, something he later acknowledged "would have been quite beyond . . . [his] powers" in 1956.[169] And yet Baldwin's postwar writing—and, in particular, *Giovanni's Room*—feeds directly into debates about the policy of assimilation and anxiety over "raceless" novels. According to Arnold Rampersad, Langston Hughes "linked what he saw as Baldwin's excesses to the trend of integration sapping the strength of black youth." In a letter to Arna Bontemps, Hughes warned that "[i]ntegration is going to RUIN Negro business—as it is apparently threatening to ruin the finest young writer of fiction [Baldwin] in the race."[170] Like Hughes, Addison Gayle in a discussion of Baldwin's essay "Stranger in the Village," complained of the "tone of assimilation, the obsession with fusing the black and white cultures," accusing Baldwin of "obliterating racial characteristics altogether."[171] For writers including Wright, Chester Himes, and Albert Murray, there was a consensus that "Baldwin was understood to have abandoned his racial heritage," troubling critics like J. Saunders Redding with "his apparently casual disdain toward the idea of a tradition of African-American literature."[172]

Criticism of Baldwin's fusion of white and black culture can be traced to his essays of the 1950s. In *Notes of a Native Son* Baldwin frequently switches register, so that it is difficult to place the authorial voice. For example, in "Many Thousands Gone," Baldwin's racial identity becomes textually ambiguous as he aligns himself with the (white) authorial voice:

> Up to today *we* are set at a division, so that *he* may not marry *our* daughters or *our* sisters, nor may *he*—for the most part—eat at *our* tables or live in *our* houses. Moreover, those who do, do so at the grave expense of a double alienation: from *their* own people, whose fabled attributes *they* must deny.[173]

The passage begins with a "we" that is at first ambiguous: it is not clear whether Baldwin refers to "we" African Americans, "we" white Americans, or a collective "we." It soon becomes clear that the "he" is the African American male subject, objectified from a dominant (white) position. In the next sentence Baldwin collapses these divisions, where "*their* own people," becomes a shared possessive adjective.

Baldwin's use of racially interchanging pronouns infuriated and bemused a number of black and white critics alike.[174] Langston Hughes, for example, bemoaned that "Baldwin's viewpoints are half-American, half-Afro-American, incompletely fused."[175] Hughes's suggestion that Baldwin's writing is somehow bastardized—neither authentically white nor black—is most acutely illustrated in the writing of the white critic, Robert Bone, in his survey of African American literature, *The Negro Novel in America*, first published in 1958. In his chapter on Baldwin, Bone's writing demonstrates profound anxieties about the ways in which *Giovanni's Room* and other "raceless" novels merge dangerously with the body of "white" American literature.

Whereas Bone lauds Baldwin's first novel, *Go Tell It on the Mountain*, for capturing "the essence of Negro experience in America," he lambastes *Giovanni's Room*, criticizing the novel's sketchiness, describing it as though it were a dismembered and deteriorating body: "The characters," writes Bone, "are vague and disembodied, the themes half-digested, the colors rather bleached than vivified. We recognize in this sterile psychic landscape the unprocessed raw material of art."[176] Although Bone's language—such as the word "sterile"—suggests a not fully articulated homophobic response, his comment that the characters are bleached rather than vivified holds the key to Bone's unease. It is rather that, for Bone, the characters are really African American, made white for the purpose of Baldwin's novel, compounded by his view that Baldwin "simply transposes the moral topography of Harlem to the streets of Paris."[177]

Bone's mistrust of *Giovanni's Room* is illuminated by his broader examination of African American literature in relation to the wider debates over assimilation and integration. For Bone, literature is the expression of experience, something that is governed by cultural and racial backgrounds:

> In choosing an appropriate vehicle for his theme, the author's first consideration must be familiarity with surface detail. . . . Every artist apprehends reality through a specific culture. Why should the Negro novelist imagine that he alone is exempt from the limitations of time and place?[178]

Bone's role as literary immigration officer is deeply problematic, not least because there is no discussion of white portrayals of black American culture. For Bone, an authentic African American literature—and the term "authentic" is one that Bone employs—is one that reflects what he calls "a Negro quality in his experience," what he elsewhere refers to as the "fidelity to his deepest experience."[179] In contrast to "authentic" black American literature, Bone claims that "raceless" or "assimilationist" novels are not only largely "extra-literary," but they are "truncated, rootless and artificial."[180]

Importantly, Bone explicitly acknowledges the relationship between "raceless" literature and the growing move toward assimilation, a fact that he fiercely contests.[181] Rather than reflecting the African American's acceptance into mainstream American culture, Bone argues that assimilation is "a means of escape . . . a denial of one's racial identity." For Bone, the "assimilationist novel" illustrates "the loss of contact with the realities of Negro life." This, Bone concludes, "amounts . . . to a kind of literary 'passing,'" what he also refers to as "a kind of psychological 'passing' at the fantasy level."[182]

Bone's pejorative use of the words "fantasy" and "passing" raises several important points that are central to a discussion of *Giovanni's Room* and Baldwin's earlier essays. By equating fantasy with (unwanted) assimilation, Bone acknowledges the ways in which fantasy can disturb the "racial order" of a racially divided literature. In other words, "raceless" novels, such as *Giovanni's Room*, threaten the stability of racial parameters, what Bone refers explicitly to as "walls."[183] By equating "raceless" novels with "passing," Bone also points to the ways in which *Giovanni's Room* upsets the boundaries that he is so adamant to defend. As Elaine Ginsberg has cogently argued:

> [W]hen "race" is no longer visible, it is no longer intelligible: if "white" can be "black," what is white? Race passing thus not only creates, to use Garber's term, a *category crisis* but also destabilizes the grounds of privilege founded on racial identity.[184]

Ginsberg points to the ways in which *Giovanni's Room* problematizes the very categories of black and white literature, something that numerous critics have explored by decoding a racialized—and, in particular, African American—character in Baldwin's second novel. The references to Joey, David's first lover,

as "quick and dark," "brown" with "dark eyes" and "curly hair," have prompted
some critics to contend that Joey's darkness represents the position of a black
gay lover, or to argue that "the question of blackness, precisely because of its
apparent absence, screams out at the turn of every page."[185] I want to argue
rather that Baldwin deliberately teases the reader, disturbing the "purity" and
"authenticity" of his "white" text through suggestion. But, by portraying a
character whose homosexuality is not visible—a character who is able to pass
in both the straight and gay worlds—Baldwin also questioned the prevailing
notion that sexuality could be readily identified by those attempting to scrutinize and categorize sexual differences.

Although I have focused on Bone at some length, most criticism of the
1950s was too appalled by the homosexual subject matter to address the novel's absence of black characters. While a handful of reviewers commended
Baldwin's sensitive treatment of homosexuality, the praise was largely
drowned out by criticism that praised the novel's style, while dismissing its
content. Charles Rolo, typical of many reviewers, begins by lauding Baldwin
as a writer "endowed with exceptional narrative skill, poetic intensity of feeling, and a sensitive command of language." But, Rolo quickly adds—in a curiously gustatory rhetoric—"[t]his endorsement is made despite the fact that
Mr. Baldwin's subject is one which I have had my fill."[186] The refusal of critics
to engage seriously with the theme of homosexuality is indicative of the prevailing attitudes to dissident sexualities, particularly in the ways that left-
wing politics during the 1950s undermined (or "contained") the political
relevance of same-sex desire. As Robert Corber has noted in his analysis of
homosexuality during the Cold War, "even supposedly progressive critics"
such as Leslie Fiedler deflected the political significance of gay male writing,
challenging its claim for a gay male identity.[187] In his review of Giovanni's
Room, for example (which I return to), Fiedler deflects the significance of the
homosexual plot, stating that "it is a basic American plot—a staple of popular
fiction." Baldwin's decision to cast Giovanni as homosexual, Fiedler contends,
is little more than a "gimmick," a substitution of "the poor but worthy girl
[for] a poor but worthy fairy."[188]

Although Fiedler is well known for espousing the centrality of homoeroticism in American literature (most notably in his 1948 essay "Come Back to
the Raft Ag'in, Huck Honey!"), critics such as Robyn Wiegman have noted
how his figuration of homosexuality (which, by 1960 he changed to "homoeroticism"), in fact cast "homosexuality as the immaturity of arrested sexual
development."[189] In "Come Back to the Raft," as Corber points out, Fiedler's
reading of The City and the Pillar, like his reading of Giovanni's Room, refused
to distinguish Vidal's novel from the mainstream of American fiction; rather,
as Corber notes, Fiedler saw "its focus on gay male experience [as] business as
usual because it supposedly conformed to the repressed and sentimentalizing
homoerotic character of American literature."[190]

The connection between *Giovanni's Room* and *The City and the Pillar* was made explicit by Baldwin's publishers. Readers at Knopf referred to the homosexual scenes in *Giovanni's Room* as "repugnant," while William Cole, in a wonderful double entendre, concluded that "[i]t was judged not the time for an out-and-out homosexual novel. There had only been Gore Vidal's."[191] Knopf's comparison with *The City and the Pillar* indicates both the boldness of *Giovanni's Room* and also similarities between the two novels that go far beyond the theme of homosexuality. Prefacing a revised edition of *The City and the Pillar*, Vidal talks explicitly of how he wanted to shatter the stereotype of homosexuals as "shrieking queens or lonely bookish boys." Instead, Vidal recalls how his "two lovers were athletes and so . . . entirely masculine that the feminine was simply irrelevant to their passion."[192] Like Vidal's protagonist, Baldwin's David is blonde and athletic (there are references to his footballing past), and like Jim Willard, David is contrasted with the negative depiction of an effeminate homosexual underworld.

The indistinguishable homosexuality of both David and Jim Willard suggests ways in which both Vidal and Baldwin were pointing toward the "naturalness" of a homosexual identity, one not defined in opposition to a dominant definition of masculinity, a point that Baldwin had made earlier in his 1949 article "Preservation of Innocence."[193] The decision of Baldwin and Vidal to cast their heroes as strong, athletic, and masculine challenged the assumptions not only that homosexuality was easily recognizable but also that masculinity was incompatible with homosexuality. But, crucially, the ability of both protagonists to "pass" as straight fed into increasing anxieties over the policing of sexual boundaries.

As various cultural critics including John D'Emilio and Estelle Freedman have noted, the postwar period in America simultaneously saw a relaxing and a tightening of sexual boundaries.[194] Nowhere was this confusing blend of sexual permissiveness and restraint more acute than in the treatment of homosexuality. The publication of Alfred Kinsey's reports on male and female sexual behavior in 1948 and 1953, respectively, shattered pervasive conceptions of sexual practice.[195] *Sexual Behavior in the Human Male* catapulted the private sexual experiences of American men into the public arena. Top of the bestseller lists in the *New York Times* for over six months, Kinsey revealed that "a considerable portion of the population, perhaps the major portion of the male population, has at least some homosexual experience between adolescence and old age."[196]

The impact of Kinsey's report was far-reaching enough to precipitate over two hundred studies on sexuality between 1948 and 1949.[197] Although Kinsey had set out to show that punishment for homosexuality was irrational and illogical, his report in fact contributed to a national homosexual panic. Crucially, Kinsey dismissed early reports that had attempted to register the degree of male and female characteristics in homosexual men and women.

Repudiating the myths that gay people could be identified by their "[f]ine skins, high-pitched voices, [and] obvious hand movements," Kinsey insisted that homosexuals could "pass" as straight, indistinguishable in appearance from heterosexual men.[198]

The increasing number of arrests for homosexuality in the 1950s points to the ways in which deviant sexuality became associated with threats to the nation's security.[199] During the hearings of the House Un-American Activities Commission in the 1940s and 1950s, the committee extended its investigations, not only to fears of communist infiltration, but, as Corber has noted, to "homosexuals and lesbians who 'passed' as heterosexual."[200] Following claims that several homosexuals had been dismissed in 1950 from the State Department, Senator Joseph McCarthy ordered a Senate inquiry into same-sex behavior, which concluded that there were "no outward characteristics or physical traits" to positively identify homosexuals and lesbians. Effeminate men and masculine women, the medical report concluded, were not necessarily homosexual.[201]

As is well documented, the report's findings were interpreted to argue that homosexuals did indeed constitute a security risk. In attempting to show that homosexuals and lesbians "be considered as proper cases for medical and psychiatric treatment," the official conclusion was that, since homosexuals were emotionally unstable, they were vulnerable to "the blandishments of the foreign espionage agent."[202] The perceived threat of homosexuality to national security resulted in the dismissal of thousands of suspected "sexual deviants." In fact, more men and women were fired from government offices under the suspicion of homosexual practice than for alleged communist connections.[203]

The complicated connections between communism, homosexuality, and miscegenation are further grouped by a prevailing rhetoric of contamination. The Senate's report, *Employment of Homosexuals and Other Sex Perverts in Government*, for example, warned that one homosexual "can pollute a Government office," echoing fears that the "red disease" could infect the American body politic or that integration would lead to the miscegenation of American life. Accompanying pervasive pollution metaphors was the concern that homosexuals, like communists, might not be identified, resulting, as Elaine Tyler May has shown, in the scrutiny of employees' sexual behavior, whether in private industry, the army, or government.[204]

The correlation between homosexual "passing" and communism was made explicit by Arthur Schlesinger, who, in his attempts to show the secrecy and conspiracy of the American Communist Party, compared the dissenters to participants of gay male subculture. According to Schlesinger, communists communicated to one another by recognizing certain signals in an analogy that explicitly drew on gay cruising, which, as George Chauncey has shown, was communicated in an articulate form of "codes of dress, speech and style."[205] Communists, Schlesinger insisted, could "identify each other (and be identified by their enemies) on casual meeting by the use of certain phrases, the names of certain friends . . . and certain silences," paralleling Vidal's description of cruising as "a quick glance . . . a form of freemasonry."[206] Similarly, in *Giovanni's Room*, concerned that people are taking bets on his sexuality, David is aware of being watched by *le milieu*, "in order to discover, by means of signs I made but which only they could read, whether or not I had a true vocation."[207]

Schlesinger's correlation between communism and homosexuality—and, in particular, the inability to identify subversive activity—points to a larger Cold War concern with the policing of racial, sexual, and political boundaries that Baldwin's second novel feeds into. At the root of these anxieties is the fear that boundaries are porous, that communists, homosexuals, or African Americans can "pass," assimilating without detection into American culture, a point made explicit by Leslie Fiedler's review of *Giovanni's Room*:

> [T]here are not even any Negroes—and this, I must confess, makes me a little uneasy. . . . It is rather the fact that he [David] encounters no black faces in his movements through Paris and the south of France, that not even the supernumeraries are colored; so that one begins to suspect at last that there must *really* be Negroes present, censored, camouflaged or encoded.[208]

Fiedler's rhetoric of suspicion—"censored, camouflaged or encoded"—calls to attention the policing and surveillance of Cold War America: a fear of spying, infiltration, and contamination that I pick up on in the following chapter where I examine Baldwin's FBI files. For Fiedler, *Giovanni's Room* only appears to have an all-white cast, but he continues to probe the text, using a language that becomes increasingly illogical and confused. How can black characters be both present and censored? Censored by whom? Does he mean that Baldwin's protagonists are really black, camouflaged by their white personas?

Fiedler's review implicitly suggests that Baldwin—as an African American—must leave a trace of his ethnicity in the white world that he describes.[209] And, like the eponymous sleuth in Twain's *Pudd'nhead Wilson*, the detective-critic can scrutinize literary fingerprints to reveal an author's racial identity. But Fiedler's anxiety also stems from his inability to locate firm racial boundaries. By insisting that there must be "camouflaged" black characters that he cannot locate, Fiedler suggests that Baldwin's scopically white (but racially "black") characters have "passed." Like Fanon, who writes of how the Jew "can *sometimes* go unnoticed," or Freud's observation that people of mixed race "resemble white people, but . . . betray their colored descent by some striking feature or other," Fiedler struggles to locate a gesture or feature that will betray the characters' "real" blackness.[210]

Fiedler's anxieties about the lack of visible black characters in *Giovanni's Room* articulate the ways in which the novel has been viewed as a hybridized or bastardized narrative, charges that were often leveled at Baldwin's genre-defying writing. Neither wholly white nor wholly black, *Giovanni's Room* underscores the ways in which the African American canon has been constructed around works that demonstrate racial authenticity. As a novel that remains on the peripheries of the African American canon, *Giovanni's Room* is also a sharp reminder of the ways in which Baldwin resisted dominant Cold War categories of black and white, gay and straight, loyalty and disloyalty. Moreover, his explorations of the key Cold War themes in his second novel can be read as part of his political trajectory from his early years rubbing shoulders with the New York Intellectuals. Although Baldwin distanced himself from formal political engagement, and while his intellectual home became Paris, not New York, his first decade as a writer merits rethinking about his contribution to, and analysis of, leftist American culture. As I explore in the following chapter, Baldwin's repeated criticism of postwar American politics and ideology—and his involvement with civil rights—meant that he was featured prominently in the Federal Bureau of Investigation's files on writers. Like his second novel, Baldwin was increasingly viewed as "Un-American," at some considerable cost, inviting a closer look at his role as a disturber of the peace.

{ Chapter 2 }

Radical Baldwin and the FBI:
From the Civil Rights Movement to Black Power

Click onto the Federal Bureau of Investigation website and you will find a wealth of information.[1] Glance at the banners on the left-hand side of the homepage and you will find all manner of useful and friendly services: fun activities for schoolchildren who can "Help Bobby Bureau Go Undercover," plus helpful advice for researchers and a smiling African American male above an announcement for jobs at the Bureau. There is an intriguing online history of the FBI that debunks the "top ten myths of the FBI": there is actually no X-Files team, but there were in fact minority agents working for the Bureau's long-serving director, J. Edgar Hoover. Delve into the archives of the "Electronic Reading Room" and you will find files arranged under topics such as "Espionage," "Famous Persons," "Gangster Era," and "Unusual Phenomena."

The near Disneyfication of the FBI results in a confusing message: There is information on current activity—such as lists of the most wanted and information on terrorism—but this serious work is muted by the tone of openness, couched in a visual and verbal rhetoric that suggests viewers are entering the virtual theme park of a friendly public service. Duck under the radar of friendly banter—"What do Jackie Kennedy, the Beatles, Albert Einstein, Gracie Allen, Thurgood Marshall, and Walter Winchell have in common? Give up?"—and you will find surprising and at times sinister examples of surveillance, exemplified by the voluminous files on civil rights leaders, including 4,065 pages on Malcolm X and 16,659 pages on Martin Luther King Jr.[2] Look a little further and you will find a 1,884-page file: that of James Arthur Baldwin.

Toward the end of Baldwin's FBI file—active between 1960 and 1974—there is an intriguing memorandum written on April 18, 1972, from the New York office that states that "although formerly an advocate of Black Power movements in the US, he has not been over the past year engaged in black extremist activities" (FBI Files, 1595).[3] Satisfied that Baldwin had retired from radical politics, the FBI downgraded the writer to "Category III of the ADEX" (Administrative Index), a list of US citizens whom the Bureau considered a threat to national security. In an addendum, however, placed directly underneath the file, an unnamed source questions the judgment of the New York office on this matter. Not only has Baldwin "been connected with several Communist Party front groups," the agent writes, but he has supported subversive causes. By way of conclusion, the notes end with the following reason for keeping Baldwin in Category IV of the ADEX: "It is believed that the subject, *due to his position as an author*, is likely to furnish aid or other assistance to revolutionary elements because of his sympathy and/or ideology" (1595, emphasis added).

The Bureau's emphasis on Baldwin's role as a writer—with the corollary that an author is, by default, radical—says much about the FBI's concerns that authors posed a significant threat to the stability of the social order during the radical period of the 1960s and early 1970s. As Natalie Robins has documented, the Bureau's long-serving director, J. Edgar Hoover, remained convinced that writers could become "Communist thought-control relay stations," because "they were more susceptible to radical propaganda than ordinary people, and more adept at communicating ideas."[4] Robins's thorough study, *Alien Ink: The FBI's War on the Freedom of Expression*, shows the extent of the Bureau's monitoring of writers from Truman Capote (110 pages), John Steinbeck (94 pages), Henry Miller (9 pages), and Richard Wright (276 pages).[5] Given this range of surveillance on noted authors, Baldwin's file seems particularly long.

The decision not to downgrade Baldwin's security status in 1972 seems surprising, particularly given the writer's relatively quiet output. What is more, by 1971, the FBI had achieved its goal of subduing black radical organizations through "the use of harassment arrests, imprisonment, murder and undercover agent influence."[6] Baldwin's last novel of the 1960s, *Tell Me How Long the Train's Been Gone* (1968), in fact explored the fraught relationship between the artist and activist in revolutionary times, a theme he returned to again in 1972 with his extended essay *No Name in the Street*. The extent of Baldwin's FBI file, which is five times larger than Richard Wright's, however, raises important questions, both about Baldwin's political activity and the reasons why the Bureau continued to monitor a writer, who, though a self-confessed "disturber of the peace" hardly constituted a national security risk.[7]

By analyzing Baldwin's files, I contend that several crucial pictures emerge. First, the files call attention to the extent of Baldwin's political activity. While biographers have previously noted the author's involvement with civil rights organizations, the files add considerable detail to these accounts, shedding light on the extent of Baldwin's energy and commitment to a wide range of political activity, particularly as the FBI files were declassified after the publication of David Leeming's and James Campbell's biographies.[8] While there are many factual errors contained in the FBI's reports, the numerous newspaper clippings and copies of Baldwin's letters to publications such as *Freedomways*, a prominent civil rights journal, constitute the closest thing we have to a political biography of the writer.

As Gary Edward Holcomb observes about the FBI files of the Jamaican writer Claude McKay (whom the FBI was convinced was a Communist sympathizer) "even bearing in mind its sometimes laughable manifestation of the banality of evil," the files are "in some ways a more reliable representation of his life during the 1920s than his own 1930s autobiography."[9] In the case of Baldwin, who claimed allegiance with no organization but supported many, the files produced a significantly fuller picture of the writer's political contributions. Furthermore, a close reading of Baldwin's files has the secondary but important function of shedding light on why the Bureau gathered so much information on African American writers during the 1960s and 1970s. As William J. Maxwell has documented, Hoover "fostered an intimate relationship between state surveillance and African American literary experimentation from the birth of the Harlem Renaissance . . . to the height of the Black Arts Movement," underscored by FBI files that were opened on writers including Lorraine Hansberry, Langston Hughes, and Amiri Baraka.[10] Additionally, since Hoover believed that the files would never be declassified, the handwritten notes that he and others added to the files also tell us much about the FBI's attitudes toward "un-American" behavior, particularly in the case of Baldwin, a high-profile African American who was increasingly unable to safeguard the "private life" that he cherished.[11] In a broader context, a close reading of Baldwin's files contributes to an understanding of the FBI's Counter Intelligence Program (COINTELPRO), which sought to infiltrate and disrupt civil rights and socialist organizations, what Noam Chomsky has described as "a systematic and extensive program of terror, disruption, intimidation and instigation of violence, initiated under the most liberal Democratic administrations and carried further under Nixon."[12]

Before charting the history of Baldwin's FBI record, it is important to clarify what a file actually is. According to Natalie Robins:

> At the point at which the documents reach anyone who has solicited them under the Freedom of Information Act, a dossier consists of separate pages of investigative reports, legal forms, interviews, memorandums, petitions, letters, articles and news clippings that have been collected and clipped together in one folder by the Federal Bureau of Investigation.[13]

Baldwin's files are presented in an approximately chronological order and offer an eclectic mix of media in what resembles a biographer's chaotic attempt to map out his or her subject. According to James Lesar, a tireless crusader for the Freedom of Information Act, Baldwin's files "were not compiled for law enforcement purposes"; instead they were "a compendium of every piece of gossip that the FBI picked up through wiretaps and other sources that relate to Baldwin," a description that strongly echoes Max Lowenthal's 1950 exposé of the FBI, *The Federal Bureau of Investigation*, where he highlighted the network of "rumors, suspicion and gossip."[14] Although Madonna may feel that she was the first celebrity to suffer at the hands of snooping paparazzi and fans rummaging through her trash, there are instances of agents (or informants) rooting through garbage bins to find evidence of Baldwin's subversive activity. One "reliable informant" reports finding Baldwin's return address on an envelope to the *China Daily News* (FBI Files, 503), a paper founded in 1940 by Chinese communists, while another report notes that the writer "received a copy of *Worker's World*," an East Coast communist publication (FBI Files, 187), supporting Robins's conclusion that most writers "were watched because of *what they thought*" rather than what they did.[15] While it may be of mild interest to know that Baldwin's application for a Diner's Club Card was rejected in 1961, it is at times hard to understand what the Bureau was trying to do (FBI Files, 190).

The Bureau's findings are a mixture of sinister surveillance and glorious incompetence, a wider characteristic of many FBI files. According to Nelson Blackstock, with reference to the COINTELPRO papers, the "files reveal some stupid FBI blunders and misestimates. The total picture, however, is of cool, calculating technicians, not crazed paranoids, going about the business of secretly combating people who are challenging the rule of the rich."[16] Although many critics conclude that the power of Baldwin's prose had dwindled by the early 1960s, it soars with piercing brilliance in comparison to some of the grammatically challenged reports. In the write-up of the meeting on June 2, 1961, on "Nationalism, Colonialism, and the United States: One Minute to Twelve," for example, the informant begins with a wonderful Freudian slip, where "Nationalism" becomes "Nationislam." "Mr. Baldwin," the informant notes, had been living in "Paris, Frances" [*sic*], recording how he "realyy [*sic*] capivtated [*sic*] the audience with his frech [*sic*] accent and the courageiousness [*sic*] of his message" (FBI Files, 29). Glancing through the files it becomes evident that Baldwin's phone was tapped on numerous occasions. He was also followed on his travels to France, Italy, and Great Britain by agents or informants posing as publishers or car salesmen (FBI Files, 891).

Despite the relentless surveillance that Baldwin endured, the Bureau's findings are remarkable for their basic mistakes, which raise important questions about the competency of the FBI's intelligence gathering at a time of international and domestic unrest. Baldwin's date of birth is frequently incorrect and one report notes that they cannot find a record of his birth, perhaps because the Bureau had not established that the author was born James Jones.[17] Baldwin the "Boston-novelist" (FBI Files, 1010) is described early on as "white, early 20s, 6', neat," a description so far removed from the writer that it must surely be in code (FBI Files, 26). Baldwin is listed as the author of *Go Tell It to the Mountain* (FBI Files, 51) and *Another World* (FBI Files, 1505), and another file reports on how he spoke about his "boyhood in the South" (FBI Files, 60). In 1968 when Baldwin was at the height of his fame, reports fly back and forth claiming the author's sister, Paula, was his wife (FBI Files, 698). Other reports are so vague that they beg the question of what FBI training these agents or informants undertook. In a report on the black American actor Otis Young, his height is "not known"; he is described as "lighter than average," with an age of 36 ("probably older"). More worryingly, the author of the report seems wrong-footed in his or her attempts to describe Otis Young's ethnicity. Young is also described as "dark—not VERY dark for a negro but darker than medium," adding that his speech "sounded like a negro, but not someone from the deep south" (FBI Files, 1684).

The description of Otis Young tells us much about the Bureau in the 1960s, particularly the assumed complicity between writer and reader of the report, which was not surprising given the paucity of black FBI agents in the 1960s. There is an approximate—but presumably ingrained—Bureau notion of what an African American sounds like and what an average complexion constitutes, as well as a conflation of black Americans with the South, with the implicit understanding that an accent would be measured in relation to the "authentic" timbre of the South.

Despite the Bureau's careful monitoring of individual subjects, Baldwin's files illustrate the ways in which the FBI in fact often overlooked the specific details of those under investigation, resorting instead to generalizations about how a homosexual, communist, or African American was expected to behave. In Baldwin's case, it was enough for the Bureau to conclude that he was linked to the Communist Party through association. In 1961 Baldwin signed a petition on behalf of the Carl Braden Clemency Appeal Committee. Although it is unlikely Baldwin knew or cared that Braden was a member of the Communist Party, Baldwin was wrongly marked down as a communist because of his signature on this petition.[18] The Bureau kept detailed records of Baldwin's political activities, including newspaper articles and interviews, fund-raising events that he attended or spoke at, and petitions or letters that he signed. Given the scrutiny of his activities, it is surprising that there is no mention of his self-confessed Trotskyite past or a suspicion that his early publications in leftist magazines might have indicated an active left-wing mind.

Before looking more closely at the Bureau's reasons for monitoring Baldwin, it is important to get a sense of the FBI's wider surveillance of African American writers and their political activity more broadly, particularly the ways in which Hoover and his team repeatedly connected civil rights activism with communist activity. As Robins has shown, Hoover's FBI "sought to pin a Red label on anyone who demanded equal rights for blacks, and all politically active blacks were considered security threats."[19] Although Hoover opened more files on writers, editors, and publishers during the 1960s than any other period (over 250), Baldwin's position as a high-profile, politically informed African American writer no doubt contributed to the level of his surveillance. Historians, including Robins and Kenneth O'Reilly, concur that Hoover, in the latter's words "had always been a racist" and most critics agree that the Bureau's director imposed a vision of conservative, white Christian America that treated any deviation as scurrilous and deviant.[20]

As a number of scholars have documented, the FBI sought to "ridicule and discredit" civil rights activists.[21] As early as 1942, Hoover had set up a thorough investigation of racial conditions (RACON), insisting that African Americans were "seeking to exploit 'the disloyal and malcontent'" in the United States by disrupting the war effort.[22] As far as the FBI was concerned, the early civil rights movement was "simply a Communist plot."[23] As Nelson Blackstock notes, "One of the things that comes through clearest in the Cointelpro papers is that the FBI reserved a special hatred for the Black civil rights movement, and black members of the SWP [Social Workers' Party] were singled out for special attention."[24] During his close monitoring of civil rights groups, Hoover frequently exaggerated the extent of Communist Party involvement in groups such as the National Association for the Advancement of Colored People (NAACP). In the case of Mary McLeod Bethune, for example, a former director of Negro Affairs for the National Youth Administration and prominent civil rights activist, Hoover "exposed" her as a Stalinist in order "to link a consensus opinion (that communists posed a serious threat to American institutions and values) with a more problematic one (that civil rights advocates posed an equally serious threat to those same institutions and values)."[25]

The FBI formed COINTELPROs against some African Americans between 1960 and 1971, although it is likely that there were similar strategic programs in the 1950s. Baldwin, for example, was targeted in 1964 as part of an operation known as the "Disruption Program Aimed at the Socialist Workers Party."[26] By 1967, a new COINTELPRO initiative was set up to "expose, disrupt, misdirect, discredit, or otherwise neutralize the activities of black nationalist, hate-type organizations or groupings."[27] Not only were there numerous examples of FBI field agents taking notes and pictures as civil rights activists were beaten but the COINTELPRO tactics of the mid- to late 1960s took a new turn as the FBI deliberately stirred up rivalry between civil rights groups that on occasion resulted in bombings and shootings.[28]

As FBI historians have shown, the Bureau targeted well-known political figures, in particular Martin Luther King Jr., Stokely Carmichael, and Malcolm X, figures with whom Baldwin worked closely. As Manning Marable has documented in *Malcolm X: A Life of Reinvention* (2011), "J. Edgar Hoover's animus toward Malcolm X . . . set into motion acts of illegal wiretapping, surveillance, and disruption by law enforcement officers that probably surpassed anything Malcolm would have imagined."[29]

Although the assassinations of Malcolm X and Martin Luther King Jr. have been well documented, a number of other black activists died under mysterious circumstances. Fred Hampton, the young charismatic Black Panther leader, was murdered in his bed. Access to subsequent files reveal that his bodyguard, William O'Neal, worked for the FBI and supplied detailed floor plans of Hampton's house, assisting in what Chomsky has described as the "gestapo-style political assassination" of Hampton and other Panthers.[30] Baldwin worked closely with a number of the Panthers, as well as King and Malcolm X, so it is not surprising that his 1972 long essay, *No Name in the Street* is shot through with moments of despair and sadness. As we will see through an analysis of his voluminous FBI file, Baldwin was frequently monitored and harassed between 1960 and 1972. With typical ebullience, Baldwin was irrepressibly vocal about his opposition to, and suspicion of, Hoover and the FBI, a factor that contributed to his continued surveillance.

Baldwin's FBI Files

Although there is no corresponding record in his files, in *The Devil Finds Work* (1976) Baldwin recollects being accosted by two agents in 1945. Noting that his color had already made him "conspicuous," Baldwin concludes that the FBI "frightened me, and they humiliated me—it was like being spat on, or pissed on, or gang-raped."[31] Baldwin's recollection of the Bureau's violation connects his sexual "perversion" (a word used by the Bureau about Baldwin and his fiction) and his racial identity to the specific ways in which he was scrutinized. This surveillance was orchestrated by Hoover, whom Baldwin describes as "history's most highly paid (and most utterly useless) *voyeur*" a description that reduces the Bureau's monitoring of its subjects to little more than a prurient gaze.[32]

Hoover and his agents first opened a file on Baldwin after he supported the Fair Play for Cuba Committee (FPCC), an organization set up by Vincent T. Lee in 1960 to petition an end to the United States' economic boycott of Cuba. Baldwin's association with the organization was brief. Richard Gibson, an organizer of the FPCC who was acquainted with Baldwin in Paris, recalled that he "tried to get him more deeply involved," adding that Baldwin "always avoided aligning himself politically," which underscores the contradictions in the FBI's surveillance of his political activity.[33] By signing an advertisement that stated the FPCC's aims in the *New York Times* (April 1960), Baldwin had unwittingly alerted the Bureau to his revolutionary potential, opening up an unusually large sequence of files that would run for nearly nineteen hundred pages.

Baldwin in fact makes an earlier appearance in Richard Wright's FBI file. The 1955 report discusses Wright's American Fellowship Group in Paris, a forum ostensibly to sponsor young writers. The informant concluded that the organization was "'leftist' in the nature of its discussions" and noted Baldwin's detachment from Wright and his group:

> According to the informant, Wright and his group were the target of attacks from one James Baldwin, a young Negro writer who was a student in Paris. Baldwin attacked the hatred themes of the [sic] Wright's writings and the attempt of the Franco-American Fellowship Group to Perpetuate "Uncle Tom Literature Methods."[34]

Baldwin, who had been living in Paris since 1948, was not a student and this basic mistake, along with the garbled account of the former's strained relationship with Wright, is typical of the many basic errors found in the files. The informant here has clearly muddled details from Baldwin's 1949 essay "Everybody's Protest Novel," in which he famously dismisses the political and aesthetic impact of the protest novel in a devastating critique of Wright's best-selling 1940 novel, *Native Son*. The informant conflates the protagonist of Wright's novel, Bigger Thomas, with Uncle Tom, the eponymous character in Harriet Beecher Stowe's 1852 bestseller. Furthermore, the misapprehension of "Uncle Tom Literature Methods"—suggesting a new school of Uncle Tom Literature—highlights the Bureau's lack of attention to, or interest in, literary analysis, as well as underscoring their lack of awareness about intra-racial literary debates.

The subsequent entries in Baldwin's FBI files offer a useful overview of his political activities, particularly during the early to mid-1960s as he became a well-known author and celebrity. A week after he appeared on the front cover of *Time* magazine, Baldwin met Robert Kennedy at his New York apartment on May 24, 1963, in a meeting that the *New York Times* described as "evidence of growing concern over criticism voiced by Negroes across the country on its handling of the civil rights issue" and which immediately heightened surveillance on the writer.[35] Baldwin brought along friends, including the actor and activist Harry Belafonte, the playwright Lorraine Hansberry, the psychologist Dr. Kenneth Clark, Martin Luther King Jr.'s lawyer Clarence Jones, and Jerome Smith, a freedom fighter, who had "probably spent more months in jail and been beaten more often than any other CORE [Congress of Racial Equality] member."[36] The meeting as Kenneth Clark recorded in an article in the *New York Post*—a copy of which was duly clipped to Baldwin's file—was not a success. Communication broke down as Kennedy expressed shock at Smith's admission that he could not conceive of fighting for his country and the meeting, in Clark's words, changed from "a dialogue into a diatribe" (FBI Files, 47). Matters got worse when Baldwin reproached Kennedy for alluding to his family's history of oppression as Irish immigrants.

The article in Baldwin's file also notes how the African Americans present "raised questions about the dubious role of the FBI in civil rights cases," something that would no doubt have infuriated the Bureau's director. A later report records Baldwin's statement in the *New York Times* of September 19, 1963, that "I blame J. Edgar Hoover in part for events in Alabama. Negroes have no cause to have faith in the FBI" (FBI Files, 106). After several articles appeared in the press about Baldwin's altercation with Kennedy, Hoover sent Kennedy (who referred to Baldwin as "a nut") dossiers on all those who attended the meeting.[37]

The ill-fated meeting with Kennedy illustrates Baldwin's willingness to get involved in civil rights issues, not just as a writer, but as a participant, or, to use his preferred term, "witness."[38] For Harold Cruse, Baldwin's contribution to the Kennedy meeting was ineffectual, evincing the writer's "intellectual inconsistencies," and his refusal or inability to engage with "sociology and economics jazz."[39] Cruse's harsh assessment of Baldwin may have been right in some ways: Baldwin was more interested in the moral complexity of politics than in the finer details. Yet, Baldwin's activities of the 1960s, as recorded in his FBI files, show the extent to which he offered his services to civil rights organizations, whether donating money, giving speeches, granting interviews, writing articles, or appearing on television. Baldwin had in fact been actively involved in civil rights from as early as 1957 when he visited the South for the first time, an experience he wrote about in "A Fly in Buttermilk" (1958) and "Nobody Knows My Name: A Letter from the South" (1959). In 1960 Baldwin returned to the South at the height of the sit-ins, forging close links with the Student Non-Violent Coordinating Committee (SNCC) and the Congress of Racial Equality (CORE), publishing two further essays: "They Can't Turn Back" (*Mademoiselle*, 1960) and "The Dangerous Road before Martin Luther King" (*Harper's*, 1961). By the summer of 1961, following the publication of *Nobody Knows My Name*, Baldwin emerged as a spokesperson for the civil rights movement, lending his charisma, inimitable rhetorical flourishes, and support to numerous organizations. Baldwin published interviews, letters, and speeches in a wide range of periodicals from *Muhammad Speaks* to the journal *Freedomways: A Quarterly Review of the Negro Freedom Movement*. With the publication of *The Fire Next Time* in 1963, a best-selling book that first appeared in two parts in the *New Yorker*, Baldwin became the most prolific African American writer of the civil rights era.

Baldwin's emerging role in the early 1960s as a high-profile commentator on the civil rights movement no doubt precipitated the number of FBI files on the writer. In 1964, for example, one of the reasons for keeping Baldwin on the Security Index is his "personal involvement in the current civil rights struggle," with the implicit acknowledgment that this involvement is tantamount to civil disobedience. Other reasons include "the inflammatory nature of his writings," and the report reaches the conclusion that any attempts to interview the writer would cause embarrassment to the Bureau, presumably because of Baldwin's "gift for publicity" and ability to use such opportunities to his advantage (FBI Files, 393).[40] Nonetheless, in reading Baldwin's files between 1960 and 1963, it is hard to see why Baldwin's ability to manipulate the media led him to be placed on the "security index" and defined as "a dangerous individual who could be expected to commit acts inimical to the national defense and public safety of the United States in time of an emergency" (FBI Files, 230). Paradoxically, the report notes that "Baldwin is against all forms of violence and shedding of blood" but elsewhere talks of the author's "dangerousness" (308). His observers were perhaps picking up on the shift in the writer's register, which became increasingly embittered as the civil rights movement became bloodier. Baldwin, who had urged his nephew in *The Fire Next Time* to accept white people "and accept them with love," now announced that "many people, even members of my own family . . . would think nothing of picking up arms tomorrow."[41]

Just as Baldwin's files reveal much about the Bureau's attitudes toward the civil rights movement, they also reveal the extent of the author's political commitment. There is a record of Baldwin speaking at the National Lawyers Guild in October 1963 (FBI Files, 132–32), an organization the FBI claims is "a communist front" (FBI Files, 145). More seriously, Baldwin is listed as a sponsor of "a rally to abolish the House un-American Activities Committee" in 1961 (FBI Files, 195). Although there are frequent memos that cite Baldwin's connection with "Communist Influence in Racial Matters," there are no firm reports on Baldwin's "red" credentials. A 1963 report, for example, acknowledges that "[c]onfidential sources familiar with various phases of CP in the New York area were unable to furnish any additional information concerning the subject" (FBI Files, 209). Yet it was enough for the FBI to justify surveillance of Baldwin because he was frequently guilty of associating with communist or suspected communist individuals or publications. He supported the Committee to Aid the Monroe Defendants, a group that the FBI claimed was formed by the Socialist Workers Party and was composed of black and white activists who supported North Carolina NAACP leader Robert Williams's call for citizens to arm themselves against the Ku Klux Klan.[42] Furthermore, according to the FBI, *Freedomways*, which Baldwin supported and wrote for, was "in the hands of a mixed group of Marxists and non-Marxists" (FBI Files, 219). Although the report is vague, the implicit suggestion is that Baldwin was again fraternizing with leftist subversives.

The FBI's interest in Baldwin during the 1960s was fueled by his visible presence, both in the United States and across the globe. Although he did not change his behavior, Baldwin was intensely aware of the Bureau's presence in his life; he complained that he was being bugged by the FBI and recorded that several agents had come to his apartment several days after his meeting with Robert Kennedy.[43] In a letter to President Kennedy's Special Assistant

Kenneth O'Donnell on June 6, 1963, Hoover noted Baldwin's allegation, dismissing it as "without foundation," adding that "we have not conducted any investigation of Baldwin and he has not been harassed in any way by Agents of this Bureau" (FBI Files, 1024). In fact, there are records of Baldwin complaining about the FBI to Clarence Jones, Martin Luther King Jr.'s lawyer, detailing how people have been "'camping on his doorstep' and watching people enter and leave his residence and have even threatened him" (FBI Files, 1040). The irony, of course, is that these complaints were being wiretapped, which was corroborated by Burke Marshall, the assistant attorney-general, who later admitted that FBI agents had visited Baldwin's apartment after his meeting with Kennedy.[44]

The FBI's relentless surveillance of Baldwin clearly affected the writer, though the extent is hard to gauge. Judging by Baldwin's frequent attacks on the Bureau, the FBI clearly infuriated him—both in the ways that they tailed him and in the way that, as Baldwin saw it, Hoover and his agents did little to prevent the iniquities on the civil rights battlefields. As James Campbell notes, Baldwin complained to his old friend Engin Cezzar in the late 1960s that he was being followed relentlessly—although it is unlikely that this is the case. More importantly, as Campbell astutely points out, "[i]n this state of mind, every conversation is at risk of being overheard, even when no one is listening. Friends may appear to act in unfriendly ways . . . and every passer-by taking innocent snapshots is working for the FBI."[45]

The fine line between paranoia and knowledge is illustrated well by Baldwin's appearance on a television program in 1963 made by the US Information Agency (USIA). After requesting a transcript of the program, Clarence Jones noticed that Baldwin's remarks about Hoover and the FBI had been deleted. Baldwin had apparently stated that "part of the problem in the civil rights movement is J. Edgar Hoover," but these remarks were erased (FBI Files, 105). The exchange between Jones and Baldwin about the censored script was wiretapped by the FBI. According to the confidential source, Baldwin had witnesses to back up his expunged comments and Jones wanted to "blow the whistle on this" (FBI Files, 105). Baldwin's comments, though censored, clearly riled the FBI's director who wrote to the director of the Office of Security to find out exactly what had been said: "It will be a matter of attacking, really J. Edgar Hoover," Baldwin stated, "and asking very rude questions such as why the FBI can find a junkie but cannot find a man who bombs the homes of Negro leaders in the Deep South. They still have not found anyone" (FBI Files, 1049).

Baldwin's comments yet again called attention to claims that the Bureau was not invested in supporting participants in the civil rights movement. Hoover's insistence on getting hold of Baldwin's comments—though they were not aired—also highlights another key reason why the author was the target of such sustained vigilance. During the 1960s, in particular, Baldwin was something of a loose cannon when it came to questioning the integrity of the FBI—and, in particular, the Bureau's director. One file notes a 1968 talk where Baldwin announced that "there probably was a CIA or FBI agent in the group attending this party but he didn't care" (FBI Files, 874). For Hoover, to be anti-FBI was tantamount to being pro-communist and, as Natalie Robins notes, "[t]here was a transgression much worse than any political one: this was the crime of criticizing J. Edgar Hoover."[46] William F. Buckley's close relationship with Hoover, for example, quickly deteriorated when the former wrote a spoof article in a 1967 issue of *National Review* where he claimed that the director had resigned after his arrest "on a moral charge"—something that was perhaps too close to home.[47]

Baldwin's expunged comments from the USIA television program only begin to tell the story of his repeated digs at the FBI's director. In his books he described Hoover not only as a "voyeur" but a "terrorist."[48] More seriously, Baldwin repeatedly criticized Hoover in every available media and the Bureau dutifully recorded these indiscretions. There is a memo from December 1963 that records how Baldwin "said that J. Edgar Hoover had warned the Negroes against allowing Communists to get into the civil rights movement" (FBI Files, 253–54) and another that he was "not interested in Hoover's statement that the Negro in his quest for equality should not fight established institutions" (FBI Files, 333). Hoover would no doubt have been interested in the high-profile occasion of Baldwin's remarks: the Annual Bill of Rights Dinner that also featured a talk from "Mr. Bobby Dillon [*sic*], the noted song writer" (FBI Files, 332).

Interest in Baldwin's attacks on the Bureau grew by June 1963 when a "decoded copy" of a teletype revealed a conversation between Stanley Levison and Clarence Jones about Baldwin's plans to embarrass the FBI. Jones is reported to have told Levison that "I have seen some statements on the FBI, but I have never seen one like this. He is going to nail them to the wall" (FBI Files, 1021–22). The reason, Jones states, is because of "the harassment of himself," adding that "[t]his is going to be like an atomic bomb when it is dropped . . . it really will because he is a name in the news" (FBI Files, 1022). Baldwin's alleged statement on the FBI did not occur; instead the Bureau became increasingly paranoid that Baldwin was intending to publish a book about Hoover and the Bureau, details that the author had let slip to journalists. A *Washington Post* article from June 21, 1964, discusses the author's proposed books at Dial Press: first, *Talking at the Gates*—"about a Southern Plantation the day that news arrived that slavery had ended"—and second, a book about the FBI in the South (FBI Files, 1249). Mention of Baldwin's book on the FBI also appeared in the *New York Herald Tribune* (July 14, 1964), this time claiming it would be serialized, like *The Fire Next Time* in the *New Yorker* (FBI Files, 1255). By July 17, there was a memorandum summarizing Baldwin's proposed exposure of the FBI with a note that "discreet checks" would be made in the publishing industry, with the hope of getting hold of the galleys (FBI Files, 1256). The same report cites from Baldwin's interview in *Playbill* where he discusses beginning "a long article about the manner in which Negroes are treated by the FBI" (FBI Files, 1256). The book about the FBI in the South, reputedly called *Blood Counters*, never appeared and former editors at Dial Press have no memory of the project.

Literary Clues

The rumors about *Blood Counters* provide fascinating insight into how the FBI expended considerable energy and resources investigating a book Baldwin never wrote, while missing the stories he actually published. According to Natalie Robins, "[t]he FBI was as interested in Baldwin's writing as it was in his life" but in fact there are surprisingly few mentions of the writer's work—and there are notable omissions.[49] There is no discussion of *Giovanni's Room* (1956), for example, despite the theme of homosexuality, even though "deviant sexuality" was directly connected to national security concerns during the Cold War era.[50] One of the most detailed reports is on Baldwin's extended essay, *The Fire Next Time* (1963), where it is noted that the author "advocate[d] integration" (FBI Files, 1043) but even here the discussion of "My Dungeon Shook" is only five lines long. Apart from a concluding comment that confirms that neither the FBI nor the director are mentioned, the most striking feature is Hoover's underlining of a passage from "Down at the Cross"—the line that says Christ is "a disreputable sunbaked Hebrew" (FBI Files, 1043). For Hoover, it seems, blasphemy was as terrible as communism.[51]

As to be expected, with a novel depicting interracial and bisexual sex, there are a number of entries on Baldwin's third novel, *Another Country*. On advice from *Partisan Review*'s attorney, William Fitelson, an excerpt from *Another Country* was printed in the magazine with asterisks covering the supposedly obscene words, which had infuriated Baldwin.[52] (The words "fuck" and "cunt" were deemed too obscene for print, and both William Burroughs's *Naked Lunch* and Henry Miller's *Tropic* books were unavailable to the public on similar grounds.) When *Another Country* was published in 1962, Hoover took note of how the novel was banned in New Orleans (FBI Files, 75) and responded to several letters from outraged citizens who sought to get *Another Country* removed from bookshelves and book clubs. For one concerned Christian in Mississippi, Baldwin's books left him or her "speechless" and "numb." Worst of all, Baldwin's books had been advertised in church magazines, prompting the letter writer to implore, "Tell me, for the sake of our God and Humanity, how and where these writings fit into Christianity" (FBI Files, 1301).[53] Later entries also record the Ku Klux Klan's criticism of the Southern Baptist Association for recommending Baldwin's book (FBI Files, 1510), while another letter from 1965 complains to Hoover that *Another Country* contains "every filthy word, compound word and phrasing that could be used to portray: Drug addiction, Sex perversion at its vilest" (FBI Files, 1628).

In his responses to the outraged readers of Baldwin's work, Hoover maintained a sense of professionalism, even objectivity, but his remarks and actions suggest he was also affronted by such writing. The above letter, Hoover notes, "is very much appreciated," adding that, since no Federal law had been violated, there was nothing he could do. What he could do, however, is make his own moral stance very clear by enclosing pamphlets "which express[ed] . . . [his] views on the widespread accessibility of obscene and pornographic literature." These leaflets included: *Combating Merchants of Filth: The Role of the FBI*, *Let's Wipe Out the Schoolyard Sex Racket!* and *The Fight Against Filth* (FBI Files, 1629).

Another FBI report compares *Another Country* to Henry Miller's *Tropic of Cancer*, presumably because of the descriptions of "sex perversion" found in both novels (FBI Files, 1620). The FBI's role as the guardian of morality and decency raises important concerns about civil liberties and censorship, as well as illustrating how Hoover's power and influence extended well beyond his role as the enforcer of federal law. Furthermore, the FBI's interest in Baldwin as a writer specifically connects the author's FBI files to key questions in analysis and textual practice. Baldwin's files reveal much about how the FBI analyzed and critiqued Baldwin and his work, but the files themselves, which are encoded, blanked-out, and catalogued in a complex organizational system, resemble difficult modernist texts that frequently resist close reading. In other words, reading Baldwin's FBI files and the FBI's reading of Baldwin link both legal and textual interpretation, connecting the role of the FBI agent to that of the literary critic, both of whom seek to decode or uncover meaning from the body or body of the text. The parallels between spies and literary critics have an established history. James Angleton, a long-standing chief of the CIA's counterintelligence staff from the 1950s to the 1970s, developed a methodology that was based on I. A. Richards's and William Empson's New Criticism. For Angleton, his formalist spycraft was "the practical criticism of ambiguity," a methodological approach that focused on textual indeterminacies, in contrast to the FBI's approach, which tended to be grounded in the "biographical-historical criticism of its own day."[54]

Officially, the FBI only took note of books that violated federal law. Yet it is well known that the director had started an "Obscene File" as early as 1925 listing works deemed to be pornographic and/or a federal offense.[55] Baldwin's file includes several references to the "Bureau Library" where books were stored, presumably because they were deemed "subversive," "dangerous," or "immoral" (1592). The titles of the books held in the Bureau Library offer an intriguing insight into the Bureau's understanding of "dangerous" literature. In fact, the mere mention that Wilfred Carty was planning to set up a Black

Studies program in 1969 warranted a mention (FBI Files, 920). In order for books to be held in the library, they presumably needed to be read. But read by whom? Some deductions are possible; for instance, in 1972, Baldwin's *No Name in the Street* and Gayraud S. Wilmore's *Black Religion and Black Radicalism* were requested by Inspector G. C. M**** of the "Extremist Intelligence Section, Domestic Intelligence Division" (1600). In other cases there are headings marked "Book Review," as in the file concerning *A Rap on Race* (1971), a conversation between Baldwin and Margaret Mead, who, as was noted in the file, "had been affiliated with several communist front organizations" (FBI Files, 1592). Despite the title of "Book Review," with its connotations of literary analysis, the file suggests how the Bureau was undertaking another form of critique; one that decodes "un-American" meaning from the texts under scrutiny. In this instance the inspector concludes that both writers "agreed they had to be clearheaded as possible about all human beings" noting one instance where the FBI is mentioned (FBI Files, 1593). Here, as elsewhere, the FBI agents attempt to decode and reveal instances of subversion, but they frequently fail to provide more than superficial readings of the works at hand. While the Bureau was clearly not attempting to produce literary analysis, the report on *A Rap* underscores the ways in which it struggled to decode subversive elements that Hoover and his colleagues insisted must be present.

In addition to the reviews of Baldwin's work, the Bureau undertook forensic investigations in order to quantify and measure subversive content. Certain reports on *Another Country*, for instance, bear headings such as "Laboratory Work Sheet" and "Specimens Submitted for Examination." Under one heading, "Result of Examination," the report notes that "[t]he book described above as specimen Q1 was not identified with material of a similar nature which has been forwarded previously to the Laboratory. Specimen Q1 is being added to the Bureau's files" (FBI Files, 1622). The language here is reminiscent of Cold War rhetoric of "germophobia" and yet it also reads as a clinical attempt at some sort of literary analysis, as illustrated by a report that comments directly on Baldwin's literary skill. *Another Country*, the Assistant Attorney General of the Criminal Division concluded in a report to the director, "has been reviewed in the General Crimes Section of this Division and it has been concluded that the book contains literary merit and may be of value to students of psychology and social behavior" (FBI Files, 1627). By drawing attention to the social value of *Another Country*, the report echoes the conclusions of Judge Clayton W. Horn in the notorious *Howl* obscenity trial in 1958. Clayton adjudged Allen Ginsberg's poem to "have some redeeming social importance," concluding that "the book is not obscene."[56] However, unlike the *Howl* trial, where expert witnesses such as Professor David Kirk testified to the literary merit of the poem, the FBI's report highlights the Bureau's roles as judge and cross-examiner.[57] This in turn raises further questions not only about Hoover's attempts to monitor obscenity but also the FBI's attempts to shape public opinion and policy related to obscenity.

The Bureau's report on *Another Country*'s literary merit, then, highlights the problematic ways that the FBI relied on their in-house literary analyses to judge the social value of books under scrutiny. Furthermore, the FBI was convinced that certain books, such as John Steinbeck's *Grapes of Wrath* (1939), contained codes that spoke to Communists and fellow travelers. There are examples of Hoover reading books literally, assuming in the case of Elizabeth Dilling's 1934 *The Red Network*, a work that accused 1,300 people of communism, that it was factual, rather than conjecture and rumor.[58] An FBI memorandum of 1942 concluded that some of William Carlos Williams's poems might be written in code, concluding that "they appear to have been written by a person who is very queer or possibly a mental case." The Bureau eventually conceded that Williams used "an 'expressionistic' style which might be interpreted as being 'code.'"[59] Other reports read like weak undergraduate essays: one, for example, concludes that Rex Stout's 1941 *Sisters in Trouble* could be "a deliberate attempt to convey a meaning other than the solution of a mystery story . . . note the almost exclusive German cast of characters."[60]

The Bureau's attempts at literary analysis suggest the ways in which agents struggled to read and interpret literature that was not plotted in line with conventional American ideals: works such as Baldwin's, which deviated from acceptable parameters and tackled themes of homosexuality, race, or violence were deemed alien or subversive. In other words the FBI readers struggled to make sense of "un-American" themes. Concomitantly, as I have suggested, the files themselves also present difficulties in terms of analysis and interpretation for the literary critic without FBI training. It is not clear, for example, why there are pages of information about other FBI targets in Baldwin's file with no mention of the author.[61] One example of the confusion generated by the files is the otherwise insightful article, "'I'm Not Entirely What I Look Like': Richard Wright, James Baldwin, and the Hegemony of Vision; or, Jimmy's FBEye Blues" by Maurice Wallace. Wallace correctly points out that the FBI tailed Baldwin in Turkey, citing from a file that comments on the author's "strange" working methods. For Wallace the file is "familiarly colonial" in the way that it frames the writer "within an anthropological . . . frame of reference."[62] The passage that Wallace cites from, however, is indeed in Baldwin's FBI file but is in fact a translation from a Turkish newspaper report—and, not, as Wallace suggests—an FBI report, illustrating the difficulties of reading the files themselves.[63] Nonetheless, despite these obstacles, the files are productive, for they yield both information about Baldwin and about the FBI's specific attempts to classify a subject who was notoriously difficult to pin down, not only in terms of genre, but also physically, given his transatlantic shuffles between the United States, Europe, and Turkey.

Baldwin's FBI files—even after being declassified again in 1998, which rendered more information visible—are also full of blanked-out sections and omissions, which are classified under the Freedom of Information Act. In addition, the "final" version of the file often differs significantly from the original report. For those without FBI training, the files present a challenge: how to interpret and decode the referencing system, which is neither chronological nor immediately logical. As Clarence M. Kelley, the director of the FBI in the 1970s, has noted, "[m]ost reports were written, rewritten, edited, scrubbed, and cleaned and pressed a dozen times before they were put in the mail. Reportorial accuracy was seldom a consideration."[64] In terms of textual practice, the files represent a particular challenge to the literary or cultural critic. They are, to borrow from the French critic Gérard Genette, a kind of palimpsest: they can be read as "hypertexts," in which the original, or "hypotext," cannot be traced, leading to a confusing layering of erasure and marginalia.[65] Not only are the director's barely legible scrawls visible on the margins of the files; there are also printed footers offering financial tips to employees working on the documents—such as, "Buy US Savings Bonds Regularly on the Payroll Savings Plans," illustrating the ways in which these forms performed simultaneous functions. In Baldwin's files, there are reports on his activity, handwritten marginalia, as well as advertisements directed at agents who are reading the files.

If the files were "cleaned"—that is, expunged of sensitive material—then it is arguably the paratextual comments that reveal the most about the FBI's opinions and comments. In wonderful irony for the Bureau's detractors, Hoover, who did not consider that the Freedom of Information Act would be introduced, believed that his numerous marginal notes on files would remain private. A notable example is Hoover's 1964 jotting, "Isn't Baldwin a well known pervert?" (FBI Files, 1256). Yet this comment, written on the margins of the typed memorandum, was not just a personal note or a rhetorical musing: the barely legible question in fact precipitated a measured response, which illustrates how Hoover's marginalia acted as a central component of the files. The official report responding to Hoover's question asserts, "it is not possible to state that he is a pervert," but notes that "he has expressed a sympathetic viewpoint about homosexuality" (FBI Files, 1259). The interest in Baldwin's sexual activity—and accompanying assumption that perversion is a synonym for homosexuality—illustrates another way in which the Bureau investigated beyond the subject's political life, scrutinizing people for what they saw as moral or immoral behavior. While this particular report on Baldwin at least has the merit of not conflating an author's fictional writing with a straightforward biographical reading, it raises the question of how far Baldwin's sexuality fueled further surveillance. In other words, did Baldwin's sexuality prompt intensified federal investigation?

While the FBI sought to discredit successful leftist black American political leaders, the preferred tactic was to "dredge up a prison or arrest record
and get it sensationalized," as in the case of Clifton DeBerry, the first African
American to run for president, nominated by the SWP in 1964.[66] As Manning
Marable has noted, Malcolm X's clean-cut lifestyle in 1958 posed a challenge
to the Bureau; though he was deemed "a potential threat to national security,
his rigid behavioral code and strong leadership skills would make him hard
to discredit."[67] The effect of the Bureau's tactics to discredit high-profile individuals is recorded in Baldwin's description of his first encounter with the
FBI, which is couched in a notably violent and sexual rhetoric, where the
author recalls feeling "humiliated," comparing the incident to being "gang-
raped." Hoover, as emblem of the FBI, is transformed from prurient voyeur to
sinister perpetrator, underscoring, as Maurice Wallace has noted, "the spec-
tacular conditions of historical black masculine identity and the chronic
effort to 'frame' the black male body, criminally and visually, for the visual
pleasures of whites."[68] And yet, Baldwin's openness about this sexuality, his
readiness to address the topic in his fiction, seemed to wrong-foot the FBI,
who had no leverage to blackmail a writer who was already openly homosexual.[69] While information about Baldwin's "homosexual parties" in Istanbul
underscores the Bureau's international monitoring of its targets—and gives
credence to Maxwell's claim that the FBI became "a pioneering archivist of
black internationalism"—the scant information reveals little that was not
publicly known about the author (FBI Files, 651).[70]

For the most part, descriptions of Baldwin within his file reveal more
about the FBI than about Baldwin himself, exposing insights about the FBI's
modus operandi and turning the gaze back to the voyeuristic reach of the Bureau's surveillance. The ten entries on Baldwin's homosexuality are intrusive,
unnecessary, and often derogatory but Baldwin's openness about his sexual
activity from the 1950s left him free from the blandishments of blackmail or
exposure. The first mention of Baldwin's sexuality is a file on May 29, 1963,
where it is noted that "[i]nformation has been developed by the Bureau that
BALDWIN is a homosexual," adding, as if the two were connected, that he
also "made derogatory remarks in reference to the Bureau" (FBI Files, 69).
Since the 1940s, it had been common to link leftism and critique of government policies with homosexuality, as in the frequently used term, "pinko,"
which implied that a person not only had communist sympathies but was also
"effete," a euphemism for homosexuality.[71]

For the most part, descriptions of Baldwin reveal more about the FBI's assumptions about how a homosexual was supposed to behave, as in the following entry, which again illustrates the Bureau's use of gossip and rumor: "It has
been heard that BALDWIN may be a homosexual and he appeared as if he
may be one" (FBI Files, 591). There is mention of how Baldwin was evicted
from a house in Istanbul for "having homosexual parties," which reveals the

extent to which they kept an eye on the writer abroad, but the information again hardly seems to merit the time and money spent (FBI Files, 651). More damaging, however, are the FBI's records of Baldwin's sexuality in relation to his civil rights work where knowledge of his homosexuality almost certainly hampered his role as spokesman for the movement. There is a transcript of a wiretap where Levison is reported to have claimed that Baldwin and Bayard Rustin were "better qualified to lead a homo-sexual movement than a civil rights movement," a point I pick up on below (FBI Files, 104). Similarly, Clarence Jones is reported to have fallen out with Baldwin in 1963, adding that "Baldwin's sexual propensities had been known," with the corollary that this would damage the civil rights movement (FBI Files, 124). As I explore in the following section, Baldwin's views on homosexuality were anything but straightforward. While the FBI surprisingly did not focus on Baldwin's sexuality, knowledge (or at least conjecture) of his queerness directly hindered his role as a spokesman for civil rights issues, which in turn raises important questions about the relationship between race and sexuality in the mid- to late 1960s.

Race, Sexuality, and Black Power

According to Joseph Beam, Baldwin's work helped rip the hinges off the closet.[72] Until the publication of *Just Above My Head* (1979), Baldwin's last novel, Beam claims that African American writers had been suffering "a kind of 'nationalistic heterosexism.'"[73] While his writing offered solace and recognition for many of his contemporary readers, it was not until the 1980s that criticism (notably the work of Andrea Lowenstein and Emmanuel Nelson) began to argue for Baldwin's central place, not only as an important African American writer, but as a black and gay artist. Since the early 1990s, a number of critics (notably Dwight McBride and Robert Reid-Pharr) have made valuable contributions to what E. Patrick Johnson and Mae G. Henderson describe as "the interanimation" between black studies and queer studies in Baldwin's work.[74]

But even as Baldwin's reputation as an important—perhaps the most important—gay black American writer of the twentieth century becomes increasingly secure, a closer examination of his work reveals numerous ambiguities, contradictions, and uncertainties that sit uneasily with his increasingly iconic status. Although Baldwin is noted for his bold portrayals of homosexual relationships, it was not until 1968 with *Tell Me How Long the Train's Been Gone* that Baldwin depicted sexual relations between two black men in a novel, and not until his last novel, *Just Above My Head* (1979), that he explored sexual love between African American men. In fact, as David Bergman has pointed out, Baldwin is careful to frame his "homosexual"

relationships through bisexuality, whether past or present.[75] Still more surprising is Baldwin's insistence that his second novel, *Giovanni's Room*, a
work that has emerged as a key work of twentieth-century gay fiction, "is not
about homosexuality."[76]

Not only did he steer readers away from the theme of homosexuality in
Giovanni's Room, but Baldwin repeatedly rejected the adjectives "homosexual," "gay," and "bisexual." "The word gay," Baldwin told Richard Goldstein,
"has always rubbed me the wrong way. I never understood exactly what is
meant by it," a view that Baldwin also forcefully echoed in an interview with
James Mossman:[77]

> Those terms, homosexual, bisexual, heterosexual, are 20th century terms
> which, for me, really have very little meaning. I've never, myself, in watch-
> ing myself and other people, watching life, been able to discern exactly
> where the barriers were.[78]

Asked by Goldstein whether he considered himself gay, Baldwin replied that
he did not: "I didn't have a word for it. The only one I had was homosexual
and that didn't quite cover whatever it was I was beginning to feel."[79]

Not only did Baldwin repeatedly disavow the terms "gay," "homosexual,"
and "bisexual," but he was deeply suspicious of the United States's (and any
other nation's) Gay Rights movement. Although he spoke in New York on
"Race, Racism and the Gay Community," in 1982, Baldwin harshly condemned public exhibitions of gay solidarity, claiming that "they're involved in
some kind of exhibition of their disaster."[80] The very negative language here
("disaster") suggests more than a suspicion of labels, suggesting a level of internalized homophobia, which I will return to.[81] Baldwin's at times unsettling
rhetoric and depiction of gay subculture has led some critics, such as Donald
Gibson, to conclude that "[t]he fact of the matter is that Baldwin's attitude
toward homosexuality is decidedly critical."[82] Similarly, Emmanuel Nelson, a
pioneer in the treatment of Baldwin's accounts of homosexuality, concluded
that *Giovanni's Room* evinced a Baldwin who had "not freed himself from the
internalization of homophobic beliefs regarding the origins of male homosexual impulses."[83] While some writers, such as Joseph Beam, may have been
inspired by Baldwin's depictions of black gay lives, others, such as the African
American gay science-fiction writer Samuel R. Delany, found his portraits far
from positive. While Delany acknowledges that Baldwin "at least, had talked
about it [homosexuality]," displaying "a certain personal honesty," he also
groups *Giovanni's Room* with negative portrayals of homosexuality, such as
the writing of Havelock Ellis.[84]

By drawing attention to Baldwin's mercurial views on sexuality, my aim is
not to undermine his central place as a key writer of black queer fiction. Instead,
I contend that Baldwin's views operate along complex circuits of desire that
make his work more challenging—and therefore more interesting—than is

often assumed. Beginning by exploring the disparity between Baldwin's prodigious examinations of sexuality in his fiction and his surprising silence in his essays, I focus on the turbulent arena of black radical politics during the 1960s. While there has been some useful and pioneering work on the ways in which Baldwin was sidelined by civil rights activists because of his sexuality, little has been done to examine his own unsettling comments on black masculinity and sexuality during this turbulent period.

For a writer who so fearlessly and tirelessly addressed issues of homosexuality and bisexuality in his fiction, Baldwin's relative silence about homosexuality in his essays seems surprising. Only in 1985 in the essay titled "Here Be Dragons," the closing piece in Baldwin's collected nonfiction, *The Price of the Ticket,* did he write about his sexuality openly. Homosexuality—although not explicitly Baldwin's—was discussed in two earlier essays, "Preservation of Innocence" (1949) and "The Male Prison" (1954), originally published in the *New Leader* as "Gide as Husband and Homosexual," later collected in *Nobody Knows My Name* (1961). Although Baldwin wrote little about homosexuality in his essays, he was more forthcoming in conversation. In an interview with Richard Goldstein, also from 1985 and published as "Go the Way Your Blood Beats," Baldwin delivered his most candid discussion of homosexuality. Three important points emerge from this intriguing interview. First, Baldwin's repeated rejection of the terms "homosexual" and "gay," a point that I have already raised; second, his insistence that sexuality is a private matter; and finally, his repeated statement that race is a more important question than issues of sexuality.

Given that he used the very public forum of the novel to explore homosexuality and bisexuality, Baldwin's insistence that "one's sexual preference is a private matter," sits at odds with his reputation as a key figure in gay literary history.[85] And yet, Baldwin's insistence on privacy punctuates his commentaries on sexuality. In his essay on Gide, for example, Baldwin reprimanded the French author, insisting that he ought to have kept his sexuality hidden.[86] Baldwin's sexuality, as he recounted to Goldstein, was "very personal, absolutely personal. It was really a matter between me and God."[87]

Jerome de Romanet reaches the reasonable conclusion that Baldwin, on the whole, "reserved the more public voice of spokesman (of the black community as a whole, of writers and artists) for his essays and formal addresses, while he often let his fictional characters discuss the more private issues of sexual politics and preference."[88] Indeed, in contrast to the paucity of essays dealing with sexuality, Baldwin's fiction is replete with depictions of same-sex desire. Why Baldwin chose to circumscribe homosexuality in his essays is a different question. One answer may lie in Baldwin's awareness that readers and critics who were uncomfortable with his fictional depictions of homosexuality and bisexuality were less troubled by the emphasis on race in his essays. While critics are divided in their appraisal of Baldwin's forte as an essayist or novelist, Emmanuel Nelson is surely right to suggest that many heterosexist critics felt more comfortable with Baldwin's relative silence on sexuality in his essays.[89]

The glaring disparity between discussions of sexuality in his essays and fiction also highlights the ways in which Baldwin was preoccupied by his roles both as an artist and as a spokesman. In the mid-1960s, in particular, Baldwin came under increasing attack by a new generation of radical black American writers, such as Ishmael Reed and Amiri Baraka, who criticized his writing—and in particular his fiction—for not being sufficiently politically engaged. Importantly, criticism of Baldwin's political ineffectiveness was directly bound to the public knowledge of his sexual orientation. Although Henry Louis Gates Jr. is careful to point out that Black Nationalism did not have a unique claim on homophobia, he rightly discusses the ways in which "national identity became sexualized in the 1960s, in such a way as to engender a curious subterranean connection between homophobia and nationalism."[90]

While I acknowledge Cheryl Clarke's admonishment that the black community is too frequently pilloried for its homophobia, it seems that Baldwin's insistence on privacy in relation to discussions of homosexuality came directly out of increasing attacks on his authority as a (homosexual) racial spokesman.[91] Despite this, Baldwin's distinctions between the public and the private spheres are difficult to constitute. Although Baldwin largely leaves his depictions of homosexuality to his fiction, his widely available novels of the 1960s hardly constitute a private sphere.

Black Nationalism, Homophobia, and the Role of the Artist

Baldwin's involvement in civil rights shifted from his role as reporter to more engaged activist. In 1957 he had been commissioned by *Harper's* magazine to write about the South, writing an emotional account about his first visit to the South and his first meeting with Martin Luther King Jr.[92] After a second visit to the South in 1960, Baldwin became more actively involved in the civil rights movement through work with the Congress of Racial Equality (CORE), an organization—along with the Student Non-violent Coordinating Committee (SNCC)—that he later joined.[93] Tired of sojourning in France, "polishing my fingernails," as he recalled, Baldwin's new involvement in the South ignited in him a new political commitment: "I realized what tremendous things were happening," Baldwin averred, "and that I did have a role to play."[94]

Baldwin's role as writer/reporter was indeed unique. Richard Wright, whose reputation in the United States had dwindled by the late 1950s, remained in France until his death in 1960, and neither Ralph Ellison nor Langston Hughes played a significant role in writing of the civil rights era. With the success of *The Fire Next Time* (1963), Baldwin commanded a large and receptive audience, as is illustrated by his ill-fated meeting with the Attorney General, Robert Kennedy. But even as Baldwin courted more involvement with the civil rights movement, there were whispers of his misinformed views, and aspersions were cast on his ability—and suitability—as a race leader. Martin Luther King Jr., for example, in a conversation secretly recorded by the FBI, expressed his reluctance at attending a television program with Baldwin. According to the FBI report, King was "put off by the 'poetic exaggeration' in Baldwin's approach to race issues."[95]

Baldwin would later explore his problematic role as writer and spokesman in *Tell Me How Long the Train's Been Gone* (1968), emphatically telling *Mademoiselle* magazine in 1969 that "I am *not* a public speaker. I *am* an artist." While Baldwin insisted that he was first and foremost a writer, knowledge and rumor of his sexuality ensured that he was excluded from full participation in the civil rights movement.[96] According to Morris Dickstein,

> The crucial charge against Baldwin had little to with his politics, or his literary craftsmanship, or even, for that matter, his precise position on the race questions. The argument was that Baldwin's homosexuality, his unconfident masculinity, is the hidden root of all his writing and completely disqualifies him as a representative spokesman.[97]

Evidence of how his sexuality undermined his authority as a racial spokesman is clearly illustrated in an issue of *Time* magazine published in May 1963. While the photograph of Baldwin on the cover testifies to a politically engaged African American writer at the height of his success, the article overtly undermines his authority as a racial spokesman. Not only does the article emphatically state that Baldwin is "not, by any stretch of the imagination, a Negro leader," but it also tacitly emphasizes Baldwin's effeminacy as a euphemism for homosexuality: Baldwin is described as a "nervous, slight, almost fragile figure, filled with frets and fears. He is effeminate in manner."[98] By framing Baldwin as weak, and by implying his sexuality, the *Time* article implicitly suggests that Baldwin is not threatening to its white readership, a point explicitly made by Calvin Hernton and Stanley Crouch. Hernton's brief discussion of the *Time* article concludes that white Americans love Baldwin because of his "lack of 'masculine aggressiveness,'" adding that he is "a sweet, exotic black boy who cries for mother love."[99]

Time's derisive caption could only have exacerbated Baldwin's problematic position within civil rights circles, where it was common knowledge that he was nicknamed "Martin Luther Queen," with the implication that a "queen" could not participate in the violent and manly battle for civil rights, which several members of King's camp expressed directly.[100] King's lawyer, for example, Clarence Jones, whose telephone was wiretapped by the FBI, stated in a conversation that the Southern Christian Leadership Conference (SCLC) had a respectable reputation and "could hardly afford to have candid homosexuals close to the seat of power."[101] As I noted earlier, King's right-hand man Stanley Levison expressed his view that Baldwin and Bayard Rustin (a King aide later dismissed for his homosexuality) were "better qualified to lead a homo-sexual movement than a civil rights movement."[102]

Although knowledge of Baldwin's sexuality directly hindered his involvement with the SCLC, by 1964 King's own message of nonviolence and Christian love was increasingly viewed as weak and ineffective. As Erika Doss has cogently documented, after the Civil Rights Act of spring 1964, notions of "conciliation and mediation" were soon rejected as ineffectual.[103] Disillusioned with the lack of political gain, both white and black activists turned their attention to the North, vying, as Doss outlines, for "consciousness raising and cultural awareness."[104] Importantly, King's southern message of tolerance was quickly dismissed. There was a new arena in the North that fostered more radical and violent ideologies.

For younger black radicals such as Eldridge Cleaver, King's message of nonviolence had become "a stubborn and persistent stumbling block in the path of the methods that had to be implemented to bring about a revolution in the present situation."[105] In contrast to King's emphasis on the "good book," Cleaver notes how Fanon's *The Wretched of the Earth* was now known as "the Bible."[106] The time for Christian love and tolerance had been exhausted. According to one member of the Berkeley campus CORE organization, "[a] new leadership is emerging which reflects the aspirations of the urban Negro. . . . Yesterday's militants—like King and Rustin are the new Uncle Toms."[107]

Baldwin's alignment with the sinking radical ship of Martin Luther King Jr.—what Cleaver referred to as his "Martin Luther King-type self-effacing love for his oppressors"—is crucial to an understanding of Baldwin's subsequent development as a writer.[108] As Cheryl Clarke and other cultural critics have shown, the mid-1960s "marked a resurgence of radical black consciousness . . . [which included] rejecting the values of WASP America and embracing our African and Afro-American traditions and culture."[109] Importantly, a rejection of white values included a repudiation of homosexuality, a phenomenon that increasingly became viewed as a white aberration.[110] Not only that, but black political action became increasingly gendered and sexualized. King, as Michelle Wallace has argued, "represented a glaring impossibility—a dream of masculine softness and beauty, an almost feminine man."[111]

This important political shift in the mid-1960s, which became the Black Power movement, resulted in an attempt to homogenize both political views and identity categories.[112] As Cheryl Clarke has noted, "[i]n order to participate in this movement one had to be black (of course), be male-orientated, and embrace a spectrum of black nationalist, separatist, Pan Africanist sentiments, beliefs, and goals."[113] Crucially, you also had to be heterosexual, and it helped if you were young.[114] For the middle-aged and queer Baldwin, it was not easy to gain membership of this club. "Baldwin, who once defined the cutting edge," Henry Louis Gates Jr. has noted, "was now a favorite target for the new cutting edge."[115] "Like Martin Luther King," Michelle Wallace averred, "Baldwin was an anachronism come the sixties; but unlike King he was not conveniently murdered, so they had to dispose of him some other way."[116] This "other way" of marginalizing Baldwin deeply affected both his depictions of homosexuality and subsequent political shifts.

As the political arena shifted dramatically from 1965, Baldwin was faced with a new strand of black radicalism. The Black Panther Party for Self Defense was formed in 1966, proselytizing a well-crafted message of potent masculinity and patriarchy, made emblematic by the masculine symbols of the panther and the gun.[117] The Black Power movement, as Michelle Wallace, has reiterated, increasingly became synonymous with "the pursuit for manhood," a point that Eldridge Cleaver made explicit in an interview with Nat Hentoff in 1968.[118] According to Cleaver, the Black Panther Party "supplies very badly needed standards of masculinity," adding that "all the young chicks in the black community nowadays relate to the young men who are Black Panthers."[119]

Cleaver's assumption about male and female heterosexuality and his emphasis on masculinity are illustrative of the Black Power movement's increasingly intolerant ideology. As Erica Doss has outlined,

> by aligning black masculinity with symbols and styles traditionally associated with potent white masculinity, the Panthers also reinscribed the most egregious forms of patriarchal privilege and domination, from machismo and misogyny to violence and aggression. Their heterosexist and homophobic brand of revolutionary black nationalism excluded black women and homosexuals, and limited the context of black liberation and black power to conflicts over the definition and manifestation of black masculinity.[120]

Doss's emphasis on the increasingly homogeneous inscription of black masculinity points to the ways in which women and, in particular, homosexuals were increasingly scapegoated during the 1960s. As Ron Simmons and other critics have convincingly argued, homophobia in the black community traditionally "reinforces a false sense of manhood."[121] By delineating what is acceptable in male black subjectivity—and what is not—homophobia, according to Robert Reid-Pharr, humanizes the aggressors: "[t]o strike the homosexual, the scapegoat, the sign of chaos and crisis, is to return the community to normality, to create boundaries around Blackness, rights that indeed white men are obliged to recognize."[122]

Reid-Pharr's view is echoed by Eldridge Cleaver's description of "Punk Hunting," an urban ritual that involves seeking out and targeting homosexuals in the community. Cleaver describes "punk hunting" as the need to "satisfy some savage impulse to inflict pain on the specific target, the 'social outcast.'" What is most revealing is Cleaver's choice of analogy. Punk hunting, Cleaver asserts, "seems to me to be not unrelated . . . to the ritualistic lynchings and castrations inflicted on Southern blacks by Southern whites."[123] By aligning himself with white lynchers—who historically sought to scapegoat alleged black sexual transgressors—Cleaver reproduces what bell hooks has referred to as black resistance's equation of "freedom with manhood." By sharing white patriarchy's belief in the "erect phallus," the Black Power movement, hooks contends, "forged a bond between oppressed men and their white male oppressors."[124]

Evidence of Baldwin's scapegoating is highlighted by a 1967 edition of the *Black Panther* newspaper, which featured Emory Douglas's cartoon, titled "bootlickers gallery." In this cartoon, photographs of Baldwin, Rustin, and King are placed subjacent to a picture of a prostrate black man, who is licking the cowboy boots of President Lyndon Johnson.[125] The framing of Baldwin parallels *Time*'s undermining of his suitability as a racial spokesman. In this cartoon, the image of a prostrate "bootlicker" illustrates the ways in which the Black Power movement increasingly came to view "passivity" (i.e., nonaggression) with Uncle Tom behavior, which in turn became synonymous with homosexuality.[126] In Amiri Baraka's poem, "Black Art," for example, he describes one "negroleader / on the steps of the white house one / kneeling between the sheriff's thighs / negotiating coolly for his people."[127] Echoing Baraka's undisguised disgust at the negro leader's passivity and kowtowing, Cleaver forcefully condemned Baldwin's third novel, *Another Country*, derogating Baldwin's depiction of Rufus Scott. For Cleaver, Rufus is "a pathetic wretch . . . who let a white bisexual homosexual fuck him in the ass . . . [and] was the epitome of a black eunuch who has completely submitted to the white man."[128]

By emphasizing Rufus's submission, Cleaver implicitly conflates black homosexuality with his dubious views on the powerlessness of African American women. More specifically, as Michelle Wallace has noted, Cleaver reduces black homosexuals "to the status of our black grandmothers who, as everyone knows, were fucked by white men all the time."[129] But if Cleaver suggests that power is enacted through fucking, then, as Wallace mischievously points out, might we not consider the black homosexual who fucks the white man as the most revolutionary of all? "If whom you fuck indicates your power," Wallace argues, "then obviously the greatest power would be gained by fucking a white man first, a black man second, a white woman third and a black woman not at all. The most important rule is that *nobody* fucks you."[130]

In Baraka's and Cleaver's framework, however, ultimate power is gained by raping white women. For Cleaver, rape is explicitly "an insurrectionary act." By raping white women, Cleaver maintains that he "was defying and trampling on the white man's law . . . because I was very resentful over the historical fact of how the white man had used the black woman. I felt I was getting revenge."[131] Cleaver's act of revenge is rooted in the African American man's historical lack of authority during slavery. As Robert Staples has documented, "[m]asculinity, as defined in this culture, has always implied a certain autonomy over and mastery of one's environment."[132] During slavery, African American men had no legal authority over their wives and children, which accentuated a sense of emasculation. According to Cleaver, the legacy of psycho-sexual damage can be redressed through the reclamation of a pre-historical era. In his essay, "The Primeval Mitosis," Cleaver draws on Plato's Symposium to evoke a pre-social era in which the essence, the Primeval Sphere, became divided; but unlike in Plato, this division is between not three, but two parts, male and female. Each part, Cleaver continues, longs for its opposite in order to create a Unitary Sexual Image. Importantly, Cleaver argues that homosexuality disrupts the timeless process of synthesis: it is "the product of the fissure of society into antagonistic classes and a dying culture and civilization alienated from its biology."[133] This point is further illustrated by the necessary, healing union with African American women ("Black Beauty"): "Across the naked abyss of negated masculinity, of four hundred years minus my Balls, we face each other today, my Queen." Cleaver maintains that it is only through "re-love" of Black Beauty that his "manhood can be redeemed."[134]

Cleaver's emphasis on the redemption and healing of a wounded masculinity not only framed "the pursuit of manhood" in exclusively heterosexual terms, but highlighted the increasingly pervasive move to redress the psycho-sexual crimes of slavery.[135] During the mid-1960s, black masculinity was further damaged by the controversial 1965 findings of what became known as the Moynihan Report. Concluding that the black family suffered from an "abnormal family structure," the report suggested that African Americans suffered less from racism, and more from the dominant presence of black women.[136]

The complicated and competing images of masculinity highlight the difficult position that Baldwin faced. On the one hand, as Lee Edelman has noted, "[o]ne need not, of course, view patriarchy as itself a desideratum in order to recognize the destructiveness of a system that enshrined the paternal privilege . . . while at the same time disavowing the meaningfulness of the paternal relation for the slave."[137] But, on the other hand, Cleaver's dichotomizing of white and black as the (white) Omnipotent Administrator and the (black) Supermasculine menial exacerbated psycho-sexual myths of the black male as primarily physical and libidinous, while at the same time replicating white patriarchal and homophobic values.

By deploying white patriarchy's dominant ideologies, Cleaver's account points toward the complex entanglement of racism, sexism, and homophobia. As Isaac Julien and Kobena Mercer have argued, black men have historically internalized and incorporated dominant images of masculinity in order to contest the powerlessness of racism. This is echoed by Alvin Poussain's discussion of the ways in which African American men have tended "to adopt the attitudes of the dominant group toward black women."[138] What both cases reveal—particularly Cleaver's justification for the raping of white women—is the diaphanous line between the empowering act of reclamation and the danger of perpetuating recalcitrant myths of black sexual appetite.

This complicated position is illustrated by the ways in which Baldwin's criticism of "black manhood" set him at odds with the Black Power movement. Whereas Cleaver celebrates "the walking phallus of the Supermasculine Menial," Baldwin vociferously repudiates this image: "It is still true alas," Baldwin wrote in 1961, "that to be an American Negro male is also to be a kind of walking phallic symbol: which means one pays, in one's personality, for the sexual insecurity of others."[139] Echoing Frantz Fanon's observation that the white gaze transforms a black man in such a way that "[h]e is turned into a penis. He *is* a penis," Hall Montana, Baldwin's narrator in *Just Above My Head*, bemoans that "its color *was* its size."[140]

Despite the depiction of the black male by Cleaver and others as "supermasculine," Baldwin continued to challenge and demystify myths of black sexual prowess. And yet, Cleaver's scabrous homophobic attack of Baldwin in *Soul on Ice* had a devastating effect on the older writer. While Cleaver is not alone in his homophobic derogation of Baldwin, the severity of his attack produced a profound effect on Baldwin's writing. As late as 1984 Baldwin still spoke of trying to "undo the damage" that Cleaver had caused.[141] Henry Louis Gates Jr. recalls Baldwin's remark that "being attacked by white people only made him flare hotly into eloquence; being attacked by black people, he confessed, made him want to break down and cry."[142] According to W. J. Weatherby, Cleaver's attack was extremely "important to Baldwin's development," a key moment that "helped to shape [Baldwin's] racial attitudes in middle age . . . making him re-examine his own situation."[143] Echoing Weatherby, Gates also notes that, in the aftermath of Cleaver's attack, Baldwin's essays "came to represent his official voice, the carefully crafted expression of the public intellectual, James Baldwin."[144] Baldwin, as Dwight McBride convincingly argues, increasingly adopted the voice of "representative race man," which in turn led to a silencing—or at least a dilution—of his depictions of homosexuality.[145]

The Question of Sex Comes after the Question of Color

According to Henry Louis Gates Jr., by the late 1960s "Baldwin bashing was almost a rite of initiation."[146] Middle-aged, homosexual, and with inconsistent political views, Baldwin stood little chance against the fiery and youthful vitality of writers such as Ishmael Reed, who famously dismissed the older writer as "a hustler who comes on like Job."[147] But even as the younger writers of the Black Power movement increasingly scapegoated Baldwin, the older writer—at least publicly—refused to fire back. In fact, from the late 1960s until the late 1970s, Baldwin was not only taciturn about the subject of homosexuality, but his language increasingly adopted a new radical rhetoric, particularly in his long essay, *No Name in the Street*, published in 1972, but begun in 1967.[148] Here I want to examine Baldwin's repeated assertions that "the sexual question comes after the question of color."[149] I want to suggest that Baldwin's move away from the subject of homosexuality came directly out of the criticism that he received from African American writers such as Eldridge Cleaver. This, in turn, led to Baldwin's increasing anxiety over his role as both an artist and a spokesman.

Despite the suggestion by Gates and Campbell that his involvement with the Black Power movement was symbolic and derivative, it is clear from Baldwin's writing from the late 1960s and early 1970s that he was both committed to radical change and then deeply disillusioned. "Since Martin's death, in Memphis," Baldwin wrote in *No Name*, "and that tremendous day in Atlanta, something has altered in me, something has gone away."[150] Gone were Baldwin's more optimistic statements about the need for love between black and white people. In an essay about the head of the SNCC, Stokely Carmichael, Baldwin described the shift in the young leader's ideology in terms that are readily applicable to Baldwin himself: "Stokely did not begin his career with dreams of terror," Baldwin wrote, "but with dreams of love. Now he's saying, and he's not alone, and he's not the first, if I can't live here, well neither will you."[151] Having fervently supported King's March on Washington, Baldwin later agreed with Malcolm X that the March was in fact "a sell-out."[152] Although Gates is a little harsh when he claims that "Baldwin's reverence for Malcolm was real, but posthumous," by 1972, seven years after Malcolm X's assassination, Baldwin's recollection of the Nation of Islam leader borders on hagiography: "Malcolm, finally, was a genuine revolutionary," Baldwin recalled in *No Name*, adding that "[i]n some church someday . . . he will be hailed as a saint."[153]

But if Baldwin's support of Malcolm was, to a certain extent, retrospective, then he was eager to lend his support to the Black Power movement that had so readily dismissed him.[154] Baldwin, as James Campbell recalls, "embraced the Panthers."[155] Striking a close and lasting relationship with the chairman of the Black Panther Party, Bobby Seale, Baldwin went on to write an introduction to his second book, and to host a birthday party for the incarcerated Panther leader Huey Newton.[156] Although the project was never completed, Baldwin also began work in Hollywood on a film script about the life of Malcolm X in 1968. This work was eventually published in 1972 as *One Day When I Was Lost: A Scenario Based on the Autobiography of Malcolm X*.[157] Baldwin's attempts to make a film about Malcolm X's life were of great interest to the FBI, who carefully monitored reports and rumors about the project. In 1968, the FBI concluded that Baldwin "had joined a growing movement of prominent individuals supporting the struggle of Oakland's Black Panther Party"

(FBI Files, 852), noting his whereabouts and publications in connection to black radical activity.[158]

By 1971, the FBI noted that Baldwin was "far less militant than in the past and apparently considerably removed from the mainstream of Black Power activities" (FBI Files, 990), a report written a month before the author's participation and speech at a meeting in London to support the Soledad Brothers (George Jackson, John Clutchette, and Fleeta Drumgo).[159] By 1972, the language of *No Name* contrasted sharply with his earlier more poetic language. Although the FBI deemed him "less militant," this was a new Baldwin radical rhetoric, albeit one that sounded unsure and borrowed. The writer who had once famously claimed that he had to appropriate white culture, invoking Chartres Cathedral, Descartes, and Shakespeare, now vehemently argued that the "South African coal miner, or the African digging for roots . . . have no reason to bow down before Shakespeare, or Descartes . . . or the Cathedral at Chartres."[160] Not only did Baldwin openly support the Panthers, proclaiming, for example, that African American prisoners had never received a fair trial, but he increasingly referred to himself as a black radical writer.[161] After *The Fire Next Time*, Baldwin's writing, according to Stanley Crouch, "began to espouse the kinds of simplistic conceptions Malcolm X became famous for."[162]

Baldwin's claim that he had, upon his arrival in Paris, lived with "les misérables" (Algerians) was a blatant rewriting of his first years in Paris, a period that he spent largely with white writers.[163] If Baldwin rewrote his past to suggest more radical political engagement, then he was no less self-conscious about his present situation. In *No Name*, only four years after Cleaver's violent dismissal of his political ineffectiveness, Baldwin refers to a disagreement with a young black militant woman, concluding that the scene "rather checked the company, which had not imagined that I and a black militant could possibly disagree about anything."[164] A few years earlier in a different context, Baldwin had been dismissed because few black militants thought he could possibly agree with them about anything. Again in *No Name*, Baldwin is anxious to inflate and maintain his new radical persona: recollecting that the British Immigration considered him to be a "persona non grata"—with the implication that he was too politically dangerous—Baldwin describes how the British authorities "had thrown Stokely [Carmichael] out a week before," in a clearly strategic attempt to stress his own revolutionary credentials.[165]

Importantly, Baldwin's language increasingly borrowed from the heterosexist and machismo language of the Black Power movement. According to the "new" Baldwin, when Bobby Seale proclaimed Huey Newton as "the baddest motherfucker in history," he "restored to the men and women of the ghetto their honor"; a statement that strongly mirrors Cleaver's declaration that "I cannot help but say that Huey P. Newton is the baddest motherfucker ever to set foot in history."[166] Although Baldwin stated that "I do not carry a gun and do not consider myself to be a violent man," he began to claim that his life had "more than once depended on the gun in a brother's holster." Dialogue, the master of words now proclaimed, was no longer possible: "it is not necessary for a black man to hate a white man, or to have any particular feelings about him at all, in order to realize that he must kill him."[167] This new Baldwinian rhetoric sounds less and less like the author of *Go Tell It on the Mountain*, and more and more like the rhetoric of black radical writers. Baldwin's comment in "Notes for Blues" that "I hate them [white people] and would be willing to kill them" echoes Calvin Hernton's conclusion that "only violence . . . will at once be the tool of liberation" or Cleaver's statement that "[i]n order to bring this situation about, black men know that they must pick up the gun."[168]

Baldwin's exhortation that it might be necessary to kill white people recollects Philip Harper's discussion of the ways in which the Black Power movement aligned liberation with an aggressive and heterosexual masculinity. Not surprising, then, Baldwin's new self-proclaimed radicalism also tempered his discussion of homosexuality as he entered the arena of black macho, a point insightfully made by Stanley Crouch, who notes that Baldwin's fascination with militancy and "increasing virulence had perhaps more than a bit to do with his homosexuality."[169] Baldwin began to dismiss "most American intellectuals," on account of what he "observed of their manhood," an observation that is framed in language reminiscent of Cleaver's derogation of Baldwin.[170] Although Baldwin did not go as far as Ossie Davis, who proclaimed Malcolm X as "our living manhood," he began to commemorate the assassinated leader as "a genuine revolutionary, a *virile* impulse long since fled from the American way of life" (emphasis added).[171] Baldwin peppered his essays with discussions of how slavery "emasculated them [slaves] of any human responsibility," arguing that "a man without balls is not a man."[172]

By repeatedly emphasizing the African American male's loss of manhood, Baldwin, as Michelle Wallace wryly points out, "had finally seen the light." Baldwin's work, Wallace argues, in fact "laid the groundwork for the deification of the genitals that would later characterize the prose of the Black Movement."[173] In short, Wallace argues that Baldwin had imbibed the black power rhetoric that the "black man's sexuality and the physical fact of his penis were the major evidence of his manhood and the purpose of it."[174] While Wallace's judgment of Baldwin may seem too pronounced, it illustrates the ways in which Baldwin was viewed as an anachronism but also how the Black Power movement was indebted to his rhetoric. Cleaver's book of essays, *Soul on Ice*, with its blend of autobiography, history, and politics was clearly inspired by the author he soon dismissed. According to Crouch, Baldwin was in fact "a seminal influence" on the likes of Carmichael, Rap Brown, LeRoi Jones, and Cleaver.[175]

Nowhere was Baldwin's influence on the Black Power movement more acute than in his play, *Blues for Mister Charlie*. According to Crouch, Baldwin's play, which was first performed in 1964, four months after the assassination of John F. Kennedy, opened up the question of nonviolence, while Baraka even claimed that *Blues* "announced the Black Arts Movement."[176] While Baraka's eulogy for Baldwin may overstate the importance of this play, contemporary reviewers were quick to point out the shift in register. In his review, Philip Roth criticized what he termed Baldwin's "sentimentalizing of masculinity," arguing that the play "is a soap opera designed to illustrate the superiority of blacks over whites." Echoing Hernton's conclusion that *Blues* demonstrated "an aggressive, a masculine Baldwin," Roth argues that Baldwin suggests that African Americans, "even studious ones, make love better. They dance better. . . . And their penises are longer, or stiffer."[177]

Why Baldwin dramatically changed his rhetoric is in part explained by his public acceptance of Cleaver's virulent attack on him in *Soul on Ice*. Rather than defending his position, Baldwin surprisingly writes that he "admired" Cleaver's book, writing—in what Gates terms "an exercise in willed magnanimity"—that Cleaver was "both valuable and rare."[178] Baldwin, we learn, understood why Cleaver felt impelled to condemn him: "He seemed to feel that I was a dangerously odd, badly twisted, and fragile reed, of too much use to the Establishment to be trusted by blacks." Although Baldwin lamented that Cleaver used his "public reputation against me both naively and unjustly," his subsequent justification of Cleaver's homophobia not only exonerates Cleaver, but he complicity borrows from his former critic's vocabulary: "I also felt I was confused in his mind with the unutterable debasement of the male—with all those faggots, punks, and sissies, the sight and sound of whom, in prison, must have made him vomit more than once."[179] By employing a rhetoric (faggots, punks, and sissies) that even the Black Panther Party had by then officially prohibited, Baldwin comes dangerously close to mimicking Cleaver's own homophobic diatribe.

While Baldwin's writing shifted dramatically during the 1960s, it is important to emphasize that he experienced deep anxieties about his role both as writer and revolutionary from the mid-1960s. Writing in *No Name*, Baldwin is clearly aware of the price he has paid in becoming a best-selling author. Baldwin acknowledges that his success had driven a wedge between himself and those he grew up with: the feeling was, Baldwin averred, "that I had betrayed the people who had produced me."[180] Although Baldwin is anxious to write himself into the history of the Black Power movement, saying "I will always consider myself among the greatly privileged because, however inadequately, I was there," he also realizes that many people will be skeptical about his role, acknowledging the suspicion that "one marches in Montgomery, for example, merely (in my own case) to sell one's books."[181] As the most visible African American writer of the 1960s, Baldwin was, as he admits, "the

Great Black Hope of the Great White Father."[182] "The conflict," Baldwin recalled, "was simply between my life as a writer and my life—not spokesman exactly, but as public witness to the situation of black people. I had to play both roles."[183]

To conclude this section, I turn briefly to Baldwin's last novel of the 1960s, *Tell Me How Long the Train's Been Gone* (1968). Despite being arguably Baldwin's least successful novel, *Tell Me How Long* is an important work, both because the voice of the thespian narrator, Leo Proudhammer, is at times inseparable from Baldwin's, and because the novel illuminates and examines Baldwin's problematic roles during the 1960s.[184]

As a successful actor, Leo is increasingly torn—like Baldwin—between his artistic and his political obligations. Compare, for example, Baldwin's acknowledgment in *No Name* that "what in the world was I by now but an aging, lonely, sexually dubious, politically outrageous, unspeakably erratic freak?" with Leo Proudhammer's conclusion that "[s]ome people considered me a faggot, for some I was a hero, for some I was a whore, for some I was a devious cocks-man, for some I was an Uncle Tom."[185] In particular, I focus briefly on the minor but important character, Black Christopher, who is Proudhammer's lover in later life. By invoking a black radical character who is both homosexual and politically engaged, I argue that Baldwin attempted, toward the end of the 1960s, to reconcile his sexuality with a more fervent political role.

Eliot Fremont-Smith's review of *Tell Me How Long* in the *New York Times* caught the prevailing critical mood. It was, the critic wrote, "a disaster in virtually every particular—theme, characterization, plot, rhetoric."[186] Aside from David Lloren's emphatic view that Baldwin "had without question . . . written the most important novel of this crucial decade in American history," and Isa Kapp's more subdued praise, most reviewers lamented Baldwin's fall from stylistic grace.[187] For Mario Puzo, this was a "one dimensional novel with mostly cardboard characters." He concluded, like Guy Davenport, that this was a work of social protest that lacked narrative skill.[188] (Davenport's description of the novel as a "pamphlet" was an uncomfortable reminder of Baldwin's dismissal of Harriet Beecher Stowe's famous work.)[189] Overall, most reviewers saw Baldwin's last novel of the 1960s as the emblem of his decline as a novelist, illustrated by Granville Hick's comment that the novel "raises perplexing questions about Baldwin's future."[190] Some reviewers, like Nelson Algren, were clearly ruffled by the descriptions of homosexuality; he tellingly writes that "the author's indignation is fired less by racism than by heterosexuality" and refers to Baldwin "sashaying" rather than writing penetrating prose.[191] Most critics, however, suggested that Baldwin's engagement with black radical politics had exerted a detrimental effect on his prose. For Irving Howe, *Tell Me How Long* was replete with "speechmaker's prose," a novel written to demonstrate Baldwin's new militant rhetoric, but one that resulted in "literary suicide."[192] Puzo concluded by suggesting that it was time for Baldwin "to forget the black revolution and start worrying about himself as an artist, who is the ultimate revolutionary," while Stuart Hall noted the hubris of the novel, writing that "it is a meditation by a middle-aged black revolutionary on a revolution he has 'witnessed' . . . but cannot, finally, share."[193]

Tell Me How Long is an angry novel, full of despair and disillusionment. Religion, far from offering solace, has become a tool of the white establishment: "Fuck Jesus," rails Christopher to Leo, "[t]hey didn't want to change their hearts, they just used him to change the *map*" (*TMHL*, 403). African Americans, like Leo's father, are now turning, not to religion, but to Black Nationalism (*TMHL*, 368). In sharp contrast to Baldwin offering love as a social and political palliative in *Another Country*, love in *Tell Me How Long* is explicitly "not enough" to deal with the racism between Leo and his white lover, Barbara (*TMHL*, 298).[194]

But if *Tell Me How Long* exemplifies a new Baldwinian rhetoric of radicalism and even protest, then there is also a self-reflexive and brutal honesty to the narrative. We find this most acutely in the infrequent episodes between Leo—the middle-aged and ailing successful black actor—and "Black Christopher," the young Pantheresque radical, whose friends dress "in their Castro berets" and "heavy boots," clutching works by Camus, Fanon, and Mao (*TMHL*, 382). "I really would like," Leo implores Black Christopher, "to know more than I do about what's going on in the streets." Christopher's reply to Baldwin/Leo is that while "these cats are out here getting their ass whipped all the time . . . [when] [y]ou get *your* ass whipped, at least it gets into the papers" (*TMHL*, 402, 403).

Although *Tell Me How Long* is more often than not dismissed and ignored by critics, the novel offers useful insight into Baldwin's assertion that race is a more important issue than sexuality. Published in 1968, at the height of black nationalist fervor—and the same year as Cleaver's *Soul on Ice*—*Tell Me How Long* was Baldwin's attempt to reconcile his sexuality with black radical politics. Although critics such as James Giles have argued that Baldwin toned down the homosexuality in his fiction to appease black critics, I want to argue that Baldwin hinted at the ideal of an erotic and revolutionary black companionship that was most keenly articulated by the white homosexual writer Jean Genet.[195] By comparing Genet and Baldwin's involvement with the Panthers, I illustrate the extent that race, sexuality, and nationality figured in the obstacles Baldwin faced that prevented his full participation in black radical politics.

Although Black Christopher is only present in *Tell Me* for a dozen or so pages, he functions as a symbolic ideal for the aging Leo. While Christopher affectionately calls Leo his "dirty old man," there is never any explicit sexual interaction between the two men (*TMHL*, 373). In fact, Baldwin is careful to distinguish the love between Leo and Christopher from the "degeneracy" of other artists, such as the "broken down British faggot" actor or "the faggot painter and his Lesbian wife" (*TMHL*, 291, 316).[196] Like most Baldwin protagonists, Leo is bisexual, and Christopher offers his "dirty old man," both physical protection and emotional security, functioning as bodyguard and mother/father figure. Crucially, by naming Leo's lover Black Christopher, Baldwin offers an explicit rebuttal to the notion that homosexuality negates or dilutes blackness.[197] Christopher, Leo ponders, "was black in so many ways—black in color, black in pride, black in rage" (*TMHL*, 68). Christopher, as his name homophonically suggests, is Leo's Black Christ, redolent with the homoeroticism of Countee Cullen's poem, "The Black Christ."[198] Christopher is Baldwin's ideal for the late 1960s: a young and beautiful radical black man who combines tenderness with aggressive political action.

Baldwin's characterization of Black Christopher is a quiet but subversive attack on Black Nationalism's homophobic and heterosexist ideology. By emphasizing the homosociality of organizations such as the Black Panthers, Baldwin suggests the thin line between companionship, eroticism, and love:

> But my own instinct, as the male relation, is that men, who are far more helpless than women . . . need each other as comrades . . . need each other for tears and ribaldry, need each other as models, need each other indeed, in sum, in order to be able to love women. (*TMHL*, 81)

Baldwin's emphasis on the need for male companionship and love is illustrated most acutely by the idealized relationship of Black Christopher and Baldwin/Leo. Importantly, this idea/ideal was not articulated by Baldwin's public voice, through his essays or his interviews during the late 1960s and early 1970s. The public voice on the relationship between eroticism and revolution came, not from an African American writer, but from a French homosexual writer, Jean Genet.

Given the vocal homophobia of the Black Panther Party, Genet's invitation to work with the Black Panthers in 1970 was remarkable.[199] Although some African American radicals, such as the playwright Ed Bullins, dismissed Genet's "faggoty ideas about Black Art, Revolution, and people," Genet's sexuality was largely accepted.[200] In contrast to Baldwin, Genet's presence with the Panthers was both highly publicized and visible. Although both Baldwin and Genet—who were friends from the early 1950s—spoke together at the American Center in Paris in 1970 to defend George Jackson and the Panthers, Genet's output was far more prodigious.[201] Whereas Genet was soliciting interviews in well-known magazines and churning out publications such as the collected essays, *Here and Now for Bobby Seale* (1970), *May Day Speech* (1970), the introduction to the prison letters of George Jackson, *Soledad Brother* (1970), and then later *Prisoner of Love* (1986), Baldwin was licking his wounds after Cleaver's vicious attack.[202]

Still more surprising were Genet's repeated references to what he described as the irresistible eroticism of the Panthers.[203] While Genet's declaration that he was "in love" with the Black Panthers curiously mirrors Cleaver's recollection that "I fell in love with the Black Panther Party," for Genet, as Jonathan Dollimore has argued, the Panther's eroticism was "inseparable from their politics and the challenge they presented to white America."[204] For Genet, not only did the Panthers, like the Palestinians, exude "a very intense erotic charge," but he intimated that the former were sexually drawn to one another.[205] According to Genet, the Panthers "consisted of magnetized bodies magnetizing one another," what he elsewhere referred to as "their whole block and tackle, [which] was much in evidence through their trousers."[206]

Genet's emphasis on black manhood does little to shatter stereotypes of black sexual prowess, a point that the French writer is only too aware of: "[i]f sexual images keep cropping up it's because they're unavoidable, and because the sexual or erectile significance of the Party is self-evident."[207] But while Genet arguably employed and even flirted with black sexual stereotypes, he also emphasized the tenderness beneath the black machismo. David Hilliard, Genet repeated, was a mother to him, recalling that the Panther's kindness was "an education in affection."[208] Genet's emphasis on the Panthers' gentleness bears a striking resemblance to Baldwin's insistence that Stokely Carmichael had set out with a message of love. Malcolm X, Baldwin noted in *No Name* "was one of the gentlest people I have ever met."[209] In *Tell Me How Long*, the militant Christopher cooks and shops for the ailing Leo, paralleling David Hilliard's role as "mother" to Genet. Genet's description of *Soledad Brother* as "a book, tough and sure, both a weapon of liberation and a love poem" could equally have come from Baldwin's pen.[210]

Despite the similarities between Baldwin and Genet, the former, as I have illustrated, was largely circumscribed by the Black Power movement. In contrast to Genet, Baldwin was seen less as a revolutionary, and more—to a certain extent—as a source of poetic inspiration: both Angela Davis and Bobby Seale borrowed from Baldwin to create titles for their books.[211] Whereas the involvement with the Panthers gave Genet a new momentum and impetus to publish, the late 1960s is generally considered as the era of Baldwin's literary demise.[212] On the one hand, Baldwin was frequently criticized for being politically too vague, on the other I also want to emphasize that, unlike Genet, Baldwin's sexuality was a direct hindrance to his contribution to black politics.[213]

Genet's contrasting reception by the Panthers illustrates the pivotal roles that race and nationality played in the Black Power movement. Genet's whiteness, French nationality, and open homosexuality were far less threatening it seems than Baldwin's black queer identity.

Whereas Genet not only claimed identification with African Americans, but stated that he was black, his nationality and color enabled him to invoke this identity at will, just as he later identified with the plight of the

Palestinians.[214] Although Genet precipitated direct political action, such as Huey Newton's open letter "The Women's Liberation and Gay Liberation Movements," in August 1970—which stated that "maybe a homosexual could be the most revolutionary"—Baldwin only solicited criticism of his sexuality.[215] The different responses to Baldwin and Genet are illustrated by the latter's account of how David Hilliard not only accepted Genet's sexuality but stated "it would be great if all homosexuals would come twelve thousand kilometers to the defense of the Panthers."[216] Baldwin, too, had traveled twelve thousand kilometers from Paris to join the civil rights struggle, but he was also African American.

The impact of the late 1960s and early 1970s on Baldwin is clearly illustrated by his first novel of the new decade, *If Beale Street Could Talk* (1974). Not surprising, given the homophobia that Baldwin experienced, this is his first novel that deals exclusively with heterosexual relationships, and his first to use a female narrator. In rhetoric reminiscent of *Tell Me How Long*, the characters, according to Michelle Wallace, "positively gush the dogma of the Black Movement."[217] In contrast to the period before 1962, the publication date of *Another Country*, Baldwin was increasingly less vocal about the subject of sexuality, both in his fiction and his essays.

In his last novel, *Just Above My Head* (1979), Baldwin boldly paved the way for African American gay writing in the 1980s, radically portraying the intense love between black characters such as Arthur and Crunch, and Arthur and Jimmy. Countering critics such as Stanley Crouch, who refused to align homosexuality with liberation, and the First National Plenary Conference on Self-Determination, which argued that "[r]evolutionary nationalists . . . cannot uphold homosexuality in the leadership of Black Liberation," Baldwin's radicalism came in his continued insistence that "all love was holy."[218] As I explore in the following chapter, Baldwin's work pioneered a dialogue between religion and sexuality, the holy and the profane, boldly challenging the puritanical view of "terrors of the flesh."

FIGURE 1 *James Baldwin frying fish for guests of his dinner party at the apartment of his host Engin Cezzar, Istanbul 1965. Photograph by Sedat Pakay © 2014.*

FIGURE 2 *His French house guest Alain joking with James Baldwin in his Hollywood Hills apartment where he resided while working on the script of* The Autobiography of Malcolm X, *which he was co-authoring with playwright Arnold Perl. The film was to be based on Alex Haley's book on Malcolm X and to be produced by Columbia Pictures. Later it was produced by Warner Brothers as a documentary after Baldwin walked out of his assignment, January 1970. Photograph by Sedat Pakay © 2014.*

FIGURE 3 *During a conversation at a friend's house, Istanbul 1964. Photograph by Sedat Pakay © 2014.*

FIGURE 4 *In a happy mood, flashing his signature laugh during his stay in Rumeli Hisar, Istanbul, 1966. Photograph by Sedat Pakay © 2014.*

FIGURE 5 *Sipping afternoon wine at a friend's house, Istanbul, 1965. Photograph by Sedat Pakay © 2014.*

FIGURE 6 *Reading, accompanied by his mentor, the painter Beauford Delaney, on the porch of his Rumeli Hisar, Istanbul house, August 1966. Photograph by Sedat Pakay ©* 2014.

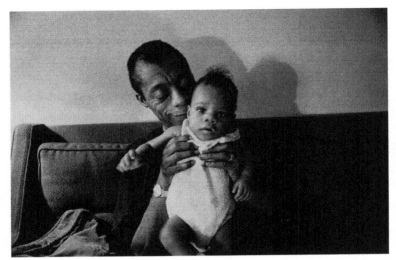

FIGURE 7 *Holding his nephew at his mother's apartment on West 71st Street, New York City, 1969. Photograph by Sedat Pakay © 2014.*

FIGURE 8 *Playing solitaire at his Hollywood Hills, California, apartment, January 1970. Photograph by Sedat Pakay © 2014.*

FIGURE 9 *Among his friends and family at a gathering at his mother's apartment, holding his brother David's hand. TV producer Ellis Haizlip is seated next to David, 1969. Photograph by Sedat Pakay © 2014.*

FIGURE 10 *Typing his novel,* Tell Me How Long the Train's Been Gone. *Rumeli Hisar, Istanbul, July 1966. Photograph by Sedat Pakay © 2014.*

Chapter 3

James Baldwin's Religion:
Sex, Love, and the Blues

So, in my case, in order to become a moral human being,
whatever that may be, I have to hang out with publicans and sinners,
whores and junkies, and stay out of the temple where they told us
nothing but lies anyway.

—JAMES BALDWIN, *A RAP ON RACE*

The essential religion of Black people comes out of something
which is not Europe. When Black people talk about true religion,
they're "speaking in tongues" practically. It would not be
understood in Rome.

—KALAMU YA SALAAM, "JAMES BALDWIN: LOOKING TOWARDS
THE EIGHTIES"

Much of the most penetrating critical work on James Baldwin has stressed the importance of reading the author's work across the different theoretical crossroads that his work traverses. Not only was he a queer, black, expatriate writer but Baldwin's work—as playwright, poet, essayist, and novelist—defies any straightforward reduction. With the advent of cultural theory, critics are now beginning to interrogate and celebrate Baldwin's manifest complexity. Yet, despite the promise of a critical framework that might tease out and illuminate the writer's vast body of work, one glaring absence remains. As friends and luminaries gathered to honor Baldwin at the Cathedral of St. John the Divine on December 8, 1987, it was the deceased author himself who reminded the congregation of the importance of religion in his life. As a recording of Baldwin singing "Precious Lord, Take My Hand, Lead Me On," filled the Cathedral, "it startled the listeners," David Leeming recalled. "He seemed to be there, still witnessing, and people were moved."[1]

Yet, Baldwin's haunting reminder of his religious past has gone all but unnoticed. Out of nearly a dozen full-length studies on Baldwin, only two books seriously consider him as a spiritual or religious writer, a factor even more surprising given claims by Hent de Vries and other scholars of a "'return to religion' in contemporary literature theory."[2] As Michael Lynch, one of the few critics to focus on Baldwin's theology, has pointed out, "[i]n spite of the profusion of biblical allusions and Christian symbols and themes throughout Baldwin's writing, the scholarship, aside from brief mention of the residual Christian content in his imagery . . . has offered no sustained treatment of his religious thought or theology."[3] While few critics would deny the continued influence of the black church on Baldwin's cadenced language, this is most often explained simply as a matter of style. Melvin Dixon places emphasis on how Baldwin manipulated "religious expression as a structural device for theme" and Harold Bloom concludes that Baldwin was a "post-Christian writer" whose "prophetic stance is not so much religious as aesthetic."[4] On the other hand, Cornel West notes that Baldwin's essays "are grounded in moralism," but he places emphasis on Baldwin's aesthetic mastery of "the rhythm, syncopation, and appeal of an effective sermon."[5]

It is arguably Baldwin himself who steered readers away from his complicated relationship to Christianity. After his vitriolic attacks on the church, notably in *The Fire Next Time* (1963) and *Tell Me How Long the Train's Been Gone* (1968), Baldwin was seen as a relentless social critic who had moved away from the institution of the church. Melvin Dixon concludes that Baldwin was "more the ironic doubter than devout believer," adding that "he had exchanged the pulpit for the pen, the sermon for the novel and the essay."[6] According to critics such as Craig Werner, Baldwin's later work rejected "purely spiritual approaches to problems" and took up "a perspective stressing social action in the face of an oppressive environment."[7] Critics noted a "comprehensive secularization" in Baldwin's work, and some began to accuse him of being "secular to his fingertips."[8]

Amid the critical silence surrounding the question of whether he was a religious writer or not, Baldwin's own voice, like the recording at his funeral, punctuates and disturbs the established critical corpus.[9] Often the moment is brief and unexpected, diluted and lost amid Baldwin's own attacks on Christianity, and yet it challenges claims that he merely exchanged the pulpit for the pen. Ernest Champion recalls how Baldwin terrified his students during his stint at Bowling Green State University in the late 1970s with his blasphemous dismissal of God. But Champion also writes about how on one occasion, Baldwin broke down while hearing a Gospel choir and was unable to remain in the room. "[T]hey are singing my life," Baldwin told Champion, "[t]hat is where it all began."[10] Again, in *Rap on Race* (1971), in a conversation with Margaret Mead, Baldwin seems to have been set off balance by the anthropologist, admitting not only that "religion has always really obsessed" him, but accepting the anthropologist's definition of him as a Christian.[11] As late as 1985, in the introduction to *The Price of the Ticket*, Baldwin confessed that "[o]nce I had left the pulpit, I had abandoned or betrayed my role in the community," a clear indication of the church's continued hold on him.[12] A closer examination of his "secular" texts, such as his final book, *The Evidence of Things Not Seen* (1985), reveals glimpses of his continued fascination with religion and spirituality.

I want to draw attention to the importance of Baldwin's spiritual development in his work alongside the impact of his religious background on his writing. In a critical era that is dominated—at least in Baldwin studies—by theoretical discussions of gender, masculinity, and sexuality, might it be that the sophistication of cultural studies is ill-equipped or simply unable to grapple with the religious? Katherine Clay Bassard's call for scholars to develop "greater sophistication in the theorizing of connections between literature and religion" has been heeded by a handful of scholars, but few engage with the relationship between religion and twentieth-century African American literature, and fewer critics again include Baldwin in their work.[13] Although Bassard's focus in *Spiritual Interrogations* is on early African American literature, her aim to foster "a deeper understanding of the ways in which sacred and secular, spiritual and political, often coexist" is particularly germane to Baldwin's writing.[14] If, as James Coleman points out, "critics who write about black novels seldom deal with religious and biblical traditions in fiction," what might Baldwin's writing reveal about the purported secularization of twentieth-century African American intellectual production?[15] Unlike Coleman who distinguishes between the "faithful vision" and lack of "faithful vision" in African American novelists, Baldwin's work complicates such divisions. As Joanna Brooks insightfully points out, Baldwin's work is shot through with references to the "threshing floor," a site that is not "an escape from struggle, but rather the beginning of struggle lived in a different, more socially demanding key."[16] One of the reasons that Baldwin has not been considered a "religious" writer may be precisely because his work seeks to redefine those boundaries between the sacred and the secular in ways that trouble conventional criticism that clings to those divisions.

In contrast to critics who see a progressive secularization in Baldwin's work, I question this prevailing critical narrative. Although Baldwin is frequently critical of black and white Christian practice and doctrine, his writing is characterized by a developing spiritual aesthetic, a feature of his work that troubles a critical autopsy of the writer as either secular or religious. Baldwin rarely used the terms "spiritual" or "spirituality" in writing or interviews, but the terms most closely describe several key moments in his work that I explore. Where possible, I have used the term "spiritual," rather than "religious," to distinguish Baldwin's explorations of transcendence that occur outside of Christian institutions. Anticipating novels such as Alice Walker's

The Color Purple or Gloria Naylor's *Mama Day*, much of Baldwin's work re-pudiates the stern patriarchy of institutional Christianity. In Baldwin's writing transcendence or ecstasy frequently occurs outside of religious worship; it is most likely to be found in the communion of friends and lovers, through playing or listening to music or making love. These moments are, as Clarence Hardy observes, imbued with "a very nearly religious cadence."[17] Baldwin's writing, in other words, frequently draws attention to the spirituality of "secular" actions and activities, what Walton Muyumba describes as the writer's "secular piety."[18]

Despite a smattering of articles on Baldwin and religion, there is no sustained critical examination of Baldwin's relationship to Pentecostalism/the Holiness movement.[19] Baldwin's at times vitriolic attacks on Christianity make sense when viewed alongside an understanding of his Pentecostal past. It becomes more productive, in other words, to see how his work diverges from, and resonates with, aspects of Pentecostalism, rather than simply labeling Baldwin as secular or irreligious. As Clarence Hardy has persuasively shown in the only full treatment of Baldwin's relationship to Pentecostalism, Baldwin's relationship to black Holiness culture is anything but straightforward. Hardy astutely points out that Baldwin's writing explores how "black evangelicalism embodies a posture of resistance against a hostile white world," echoing James Tinney's claims of the radical political implications of Pentecostalism. And yet, as Hardy argues, the black evangelical church falls short; for Hardy, its "redemptive value ultimately fails to overcome the extent to which Christianity has contributed to African disfigurement."[20] Hardy shows through his reading of Baldwin's work how the writer not only rejected white Christianity's demonization of the black body ("the creation of the devil 'flung into hell' as punishment for acting against God's will") but also how he lambasted the black church's inability or unwillingness to counter a deeply embedded black self-loathing.[21] Over the course of his life, Baldwin was increasingly critical of the black church's involvement in racial politics during the period of the civil rights movement.

Hardy's valuable work adds much to clarify Baldwin's complicated relationship to Pentecostalism (although he uses the term "Holiness" rather than Pentecostal). In contrast to Hardy's work, I am not concerned with the strengths or weaknesses of this Holiness tradition; rather I explore the importance of the black church on Baldwin's writing throughout his career. The church, Baldwin recalled in the late 1970s, "was how we forged our identity."[22] More specifically, I want to consider how Baldwin's writing was shaped by key features of Pentecostalism, a marginalized denomination that sought distance from mainstream Protestantism, striving for what believers see as a quest for a purer or more authentic spirituality. Grounding Baldwin's anti-institutional views in an understanding of Pentecostalism may illuminate his more puzzling comments on the church. As Patricia Schnapp astutely writes,

"Baldwin has never had any argument with the gospel as such. What he has criticized is rather, institutionalized Christianity as embodied in the churches and the failure of nominal Christians to live up to the moral tenets of their religion."[23]

While it would be hard to argue that Baldwin remained uncritical of Pentecostalism, his writing is shaped by some of the faith's distinguishing features, particularly the theme of exile and the emphasis on salvation as an individual matter. Thus, while Sondra O'Neale rightly concludes that "one cannot ascertain whether or not Baldwin is a 'religious' writer because his works do not reflect the traditional treatment of Christianity in black American literature," his portrayal of spirituality in fiction and nonfiction begins to cohere with an understanding of Pentecostalism.[24]

Baldwin's Pentecostal Past

In her excellent cultural history of the Holiness movement, *Saints in Exile*, Cheryl J. Sanders notes that numerous articles and books draw on Baldwin's description of conversion in *Go Tell It on the Mountain* "as their major source of information" about Pentecostalism.[25] Sanders's observation is surprising given that few literary or cultural critics refer specifically to Baldwin's Pentecostal past. In fact, aside from David Bergman's brief discussion of Pentecostalism in his chapter, "The Agony of Gay Black Literature" and Clarence Hardy's discussion of Holiness culture in *James Baldwin's God*, few if any critics distinguish Baldwin's Pentecostalism from Protestantism.[26]

Baldwin's involvement with Pentecostalism began in his early teenage years when he accompanied friends to Mother Rosa Horn's Mount Calvary Assembly of the Pentecostal Faith of All Nations in Brooklyn. Previously, Baldwin had attended various Baptist churches with his father, including the Abyssinian Baptist Church on 138th Street, run by the famous preacher and congressman, Adam Clayton Powell. After a short spell at Mother Horn's church, Baldwin moved with his friends to the Fireside Pentecostal Assembly, where, at the age of fourteen, he became "a Holy Roller Preacher."[27] As Baldwin recalled in *The Fire Next Time*, he was fourteen when he underwent "a prolonged religious crisis," adding that "I use the word 'religious' in the common, and arbitrary sense, meaning that I then discovered God, His saints and angels, and His blazing Hell."[28] A close reading of *Fire* reveals that Baldwin's religious experience was anything but arbitrary; his long essay in fact suggests that he had by no means "got over" his church upbringing. While he would refer to the church in *Fire* as a "gimmick," his writing would repeatedly counter this view.[29] In "To Crush a Serpent," for example, one of his last essays, Baldwin made no attempt to mask the sincerity of his early years. Noting that "the depth of his [a young minister's] faith is a mighty force," Baldwin recalled that when he was in the pulpit, he "believed."[30]

For a writer who would become preoccupied with the themes of exile and alienation, Baldwin's decision to move from the mainstream Baptist church to the marginalized tradition of Pentecostalism seems in keeping with his future literary interests.[31] Although Joseph Washington has argued that African Americans "have never been included in the mainstream of American Protestantism," Pentecostalism has historically been greeted with "suspicion and disapprobation" by the African American mainstream.[32] One major factor was the Pentecostal belief not only in glossolalia and xenoglossy but also in the power of the Holy Spirit to heal the sick, a practice that led to charges of paganism, heathenism, and even heresy.[33] In a number of social histories of African American religion, including E. Franklin Frazier's influential *The Negro Church in America* (1964), Pentecostalism is listed variously under "Negro Cults in the City" and "Organized Religion and the Cults."[34] Mother Horn, in particular, as Frazier notes, was notorious for her claims of not only healing the blind but for raising thousands of people from the dead.[35] In contrast to the middle-class respectability of preachers like Adam Clayton Powell, a large number of Holiness church preachers were untrained. Many, as Frazier notes, were accused of being "exploiters and charlatans."[36] Pentecostal congregations were frequently described in terms that smacked of class snobbery, illustrated by Joseph Washington's description of storefront congregations as "a membership that is less than lower-class in status, with untrained charlatans for leaders, and worshippers who do not only 'shout' but speak in strange 'tongues.'"[37]

Despite the criticism leveled at Pentecostal churches, advocates stress the denomination's deliberate exile from mainstream Protestantism. Zora Neale Hurston, one of the earliest commentators on the Pentecostal church, wrote that the Sanctified Church was a "protest" against the emphasis on wealth and money in the rising black middle-class churches.[38] As Sanders notes, the early Pentecostal churches, formed at the turn of the century, "'came out' of the mainline black denominational churches and sought 'the deeper life of entire sanctification' and Spirit Baptism."[39] Like Baptists, but unlike mainstream Protestantism, the Holiness movement placed emphasis not on religion mediated through the preacher but on a direct experience with God. In so doing, as Robert Anderson has noted, "[t]he Pentecostals created a kind of anti-Establishment Protestantism that was anticlerical, antitheological, antiliturgical, antisacramental, antiecclesiastical, and indeed, in a sense, antireligious."[40] In relation to Baldwin, the Saints' dialectical identity of "being in the world, but not of it" is often explained through the paradigm of exile, a dominant theme in Baldwin's writing.[41]

According to some theologians, the Pentecostal movement was an attempt "to preserve or restate what was believed to be the old-time religion, and as such it was an authentic expression of that older, folkish culture."[42] According to Hurston, Pentecostalism was not, as many claimed, "a new religion," but "the older forms of religious expression asserting themselves against the new," a point that Baldwin picks up on when he claims that the "essential religion of Black people comes out of something which is not Europe."[43] As far as Baldwin is concerned, this movement away from an established church institution is fundamental to his emphasis on personal salvation that need not be mediated through the institution of the church. While Pentecostalism is also institutional and authoritarian, Baldwin's work most closely approximates a Christocentric view of Christianity, a theme that characterizes the Holiness movement.[44]

The deliberate movement away from established Protestant traditions to an "old-time religion" characterizes Pentecostalism as both a new and an ancient form of worship. Historically, the formal birth of Pentecostalism is marked by the Azusa Street revivals in 1906, an event that precipitated the formation of the Holiness Church.[45] And yet Pentecostalism, according to a number of critics, in its attempts to rescue a more authentic religion, can be traced back to much older African religions, a point I discuss in the final chapter. Hurston famously claimed that the Pentecostal church was an attempt to reintroduce an earlier African religion that was lost during slavery.[46] Like Hurston, James Tinney argues that Pentecostalism shares at least three distinct Africanisms, including dance, percussion, and speaking in tongues.[47] In fact, according to Tinney, not only do "few [theologians] express doubt about the Blackness of Pentecostalism," but "nowhere is there a religion [Pentecostalism] which is as truly Afro-American as this."[48]

Despite Tinney's claims about Pentecostalism's African derivation, historians have been divided on the question of whether African cultural traits survived the legacy of slavery. John Philips, for example, disputes the claims of "the uniquely African elements of Pentecostal and Holiness worship practices," arguing that black Pentecostal services closely mirror those of white Holiness practices.[49] Franklin Frazier likewise concludes that it is "impossible to establish any continuity between African religious practices and the Negro church in the United States." And yet, while his conclusion is more cautious than Hurston's claim that "shouting is a survival of the African 'possession' by the gods," he concedes that it "most likely reveal[s] a connection with the African background."[50]

While the origins of shout songs, or ring shouts, are contested, most critics agree on their central place in the Holiness movement and their impact on black culture. In fact, according to critics such as Sterling Stuckey, ring shouts and shout songs are not only fundamental to jazz, but they "continued to form the principal context in which black creativity occurred."[51] As a number of cultural critics have noted, Pentecostalism revolutionized black religious music by incorporating the secular sounds of blues and jazz

into their services.[52] For Hurston, the Holiness movement was "a revitaliz-
ing element in Negro music" to the extent that listeners could not distinguish between a jazz performance and a Pentecostal service.[53]

Hurston's observation underscores the Holiness movement's complicated
relationship to blues and jazz. For, while the shout song may be evidence of
surviving African traits, it is also a central component of jazz and blues, a
medium historically rejected by the Holiness movement for being too secular.
The anthropologist Morton Marks, for example, has argued that the en-
tranced performances of soul singers such as Aretha Franklin and James
Brown are virtually indistinguishable from the "shouts" in church services.[54]
In addition, many of the most influential jazz artists, such as John Coltrane
and Ray Charles, not only grew up in the Sanctified tradition, but forged a
new hybrid between the secular world of jazz and the spirituality of Pentecostalism. One notable example is Baldwin's own song at his funeral, "Take My
Hand Precious Lord," which was written by Thomas A. Dorsey, who pioneered the crossover from blues to gospel.[55]

The Holiness movement's ambiguous attitude toward jazz and blues is illustrated by both their acceptance and repudiation of this secular music. On one
hand, as Baldwin explores in both *Go Tell It on the Mountain* and *The Amen
Corner*, jazz is deemed unholy and prohibited. Yet, on the other, historically,
the Holiness movement was the first black Protestant denomination to employ
the "tools of the devil" (the horn, piano, tambourine, and drum) into their
service.[56] The links between Pentecostalism and jazz are also evident in the
form of worship. Not only are ministers encouraged to extemporize, rather
than prepare their sermons, but preaching in the Holiness churches is viewed
as a climatic "performance." For critics such as Joseph Washington, Pentecostal services are unstructured and unconventional; he describes them as "a time
of carelessness, like that which comes over participants in a jazz session who
are caught up in the rhythm."[57] For Baldwin, it is precisely the link to jazz—the
possibility of extemporized transformation—that characterizes his work.

Baldwin's Personal Theology

I want to turn now to Baldwin's writing about religion and spirituality in
order to argue that his work is in fact characterized by a developing spiritual
aesthetic. Like Michael Lynch, who claims that the writer's work "develops
more as a corrective to than a repudiation of Christian theology as understood and practiced," I contend that Baldwin's writing is frequently critical of
mainstream Christian practice, but that it is also punctuated with frequent
meditations on the spirit of the early church, a fundamental concern of and
inspiration for Pentecostalism.[58] To explore Baldwin's writing on spirituality,
I focus on three main areas, drawn from a variety of Baldwin's fiction and

nonfiction. First, I locate Baldwin's critique of the white church in a historical context. Second, I examine Baldwin's criticism of the black church's lack of love and what Baldwin sees as a negation of agency. Third, I examine Baldwin's call for Christianity to return to what Lynch terms "the spirit of the early church."

For many critics, Baldwin's virulent and acerbic critique of the white church in *The Fire Next Time* is ample proof of his secular birth. In fact, *The Fire Next Time* has been instrumental not only in perpetuating Baldwin's secular image but also in precipitating a revision of critical thinking about his earlier work. As Rolf Lunden has insightfully pointed out, critics repeatedly failed to interpret *Go Tell It on the Mountain* as an indictment of Christianity or an ironic commentary until the publication of *Fire* in 1963.[59] Baldwin's two essays that became *The Fire Next Time* became something of a turning point in writing about the civil rights movement. It is important, therefore, to read his criticism of the church in this context. Baldwin's essay "Down at the Cross" begins with his recollection of how, at fourteen, he experienced "a prolonged religious crisis," explaining that he "discovered God, His saints and angels, and His blazing Hell."[60] As Baldwin points out, for a young impoverished African American in Harlem, there were not many options for survival. "Some went on wine or whiskey or the needle," Baldwin recalls, while "others, like me, fled into the church."[61] As Baldwin's use of the word "fled" suggests, the church was viewed as a place of safety, or a "gimmick" as he referred to it in the same essay.[62] Despite Baldwin's skepticism, there are moments where he attests to the power of his ecumenical experience, most strikingly in a description of his conversion, described by the author as "the strangest sensation I have ever had in my life."[63] In a remarkable description, Baldwin captures the awe and terror of this transformative moment. Unexpectedly, Baldwin finds himself on his back with the saints above him, filled with an anguish that "cannot be described." When he attempts to relive that moment, Baldwin couches it in apocalyptic terms where the spirit "moved in me like one of those floods that devastate counties, tearing everything down, tearing children from their parents and lovers from each other, and making everything an unrecognizable waste."[64]

Crucially, Baldwin rhetorically brings the reader down to earth as he reflects on his experience. "But God—and I felt this even then, so long ago, on that tremendous floor, unwillingly—is white." At the very moment that he is "saved," Baldwin has another epiphany, suggesting that his political consciousness was born: "And if His love was so great, and if He loved all His children, why were we, the blacks, cast down so far? Why?"[65] This experience of conversion, I would suggest, had a profound effect on Baldwin's writing; the experience on the threshing floor is described without irony and there is an acknowledgment of the power of the Holy Spirit. The church, Baldwin writes, was a place that he continued to find "exciting," adding that "[i]t took a long time for me to disengage myself from this excitement, and on the blind-est, most visceral level, I never really have, and never will."[66]

By calling attention to the historical inequality of suffering between white and black Christians, Baldwin anticipates and feeds into the work of black humanists who have questioned the appropriateness of theodicy to explain African American suffering. Paralleling the work of African American theo-logians such as William R. Jones, Baldwin vehemently opposes the recalci-trant acceptance of "the divine right of suffering."[67] Writing over twenty years after *Fire* in his last published article, Baldwin again returned to this theme, expressing his "profound and troubled contempt" for white Christians who invoked the curse of Ham to justify slavery.[68]

Baldwin's critique of the white church is also the legacy of African Ameri-can commentators who, as Cornel West has noted, were forced to adopt what he terms a "dialectical methodology." By refusing to believe the premises out-lined by white theologians, African Americans have historically "digested, decoded, and deciphered," white Christianity's official line.[69] Baldwin's early realization in *The Fire Next Time* that "the Bible had been written by white men" and that it had been used to justify slavery anticipates the work of Afri-can American theologians such as James Cone, who have forcefully argued that "the white church's involvement in slavery and racism in America simply cannot be overstated."[70] Like Cone, Baldwin rails against Christianity's com-plicity in the mechanisms of slavery and colonialism, arguing vehemently that "[t]he spreading of the Gospel . . . was an absolutely indispensable justifi-cation for the planting of the flag."[71] For Baldwin, armed with the knowledge of (white) Christianity's relationship to colonial history, his position as a min-ister became increasingly problematic. "[I]t began to take all the strength I had not to stammer, not to curse," Baldwin recalled, "not to tell them [the congregation] to throw away their Bibles and get off their knees and go home and organize, for example, a rent strike."[72]

As Clarence Hardy has cogently outlined, *The Fire Next Time* is Baldwin's most explicit critique of Christianity's prolonged vilification of the black body.[73] Baldwin's criticism of the church implicitly attacks what Cone terms the "white lie" of Christianity. By persuading slaves that "life on earth was insignificant because obedient servants of God could expect a 'reward' in heaven after death," the (white) church was complicit in attempts to deter and contain black insurrection and rebellion.[74] But Baldwin was also increasingly dismissive of what he saw as the black church's ineffectuality, a criticism that parallels his growing disillusionment with more moderate measures to combat racism. In *Blues for Mister Charlie*, this despair is played out dramat-ically by the resignation that racial injustice will "end with the Bible and the gun," a clear indication of the need for direct action.[75] Following Baldwin's recollection in *Fire* that he wanted to implore his congregation to drop the Bible and become politically engaged, in *Tell Me How Long the Train's Been*

Gone (1968), the church is seen as politically impotent. In the face of unrelenting racism and brutality, religion is depicted as little more than a lie, illustrated by the desperate curses that so many Baldwin characters utter. In *Another Country*, Rufus curses God before hurling himself off the George Washington Bridge; in *Tell Me How Long the Train's Been Gone*, a beaten and dejected Caleb recalls that he "hated God"; and in *Just Above My Head*, God becomes "a very sick dude."[76]

Baldwin's continued pillorying of the church's political impotence is surprising given the birth of a progressive black theology in the mid-1960s.[77] In an open letter to the *New York Times* in 1966, the newly formed National Committee of Negro Churchmen (NCNC) openly declared their support for Black Power, insisting, as their chair Gayraud Wilmore later stated, that "the rising crescendo of voices from the pulpit and pew demand that black churchmen reexamine their belief; that unless they begin to speak and act relevantly in the present crisis they must prepare to die."[78] Despite the black church's growing political commitment, Baldwin critiqued its effectiveness, insisting that, since it failed to attract young people, "its social usefulness is at least debatable."[79]

If Baldwin was critical of the church's role as an effective political organ, he also lambasted the church for its inability to foster love, most explicitly illustrated in *The Fire Next Time*, where he forcefully states: "I really mean that there was no love in the church," adding that it "was a mask for hatred and self-hatred and despair."[80] What little love there is in the church, Baldwin argues, is inauthentic, since it is induced, not by unconditional love, but by fear of a wrathful God: people "ought to love the Lord *because* they loved Him, and not because they were afraid of going to Hell."[81] This terror of damnation, Baldwin contends, in fact obstructs the path to salvation, which "is not precipitated by the terror of being consumed in Hell." Rather, for Baldwin, salvation is "accepting and reciprocating the love of God," which leads, not to separation, but to "union."[82]

Baldwin's emphasis on union extends to the role that the church plays in the community. For Baldwin, the black church remains hypocritical, as it is unable or unwilling to extend the message of love to black and white alike. Recalling his indignation in *The Fire Next Time* at a pastor's command not to give up his chair to a white woman, Baldwin writes despairingly of the church's edict: "what was the point, the purpose, of *my* salvation, if it did not permit me to behave with love towards others, no matter how they behaved towards me?"[83]

In his last book, *The Evidence of Things Not Seen* (1985), Baldwin again returned to this theme, reflecting on how the church had the potential to offer love and support to individuals, but chose instead to eject them from the community. Baldwin recollects how Billy, a seventeen-year-old member of his congregation, was ostracized by the church, having "backslid" and "gone

back into the world." Disobeying the church's injunction not to communicate with Billy, Baldwin recalls his decision with both anger and indignation: "I was acting, after all, on the moral assumptions I had inherited from
the community that had produced me. I had been told to *love everybody*."[84]
His disobedience in communicating with the "fallen" Billy serves to illuminate the reasons for the author's exile from the institution of the church. Not
only did Baldwin rail against white Christianity, stating that "I became a
Christian by not imitating white people," but he also viewed all institutionalized religion as hypocritical and ineffectual.[85] In line with the early Pentecostal ethos, Baldwin told Margaret Mead that "the Christian church is
meaningless. The *Christian church* as church."[86] In a vehement outburst
against the church, Baldwin stressed that "in order to become a moral
human being . . . I have to hang out with publicans and sinners, whores and
junkies, and stay out of the temple where they told us nothing but lies
anyway."[87]

Baldwin's distrust and disillusionment with the institution of the church
is illustrated through characters such as Arthur in *Just Above My Head* and
Luke in *The Amen Corner*, both of whom represent a spiritual authenticity
that stems from outside of the church. Yet, neither Luke nor Arthur can ac-
curately be described as secular, since both protagonists are musicians, suggesting a more authentic spirituality that can be found through jazz and
gospel. By illustrating the power of music, a medium that fosters an open
community that contrasts sharply with the stifling division of institutional
piety, Baldwin suggests the close relationship between blues, jazz, gospel, and
spirituality.

Historically, there is a close, albeit complex, relationship between the
Holiness movement and jazz, a connection Baldwin makes in *The Fire
Next Time* during his recollections of preaching: "I would improvise from
the texts like a jazz musician improvises from a theme. I never wrote a
sermon. . . . You have to sense the people you're talking to. You have to respond to what they hear."[88] This connection between spirituality and
music, according to James Campbell, became a central theme in Baldwin's
later years. Campbell notes that while Baldwin "was not a believer in the
sense of subscribing to a particular faith, or belonging to a specific church,
his life was based on a faith that can only be called religious. . . . His scrip-
ture was the old black gospel music."[89]

Campbell's observation is corroborated by a striking example of Baldwin's
love of church music, which pierces the often acerbic prose of *The Fire Next
Time*:

> There is no music like that music, no drama like the drama of the saints
> rejoicing, the sinners moaning, the tambourines racing, and all those
> voices coming together and crying holy unto the Lord.[90]

Much has been written on Baldwin's pioneering use of the blues and jazz in prose and his repeated references to himself as a blues singer. Consider, for example, the plethora of Baldwin's titles that draw on African American music: *Go Tell It on the Mountain, The Amen Corner*, "Sonny's Blues," *Blues for Mister Charlie, If Beale Street Could Talk*, and *Just Above My Head*. In contrast to institutional piety, which he chastises for its emphasis on refuge and safety, Baldwin asserts that jazz and blues can only be truly heard by those who have suffered, as he makes clear in his essay, "The Uses of the Blues." Ray Charles, according to Baldwin, "is a great tragic artist, [who] makes of a genuinely re-ligious confession something triumphant and liberating. He tells us that he cried so loud he gave the blues to his neighbor next door."[91]

Baldwin's commentary on Ray Charles is important as he makes it clear that music is not so much a substitute for religion, but a spiritual medium that has the ability to reach out to others. In his recollection of Aretha Franklin's concerts, Baldwin recalls how the singer turned her performance at the Apollo Theater into "a gospel church service," adding "[a]nd that's true reli-gion."[92] Although Ralph Ellison would complain in the late 1950s that musi-cians such as Horace Silver "don't even know the difference between a blues and a spiritual," Baldwin's writing imbues the historically secular blues with a spiritual quality that can affect change and even transcendence.[93] In "Son-ny's Blues," Baldwin's most anthologized story, the narrator begins to under-stand what the blues musician is communicating in language that echoes his description of spiritual awakening: "the man who creates the music is hearing something else, is dealing with the roar rising from the void and imposing order on it as it hits the air." In this description and elsewhere, Baldwin sug-gests that the musician is able to transform pain and absurdity, not into lan-guage like his own work as a writer, but another kind of narrative, "another order, more terrible because it has no words, and triumphant, too, for that same reason."[94]

In Baldwin's first novel there is a brief but telling scene where Gabriel is introduced to John Grimes for the first time. As the baby is presented to his future stepfather, he turns, not to Gabriel, but toward the sound of the gram-ophone playing a blues record down the hall.[95] In *The Amen Corner*, Marga-ret, like Gabriel, forbids her son David to play blues records. "The way that box is going, you wouldn't hear the Holy *Ghost* come in," Margaret says about Luke's old record playing in her son's bedroom. "Turn it off! Turn it off!"[96] And yet, as Baldwin suggests through David, a budding but clandestine jazz musician, there is little to separate the music heard in the church and the jazz played downtown in bars. "Standing outside of the church," Zora Neale Hurston wrote about a jazz pianist in Jacksonville who played for Sanctified church services and at parties, "it is difficult to determine just which kind of engagement he is filling at the moment."[97] Echoing Hurston's obser-vation, David tells Luke that he knows that the men who come back to the church are not there for the Holy Ghost, as his mother believes, but to hear him play the piano.[98]

Baldwin's writing on music points to the transformative qualities of music, a force all the more powerful for being not only democratic (jazz clubs, streets, records) but also an experience that can be shared. Although his writing about the transformative powers of music is written in a suggestively spiritual way, Baldwin hints through his iconoclastic character, Luke, that spirituality need not be restricted to the church. Luke, dying of tuberculosis, implores his son not "to get away from the things that hurt you," echoing Baldwin's criticism of America's inability to confront pain and suffering.[99] According to Luke, "[y]ou got to learn to live with those things—and—use them," and indeed his music and understanding of suffering and love transform Margaret.[100] At the end of the play, Luke dies and Margaret, extemporizing her sermon like a jazz musician, leaves the church, finally understanding what Baldwin wrote much later about the blues: that "the acceptance of this anguish one finds in the blues, and the expression of it, creates also, however odd this may sound, a kind of joy."[101]

In Baldwin's work the figure of the musician increasingly represents a move toward an anti-institutional spirituality. While earlier figures such as Rufus in *Another Country* were not able to articulate their pain through music, the characters in Baldwin's last novel, *Just Above My Head*, emphasize the importance of spirituality that is forged and experienced outside of the church. *Just Above* is an important novel, not least because it tempers the critical consensus on Baldwin's increasing secularity. This last novel suggests the author's distinction between institutionalized religion and spiritual authenticity, something Baldwin explores explicitly through the character of Florence. While she is both loving and affirmative, she "doesn't like to go to church," since "the people don't have any spirit . . . they've lost the true religion."[102] True religion, or spirituality, remains a crucial tenet of Baldwin's work; it rarely surfaces through traditional religious practice. Instead Baldwin points to the spirituality of love, friendship, and creative expression.

Love Is in the Air

Although Baldwin was lambasted by critics who claimed that he extolled the power of love in *Another Country* rather than offering concrete political solutions, I want to suggest that Baldwin's developing notion of love is key to an understanding of his life and work. Like Robert Genter, who argues that "Baldwin's major contribution to the cultural politics of modernism was his reinvention of love as a guiding social principle," I want to stress the importance of love in the writer's work.[103] First, however, it is important not to confuse Baldwin's emphasis on love with an emphasis on sentimentality, a feeling that he explicitly warns against.[104] Second, his definition of love is explicitly active and political. Echoing Cornel West's warning that a "love ethic has nothing to do with sentimental feelings or tribal connections," and Martin Luther King Jr.'s insistence that "love is not to be confused with some sentimental outpouring," Baldwin explicitly points out that, by focusing on love, he does not "mean anything passive."[105] Instead, he means "something active, something more like a fire . . . something which can change you . . . I mean a passionate belief, a passionate knowledge of what a human being can do."[106] Like King who spoke of love as "a force," Baldwin wrote that he conceived of God "as a means of liberation," but also that "[l]ove is a battle, love is a war; love is a growing up."[107] Love, for Baldwin and King, as George Shulman points out, "is then a political practice, not movement beyond it," what Genter describes as "a disruptive force, one that did not provide comfort, stability, or solidarity but one that challenged, if not dismantled, the boundaries of the self."[108]

Baldwin's most radical rewriting of Christian—or at least spiritual identity—can be found in his emphasis on salvation and redemption, which comes not through God, but through a love that is founded on the sharing of pain. In contrast to characters such as John Grimes who agonize on the threshing floor at the mercy of an Old Testament God, Baldwin's later work suggests the possibility of salvation through support and love of another, a theme clearly articulated by Leo Proudhammer in *Tell Me How Long*: "some moments teach one the price of the human condition: if one can live with one's pain, then one respects the pain of others, and so, briefly, but transcendentally, we can release each other from pain."[109] By using the language of religious conversion ("transcendentally") Baldwin explicitly replaces salvation through prayer with what Leo refers to repeatedly as "the touch of another: no matter how transient, at no matter what price."[110]

Baldwin's emphasis on "touch" is both physical and spiritual, suggesting being moved (to be touched) but also the physical act of reaching out to another. By emphasizing the physicality of touch, Baldwin continues his critique of the way in which American Puritanism prohibits and inhibits both bodily and spiritual contact, what he explicitly refers to as the damage caused by "a fear of anybody touching anybody."[111] In order to redress this, Baldwin insists that we must overcome our "terror of the flesh," what he also calls "a terror of human life, of human touch."[112] As he repeatedly stated, "*Nobody* makes any connections," resulting in "this truncated, de-balled, galvanized activity which thinks of itself as *sex*."[113]

For Baldwin, the original spirit of the church has been lost, hijacked by the puritanical fervor of St. Paul who warned that it is better "to marry than to burn."[114] In *The Fire Next Time*, Baldwin explicitly inveighs against those Christians who have conveniently forgotten the origins of the early church. "The real architect of the Christian church," Baldwin reminds his readers—in a line that later infuriated Hoover—"was not the disreputable, sun-baked Hebrew who gave it his name but the mercilessly fanatical and self-righteous St. Paul."[115] Continuing this theme some twenty years later, Baldwin railed against the present-day "Moral Majority" arguing that they

> have taken the man from Galilee as hostage. He does not know them and they do not know him. Nowhere, in the brief and extraordinary passage of the man known as Jesus Christ, is it recorded that he ever upbraided his disciples concerning their carnality. These were rough, hard-working fishermen on the Sea of Galilee. Their carnality can be taken as given, and they would never have trusted or followed or loved a man who did not know they were men and who did not respect their manhood.[116]

For Baldwin, Christianity's mortification—or terror—of the flesh has stunted the opportunity for love, a condition he examines in *The Fire Next Time*, observing that "it is also inevitable that a literal attempt to mortify the flesh should be made among black people like those with whom I grew up. Negroes in this country . . . are taught really to despise themselves from the moment their eyes open on the world."[117] In his fiction, particularly in *Just Above My Head*, Baldwin would stress the religiousness of love between men, but his essays draw attention to the ways in which the Puritanism of the black church has contributed to a wider self-hatred. While Baldwin is deeply critical of white society's demonizing of the black American subject, he frequently calls the black church to task for being apathetic and ineffectual. In his recollections of becoming a minister, Baldwin makes the connections between spiritual and sexual awakening explicit. Harlem, as Baldwin recalls, was a place where "the wages of sin were visible everywhere." As a young boy, Baldwin recalled how he was vulnerable to sexual molestation, which made him feel like "one of the most depraved people on earth," which in turn caused him to flee to the safety of the church.[118] Baldwin's early teenage years, as David Leeming notes, were a period in "which he was to be nearly overwhelmed by sexuality, and, almost at the same moment, by religion."[119]

Baldwin's recollections of his entrance into the ministry illustrate the paradoxical nature of the church. On the one hand, Baldwin is critical of the church's prohibitions of the flesh, but on the other, he is also deeply aware of the physicality of worship; how spirituality is inextricably linked to the body. Recalling his early days as a young preacher, Baldwin notes how he attempted to love his congregation "more than I would ever love any lover and, so, escape the terrors of this life." But this refuge, Baldwin recalls, was not possible. Aware that his status led others to think of him as a "sexual prize," Baldwin emphasizes the carnality of congregations that are made up "of men and women."[120]

Baldwin's frequent allusions to the connections between spiritual and sexual energy are forcefully illustrated by his initiation into the church. As he joins the charismatic Mother Horn's church, Baldwin is struck by the similarity between the church and the sexual depravity of the streets. Mother Horn's first question "[w]hose little boy are you?" was, Baldwin recalled, the same question asked by pimps and racketeers. Moving to the church, Baldwin recalls, was "a spiritual seduction," not far removed from the sexual activity of the streets.[121] Even the moment of conversion, as David Leeming notes, led Baldwin "to sense the sexual roots of the terrifying release he had experienced on the church floor as Mother Horn and the saints had labored over him."[122]

Not surprisingly, some critics have picked up on Baldwin's exploration of the tensions between the Word and the flesh. John S. Lash, for example, maintains that Baldwin, though rejecting the formal strictures of the church, "transfigure[d]" his earlier beliefs into "the fear and admiration and worship of the male sex organ," what Lash terms, "a modern cult of phallicism."[123] However, in contrast to Lash's insistence that he substituted sex for religion, I would argue that it is the relationship or the similarity between sexual and spiritual encounters that concerns Baldwin. Whereas Lash concludes that Baldwin "writes well about sex and he writes well about religion . . . [but] he cannot fuse the two," it is precisely this fusion, this tension between the sexual and the spiritual, that Baldwin explores.[123]

Rather than transfiguring the religious into the sexual, Baldwin urges his readers to reexamine what is generally held sacred. This entails, far from a repudiation of the sacred, a need to accept the sensual side of religion. However, as Baldwin makes clear:

> The word "sensual" is not intended to bring to mind quivering dusky maidens or priapic black studs. I am referring to something much simpler and much less fanciful. To be sensual, I think, is to respect and rejoice in the force of life, of life itself, and to be *present* in all that one does, from the effort of loving to the breaking of bread.[124]

Baldwin's clarification of the term "sensual" is vital to an understanding of his spiritual aesthetic. Baldwin is highly critical of sexual encounters that are devoid of spirituality; in his writing, spirituality is rarely experienced between God and the believer, but through a union, often sexual, between two people. At times, as I explore a little later, this relationship is ushered in through gospel music, a medium, as Reid-Pharr notes, which "presupposed a personal relationship with one's god, a relationship uncannily similar to that between lovers."[125]

In *Nothing Personal*, Baldwin makes explicit his implicit suggestion that people, not gods, save people: "I have always felt that a human being could only be saved by another human being. I am aware that we do not save each other very often. . . . And all that God can do, and that I expect Him to do, is lend one the courage to continue one's journey and face one's end."[126] In his fiction and essays, this message is repeatedly played out: Baldwin stresses that individuals need to take responsibility to save one another and he remains deeply critical of religion's passivity. In "To Crush the Serpent," Baldwin again emphasizes the way in which spirituality is not just an abstract act of faith between believer and God, but an active connection between people. Writing that there is "absolutely no salvation without love," Baldwin emphasizes that salvation connects, "so that one sees oneself in others and others in oneself."[127]

In the Beginning Was the Word

I want to trace Baldwin's examination of religion and spirituality in his fiction, beginning with a reading of *Go Tell It on the Mountain* and the short story, "The Outing," two narratives that are formally located within the arena of the church. I then turn briefly to Baldwin's last two novels, *If Beale Street Could Talk* and *Just Above My Head*. By juxtaposing Baldwin's early and later work, I maintain that his views on religion and spirituality developed but retained essential similarities. In contrast to critics who have noted "secularization" in his later work, I locate a deep-rooted emphasis on the need for spiritual growth. My reasons for doing so are threefold. First, the tensions between religion and sexuality are one of the most central themes in Baldwin's work, themes that cohere and illuminate his fiction. Second, Baldwin's critique of the church's division between spirit and flesh is radical in the sense that it attempts to redefine the essence of authentic spirituality. Third, by focusing on this central theme, I show the coherence between Baldwin's reputedly "religious" work (that is, his early fiction) and what has generally been noted as his "secular" work—that is, his fiction set outside the boundaries of the church.

While a handful of critics have noted how Baldwin infuses his descriptions of sex with religious language, little work has been done on this important area.[128] Often Baldwin is accused of either confusing homosexuality with religion or of elevating same-sex desire to the ecstasies of religious rapture. Ralph Ellison, for example, commenting on *Go Tell It*, bemoaned that Baldwin "doesn't know the difference between getting religion and going homo."[129] Robert Bone insightfully observes that "the language of the store-front church persists ... primarily when he [Baldwin] tries to heighten or exalt the moment of sexual union," but the reasons are left unexplored.[130] Instead, Bone accuses Baldwin of over-poeticizing homosexuality, endowing it with "mythic significance." Disregarding the reasons *why* Baldwin uses religious language in sexual discourse, Bone writes disparagingly of *Another Country's* Eric as "the high priest of ineffable phallic mysteries," foregrounding Stanley Crouch's conclusion that Baldwin's fiction presents an unconvincing "alternative order in which homosexuals served as priests in a religion based on love."[131]

In contrast to Bone's insistence that Baldwin proselytizes "salvation through sodomy," I agree with Howard Harper that Baldwin's work is not "a plea for homosexuality."[132] Rather, as Harper concludes, it "is the love rather than the sex which is important." And it is love, often sexual, but infused with spirituality, that Baldwin insists upon, what he refers to in *Blues for Mister Charlie* as "the holy and liberating orgasm."[133] Michael Cobb's perceptive reading of *Go Tell It on the Mountain* in *God Hates Fags: The Rhetorics of Religious Violence* convincingly argues that Baldwin's work illustrates how "religious language . . . simultaneously hides *and* articulates the queer within . . . more 'normal' and recognizable narratives."[134] Cobb recognizes the importance of Baldwin's use of religious rhetoric and the ways in which it articulates, sometimes obliquely, forbidden queer desire. Cobb's reading of Baldwin's queer religious rhetoric is productive, but I contend that Baldwin explores the tensions and dynamics between the spiritual and the sexual across multiple sexual identities—something not limited or constrained to a specifically queer sexual identity.

Looking back on the completion of his first novel, Baldwin recalled that he "had come through something," as he finally finished the project that had taken him ten long years to complete.[135] *Go Tell It* was, Baldwin recalled, an attempt "to re-create the life that I had first known as a child and from which I had spent so many years in flight."[136] Baldwin's recollection that he had "come through something" suggests, as Cheryl Sanders has remarked, that the completion of *Go Tell It* was something akin to the experience of religious conversion: an attempt, both to come to terms with and to exorcise his Sanctified past.[137] In the process of "coming through," a phrase that draws on John's own tortuous salvation on the threshing floor, Baldwin attempted to lay his past to rest with an earlier draft titled "Crying Holy" (one of the characteristic expressions of the Pentecostal worship experience), followed by three thematically similar short stories: "In My Father's House," "The Death of the Prophet," and "Roy's Wound."

While these different versions of what would eventually become *Go Tell It on the Mountain* are all characterized by a young protagonist's tortuous relationship with his stepfather, early readers of "Crying Holy" (Baldwin's most substantial draft version of the story) noted its explicit homoeroticism. The poet Harold Norse, a friend of Baldwin's from his Greenwich Village days, recalls that "Crying Holy" was not only "beautifully written," but "[i]t was the first time I had seen the subject of homosexuality in a contemporary novel."[138] Similarly, Emile Capouya, a school friend of Baldwin's who read a similar draft, describes how the original story ended with John saying (in effect) "I want a man."[139] Baldwin, according to Norse, was pessimistic about getting his novel published: "Who'd ever take it? . . . Who wants a novel about a black boy anyway, much less a queer one?"[140] Although Baldwin toned down the explicitly homosexual relationship between John and Elisha in *Go Tell It*, it remains, as critics have begun to argue, "deeply buried" within the narrative, a point that Baldwin acknowledged, noting that it "is implicit in the boy's situation" and "made almost explicit" in his tentative relationship with Elisha.[141]

Michael Cobb, in particular, has noted the "complicated relations between queerness, blackness, and religious rhetoric" in Baldwin's work.[142] Cobb argues that the queerness of the story is there but deflected or sublimated, "told, however indirectly and violently through a more recognizable drama of pain and violence: the drama of race."[143] As Cobb suggests, Baldwin would have been unable to deal with blackness and queerness in 1953 and his first major works—novels and essays—deal with the subject of race, then sexuality; but they never deal with the two subjects together. After *Go Tell It on the Mountain*, Baldwin would publish *Giovanni's Room*, a significant novel about homosexuality but one without any black characters. Again, Baldwin's first major essay on race, "Everybody's Protest Novel," was followed, in the same magazine, by "Preservation of Innocence," a bold examination of homosexuality that does not deal with race.

Contemporary reviewers of *Go Tell It on the Mountain*, however, failed to pick up on the homoeroticism of the novel. If the novel was described as excessive (often a euphemism for homosexual), this was because it drew too heavily on the rituals of the church. Baldwin's editors, for example, took exception to what they saw as the excessive religiosity of the novel. William Cole, while noting that the "novel [is] rich and poetic," reported that "[s]ome of the long 'Come to Jesus!' passages should be cut," a comment that Baldwin reprinted with indignation in the introduction to *The Amen Corner*.[144] Similarly, although early reviewers of *Go Tell It* praised Baldwin's fluid style, describing it as "essentially a religious novel," there was no mention of the novel's homoeroticism.[145]

Baldwin's first novel is characterized by a series of powerful tensions that reverberate throughout the narrative: the awe of conversion conflicts with anger at the hypocrisy of the church while the power of the spirit is paired with a refusal to renounce, mortify, or ignore the body. Cobb's perceptive reading of *Go Tell It* illuminates the complicated nexus of race, religion, and sexuality, but I read Baldwin's first novel as a wider exploration of the tensions between the spiritual and sexual relationships, whether gay, straight, or bisexual. Baldwin's whispered descriptions of queer desire and religion no doubt troubled conservative scholars in the past, but it is his explorations of love that continue to perplex contemporary critics.[146]

Baldwin's first novel is also a remarkable exploration of loneliness told through the bulging eyes of the fourteen-year-old John Grimes. Bowed down with the expectation that he will become a preacher like his father, John Grimes is cut off from the pleasures of childhood. Even the simple joys of playing with a ball fill John with a feeling of guilt and retribution.[147] In John's fiercely religious world, the body is something to be ignored, repressed, and even re-viled. In the sermons that the young protagonist hears from Father James, John is constantly reminded that "the Word was hard, that the way of holiness was a hard way."[148] In the Pentecostal Harlem community where John and his family worship, there is no room for deviation from the hard way of the Lord. As Sister McCandless points out, "You is in the Word or you *ain't*—ain't no half-way with God."[149] Baldwin paints a picture of an isolated and claustrophobic community far removed from the bustle and cosmopolitan vitality usually associated with Harlem. In the Pentecostalists' eyes, the world outside of the church is "Broad-way," a place of sin "where the unconquerable odor was of dust, and sweat, and urine and home-made gin."[150]

In Baldwin's narrative, it becomes clear that such neat divisions as broad and narrow ways, the Word and the flesh, sinner and saved are not only dam-aging but—and this is crucial in his writing—they are fabrications that are always threatening to break down. This is most explicit in the ways that his work explores the tensions between religion and sexuality. As John cleans the church, his thoughts turn from the abstractions of the Lord to "the odor of dust and sweat" that overwhelms his senses.[151] Worship, Baldwin illus-trates, requires the body as well as the spirit to participate: when "praying or rejoicing, their bodies gave off an acrid, steamy smell, a marriage of the odors of dripping bodies and soaking, starched white linen," an earthy and sensual odor that is reminiscent of the smells of dust, sweat, and gin found on Broadway.[152]

Baldwin is at pains to point out the power of the body beneath the holy robes. When the pastor's nephew Elisha is "saved," his most spiritual moment is marked, not by his spiritual rebirth, but by the physicality of his trembling body, as "his thighs moved terribly against the cloth of his suit."[153] When Elisha is later publicly reprimanded for "walking disorderly" with Ella Mae, Baldwin describes how her "white robes now seemed the merest, thinnest covering for the nakedness of breasts and insistent thighs."[154] During the church service, Baldwin suggests that sexual energy and desire is at times in-distinguishable from religious ecstasy, illustrated by his description of Elisha on the piano: "At one moment, head thrown back, eyes closed, sweat standing on his brow, he sat at the piano, singing and playing; and then . . . he stiffened and trembled, and cried out. *Jesus, oh Lord Jesus!*"[155] Here the religious ec-stasy that Elisha experiences is infused with sexual energy, written in a lan-guage that closely mirrors Ida and Vivaldo's lovemaking in *Another Country*: "he was aching in a way he had never ached before, was congested in a new way. . . . *Come on come on come on come on. Come on!*"[156]

Baldwin does not only suggest that sexual and religious ecstasy are similar but, in a more radical move, that spirituality is fueled by sexual desire. In the description of Elisha, for example, his moaning fills the church and infects the congregation so that "the rhythm of all the others quickened to match

Elisha's rhythm," climaxing with "a great moaning [that] filled the church." As if defying the reader not to link the sexual with the holy, the next line reads: "[t]here was sin among them."[157] Similarly, during flashbacks to Gabriel's life as a young married preacher in the South, Baldwin suggests that the power of his sermon—one that is remembered for years to come—is fueled, not by his religious fervor, but by sexual tension. As Gabriel preaches, trying to stave off his desire for Esther, his sermon, directed at his object of desire, sweeps through the congregation and rocks the church. When he finally succumbs to his desire, Gabriel feels the "mystery" and "passion" in her body, a description of sex couched in religious rhetoric.[158]

Gabriel's severity—even cruelty—in later years, Baldwin suggests, stems from his renunciation of the body, compounded by the guilty memory of his adultery. In *Go Tell It*, Baldwin explores the latter theme through an episode where John sees his father's nakedness, linking this to the curse of Ham. Baldwin links the account in Genesis—where Noah curses Ham's son, Canaan, after Ham sees Noah naked—to the enslavement of the Canaanites, a story often associated with black American slavery. Throughout the novel John is troubled by his burgeoning sexual desire and the fear of eternal damnation, what Baldwin describes in his short story "The Outing" as "the sordid persistence of the flesh."[159] As John imagines the body of a woman on the ceiling of his bedroom, this momentary image of sexual desire is quickly usurped by fear, dreaming that he has awoken on Judgment Day "left, with his sinful body, to be bound in hell a thousand years."[160]

In both *Go Tell It* and "The Outing" Baldwin suggests that his protagonists are able to find solace and comfort through love for other boys but the queerness of such desire is muted, whispered rather than fully articulated. Baldwin writes of John, "[i]n the school lavatory, alone, thinking of the boys, older, bigger, braver, who made bets with each other as to whose urine could arch higher, he had watched in himself a transformation of which he would never dare to speak."[161] In a later passage, echoing the "unspeakable" thoughts that he has as he thinks of other boys, John literally reflects on his sin, as he "stared at his face as though it were . . . the face of a stranger who held secrets that John could never know."[162]

The references to queer desire are important, particularly in the way that Baldwin connects religious transformation with sexual desire. In Baldwin's descriptions of John and Elisha in *Go Tell It* and David and Johnnie in "The Outing," sexual desire is inextricably linked to religious transformation. Crucially, both of these accounts are rendered in a language that is religious in its intensity and vocabulary. In other words, it is not simply that the four boys find love or desire instead of spirituality, but that they cross the river of spiritual belief with the help of another person.

In both "The Outing" and *Go Tell It on the Mountain*, Baldwin presents his protagonists with an alternative to the Puritan strictures of the Pentecostal church. Baldwin's short story in particular clarifies many of *Go Tell It*'s important but understated explorations of sexual and religious love. At first glance, "The Outing" reads as a shorter version of *Go Tell It*. We quickly learn about the protagonist, Johnnie, and his embittered relationship to his deacon father, Gabriel. Like *Go Tell It*, the narrative is framed by the church, but in "The Outing" the plot unfolds on a church outing, as the congregation sail down the Hudson River.

The central difference between the two stories is in the close friendship that John (*Go Tell It*) and Johnnie ("The Outing") foster. In *Go Tell It*, John is strengthened by his admiration for Elisha's piety and manliness, "wondering if he would ever be as holy as Elisha."[163] In "The Outing," the central friendship is between David and Johnnie, names that suggest the biblical love between David and Jonathan. In both versions, Baldwin suggests that a truly authentic religious experience must be accompanied by love.

In *Go Tell It*, John discovers the possibility of redemption through love after a brief encounter with Elisha in the church. As John is cleaning the church, he playfully wrestles with Elisha until the tussle becomes more and more intense. John watches "the veins rise on Elisha's forehead and in his neck," feeling his "breath" on him. Echoing Baldwin's descriptions of the congregation's physicality, "the odor of Elisha's sweat was heavy in John's nostrils . . . and John . . . was filled with a wild delight."[164] As the sweaty pair disentangles themselves after the climax of their struggle, Elisha asks "I didn't hurt you none, did I," suggestive of a tender postcoital address, paralleling the tender whispers between David and Johnnie in "The Outing": "'Who do you love?' he [David] whispered. 'Who's your boy?' 'You,' he muttered, 'I love you.'"[165] In contrast to the Saints who long to soar "far past the sordid persistence of the flesh," Baldwin emphasizes the irrepressible body beneath the veneer of the holy robes.[166] This point is further illuminated in *Go Tell It* when, at the very moment when John is in agony on the threshing floor, as "the Holy Ghost was speaking," John feels "a tightening in his loin-strings" and crucially, "a sudden yearning tenderness for Elisha," a feeling Baldwin describes as "desire, sharp and awful."[167]

John's yearning for Elisha in the depths of his agony anticipates Baldwin's insistence that "a human being could only be saved by another human being."[168] In "The Outing," Baldwin makes this even more explicit as Johnnie feels the awful terror of the Lord. As Johnnie feels overwhelmed by the timeless cacophony of wailing and fire, at the very moment when he seems to give in to the Lord, "Johnnie felt suddenly, not the presence of the Lord, but the presence of David; which seemed to reach out to him, hand reaching out to hand in the fury of flood-time, to drag him to the bottom of the water or to carry him safe to shore."[169] Rather than turning to God, Johnnie is "saved" by the love of David. He feels "such a depth of love, such nameless and terrible joy and pain, that he might have fallen, in the face of that company, weeping at David's feet."[170] As Baldwin's near apocalyptic descriptions of conversion suggest, he is not concerned with categories that divide, but in moments that tear these walls asunder. Baldwin challenges the divisions between the body and the flesh, or indeed the oppositions of love/desire and spirituality. In Baldwin's writing, he frequently suggests that love *is* spirituality.

Baldwin's descriptions of the boys' conversions are free from irony, emphasizing the overwhelming power of religious conversion. As Joseph A. Brown has noted, Baldwin "does not destroy the religious universe. Rather, he writes of a reality disconnected from true liberation, true freedom, true wholeness (holiness)."[171] Thus, as Brown continues, though Baldwin describes the conversions as both erotic and holy, he "has 'secularized' the images only in the minds of those who think there can be a dichotomy between the heavenly and the mundane" and also, I might add, between the body and the spirit.[172]

In a revealing scene in *Go Tell It*, John Grimes dreams of a life that is unfettered by the strictures of the church:

> In this world John, who was, his father said, ugly, who was always the smallest boy in the class, and who had no friends, became immediately beautiful, tall, and popular. . . . He was a poet, or a college president, or a movie star; he drank expensive whisky, and he smoked Lucky Strike cigarettes in the green package.[173]

In both *Go Tell It* and the short story, "The Outing," this dream of secular success remains but a fantasy. John's choices in *Go Tell It*, like those of Johnnie and David in "The Outing," are governed by the church. In short, there is no society, no reality outside of religion's watchful eye. It is only in Baldwin's short story, "The Death of the Prophet," a microcosm of *Go Tell It*, that the protagonist, Johnnie, upon reaching adolescence, flees the stifling world of the church.

"The Death of the Prophet" is a minor but important story, since it anticipates and connects Baldwin's later protagonists who move outside of the world of formal religion. As Johnnie watches his dying father, Baldwin describes him in the throes of both release and terror. Free from his father's tyrannical Old Testament wrath, Johnnie is at last "the man, the conqueror, alone on the tilting earth."[174] But with this freedom, as later suggested by John Grimes's dream in *Go Tell It*, comes fear and guilt. Although Johnnie has made his home "in the populous Sodom," savoring the forbidden delights of films, plays, smoking, and drinking, the path to the broad way is not straightforward. "The joys of hell," Johnnie discovers, "are as difficult to discover as the joys of heaven and are even more over-rated." At the end of the story, as Johnnie leaves his deceased father, he watches the cloud envelop the sky, "burning, like God hanging over the world."[175]

In "Prophet" Johnnie's escape into the secular world is described by Baldwin as both necessary and terrifying, and, like Johnnie, Baldwin's novels move away from the arena of the formal church. In *Giovanni's Room, Another Country, Tell Me How Long the Train's Been Gone, If Beale Street Could Talk,* and *Just Above My Head,* Baldwin's protagonists struggle in the urban metropolises of the secular world. By moving his fiction from the church to the city, Baldwin's writing becomes, not more secular, as many critics have noted, but increasingly suspicious of the church's social effectiveness and its spiritual authenticity. In *Giovanni's Room,* the eponymous protagonist curses God on the death of his newborn child. In *Another Country,* the one mention of "MOUNT OLIVE APOSTOLIC FAITH CHURCH" is subsumed into the merciless landscape of the city, offering no solace to the agonized Rufus.[176]

Increasingly, Baldwin depicts the black church as an anachronistic and ineffective weapon against the ravages of modern life. In *Tell Me How Long,* Black Christopher rails against Christianity's justification of slavery, while Leo recalls that the church threw him out.[177] Those that remain in the church are either destroyed by it or so hypocritical that they are beyond redemption. Jerry in *Tell Me How Long* recalls that his mother is so "fucked up" because she believes what the church tells her.[178] Likewise, Caleb in *Tell Me How Long* finds the Lord but loses his capacity for love. But Baldwin reserves his harshest condemnation for those who adhere blindly to the church's tenets, a charge leveled by Hall Montana in *Just Above My Head*: "[t]he most dreadful people I have ever known are those who have been 'saved.'"[179] Thus, Fonny's mother in *If Beale Street* is depicted as a cold and loveless woman who refuses either to support her son or to accept her grandchild since s/he was conceived outside of the church.

Despite Baldwin's virulent critique of those who remain in the church, his fiction continues to argue for the necessity of an authentic spiritual commitment, like Florence in *If Beale Street* who eschews the façade of the modern church in search of a more meaningful spiritual experience. Echoing his insistence that he had to leave the church in order to become a real human being, Baldwin's protagonists seek spiritual sustenance away from the hypocrisy of the church. Thus, when Leo in *Tell Me How Long* is told by Caleb that it is a sin not to praise the Lord, his reply is "can't we . . . each praise God in our own way?"[180]

While his fictional work both moved outside of the church and rejected its formal doctrines, Baldwin not only continued to emphasize the importance of spirituality in his fiction but also attempted to redefine his own notion of spirituality. In particular, Baldwin increasingly suggested that redemption could, and indeed must, be achieved through mutual love and companionship. By emphasizing the sanctity of sexual love (as opposed to sex), Baldwin developed what he had hinted at through the stunted attempts of John and Elisha in *Go Tell It* and Johnnie and David in "The Outing." As Trudier Harris has insightfully argued, it "would have been the height of blasphemy for John Grimes [*Go Tell It*] to see God reflected in another human being"; but by moving outside of the church, particularly in *If Beale Street* and *Just Above My Head*, Baldwin moved from traditional religion to a new humanist religion of love, where redemption is found in one another.[181]

Baldwin's last two novels, *If Beale Street* and *Just Above My Head*, are both love stories. *If Beale Street*, narrated by Tish, tells the story of her lover, Fonny, who has been falsely accused of rape. Tish's story recounts her struggle to support her lover while pregnant, faced by the impenetrable justice system. Baldwin's last novel, *Just Above my Head*, is the tale of a great gospel singer, Arthur Montana, and is a love story on two levels. Narrated by Montana's brother and manager Hall, the story is both "a love song" to his brother and the story of the love between Arthur and Jimmy. I want to conclude this chapter by exploring how Baldwin creates what Harris astutely refers to as an attempt "to recapture the essence of Christianity" rather than a rejection of spirituality. Moving away from what he sees as the distortions and hypocrisies of Christianity, Baldwin attempts to unearth "the essence of love."[182]

Love, particularly in Baldwin's later fiction, becomes the backbone of a more authentic spiritual existence. In *If Beale Street*, in particular, this is emphasized through Baldwin's depiction of the love between Fonny and Tish. In contrast to the hypocrisy and the inconstancy of the church, Fonny and Tish's love is described explicitly as a "revelation."[183] As Harris rightly points out, their experience of love initiates a transformation, drawing on the songs of religious conversion: "I looked at my hands, my hands looked new. I looked at my feet, they did too."[184] Although their relationship takes place outside of the church and out of wedlock, Baldwin emphasizes their authentic spiritual commitment to one another: "[w]hen two people love each other, when they really love each other, everything that happens between them has something of a sacramental air."[185] The sanctity of love is reiterated in *Just Above My Head* when the narrator Hall wonders at the love between Jimmy and Arthur: "it had something to do with their vows, with their relation to each other: but it was more, much more than that. It was a wonder, a marvel—a mystery. I call it holy."[186]

In both *Just Above My Head* and *If Beale Street*, Baldwin suggests that love can only be attained through acceptance of the body as well as the spirit. While acknowledging that the body is formed "in the womb, with your mother's shit and piss," referring elsewhere to the "inconvenient" but "sacred flesh," Baldwin insists on the sanctity and acceptance of the body.[187] In *Giovanni's Room*, David's inability to love is hindered by an insistence on purity: he will not allow Giovanni to touch him, believing in the purity of his body. It is only at the end of the novel, when David has experienced both love and loss, that he understands that his salvation is hidden in his flesh, a theme that anticipates Baldwin's later work.[188] In contrast to David, Baldwin's later protagonists make no such distinction between body and soul. Thus, Jimmy recalls that "[e]very inch of Arthur was sacred to me. And I mean: sacred."[189] In *If Beale*

Street, the sticky mess of blood and sperm becomes not a sign of shame but evidence of a wondrous act: "some strange anointing. Or . . . a tribal rite."[190] Again, in contrast to John Grimes in *Go Tell It*, who feels shame at his onanism and sexual dreams, Baldwin pictures Fonny masturbating alone in prison but full of love, concentrating "as though in prayer."[191]

Reinterpreting the church's emphasis on nakedness as both foul and terrifying in *Go Tell It*, Baldwin's later fiction insists upon its sanctity. In *Just Above My Head*, Baldwin explains this through Arthur's first experience with a man. In contrast to the biblical emphasis on shame, Arthur concludes that "this is what lovers do for each other—by daring to be naked, by giving each other the strength to have nothing to hide."[192] Elsewhere in the novel, this theme is reiterated by Hall, who wonders "if I would find in myself the strength to give love, and to take it: to accept my nakedness as sacred, and to hold sacred the nakedness of another."[193]

Baldwin's repeated references to nakedness rework the Old Testament notion of standing naked before God in order to be saved. In *Go Tell It*, for example, John imagines with dread the moment when he will "come to die and stand naked before the judgment bar," just as Gabriel depicts the sinner who "saw himself in all his foulness naked before God's glory."[194] In Baldwin's later fiction, nakedness is not only holy, but the fear of judgment is replaced by the act of complete surrender to another lover. Thus, authentic sexual love becomes itself an act both of revelation and of redemption. In *Just Above My Head*, this is most keenly illustrated by the description of Crunch making love to Julia, a former child preacher. Crunch, we learn, wanted to "drench and heal her soul. He, as it were, prayed with her, longing to give her all that she needed."[195] Betrayed by the church, Baldwin suggests that Julia's true conversion begins with her relationship with Crunch, a sexual act that explicitly heals and transforms her. After making love, Julia feels that she has been "saved," a theme that also punctuates the relationship between Fonny and Tish in *If Beale Street*. The first time the couple makes love, Tish recalls that Fonny "rode deeper and deeper not so much into me as into a kingdom which lay just behind his eyes," adding, "something broke . . . in me."[196]

Tish's recollection that "[i]f his arms had not held me, I would have fallen straight downward, backward, to my death," is strongly reminiscent of John Grimes's agonized conversion on the threshing floor.[197] But in contrast to John, who feels "like a rock, a dead man's body," "screaming, at the very bottom of darkness," Tish and Fonny see revelation in one another.[198] Making love to Fonny, Tish notes, "brought me to another place," adding that "I had crossed my river," in a language evocative both of crossing the threshing floor and of crossing the river Jordan.[199] In *Just Above My Head* Baldwin again uses religious language to distinguish an authentically spiritual sexual experience. As Arthur and Crunch make love, Baldwin explicitly frames their experience within a religious language: "[t]hey were beginning to know each other; the biblical phrase unlocked itself and held them in a joy as sharp as terror."[200]

Baldwin's emphasis on the sanctity of spiritual/sexual love is clearly distinguished from sexual gratification. "[S]ex is only sex," Baldwin wrote in "The Male Prison," and it does not take long before we discover "that there are few things on earth more futile or more deadening than a meaningless round of conquests"; or, as he wrote in "Here Be Dragons," "love and sexual activity are not synonymous," adding that "[t]here is nothing more boring . . . than sexual activity as an end in itself."[201] In *Just Above My Head*, this distinction is made clear by Hall who, recalling a succession of lovers, realizes that "if there's no future for you, if fucking doesn't becomes something more than fucking, then you have to forget it. And then you're worse off than . . . before."[202] Later in the novel, Hall returns to this theme, emphasizing the need for spiritual, not just physical gratification: "without love, pleasure withers quickly, becomes a foul taste on the palate, and pleasure's inventions are soon exhausted. There must be a soul within the body you are holding, a soul which you are striving to meet, a soul which is striving to meet yours."[203] The distinction between sexual gratification and spiritual sexual love is a theme that characterizes Baldwin's fiction. When Hall falls out of love with Martha, this moment is suggested by the loss of spiritual connection in their lovemaking: "We had fucked hard, hot, and hungry, but we had not made love, something was gone."[204] In contrast, Hall's lovemaking with his wife, Ruth, is described with a spiritual intensity: "after a pause . . . I shot it all into her, shot the grief and the terror and the journey into her," and again, "I kiss her legs her thighs . . . I at least, thank God that I come out the wilderness. My soul shouts hallelujah, and I do not thank God."[205]

Love Is in the Air

[M]y ancestors counseled me to *keep the faith*: and I promised,
I vowed that I would. . . . The music is everywhere, resounds, no
sounds: and tells me that now is the moment, for me, to return to the
eye of the hurricane.

—JAMES BALDWIN, "EVERY GOOD-BYE AIN'T GONE," *THE PRICE
OF THE TICKET*

To conclude this chapter I examine the ways in which Baldwin uses music—and, in particular, gospel music—to form a bridge between traditional notions of religiousness and his new definition of spirituality. "[M]usic," Baldwin stated in his last interview, "was and is my salvation."[206] While gospel music has its roots in the Sanctified church, its historical dissemination into secular life—while retaining a spiritual foundation—offers a useful analogy for Baldwin's redefinition of spirituality.[207] In *Just Above My Head*, Baldwin illustrates this point by showing how Arthur brought the spirit of the church—through gospel music—wherever he went: "And yes, the church, wherever it was, whatever it was, a football field in Montgomery, Alabama, a stadium in Tokyo, a music hall in Paris, Albert Hall in London, or as far away as Sydney: rocked."[208] Significantly, Baldwin explicitly points out that Arthur had neither been saved nor baptized.[209] And yet, recollecting Ida's singing in *Another Country*, for those who hear Arthur sing, "there was something frightening about so deep and unreadable a passion in one so young. Arthur's phrasing was the key—unanswerable; his delivery of the song made you realize that he knew what the song was about."[210] By emphasizing that Arthur has no formal connection to the church, Baldwin becomes increasingly explicit that authentic spirituality and redemption can be—and indeed must be—found outside of the church. Gospel music becomes, for Baldwin, the ideal medium to express this belief. For those who sing gospel music, Baldwin contends, "aren't singing gospel—if you see what I mean":

> When a nigger quotes the Gospel, he is not quoting: he is telling you what happened to him today, and what is certainly going to happen to you tomorrow. . . . Our suffering is our bridge to one another. Everyone must cross this bridge, or die while he still lives—but this is not a political, still less, a popular apprehension.[211]

Gospel music, therefore, becomes in *Just Above* a medium in which Baldwin explores the possibilities of connections between people. A way to share and explore love and suffering that was unavailable to Rufus in *Another Country*. It is a theme that Baldwin had explored in "Sonny's Blues," where the narrator declares that "the tale of how we suffer, and how we are delighted, and how we may triumph is never new, it always must be heard."[212]

In *Just Above*, gospel music becomes a symphony of love. Just as the same gospel songs become re-created, renewed through each voice that sings them, so Baldwin recomposes and redefines the songs in his novel. In *Just Above*, gospel music becomes an expression, not just of God, but a way of reaching out, connecting to lovers:

> Maybe all gospel songs begin out of blasphemy and presumption—what the church would call blasphemy and presumption: out of entering God's suffering, and making it your own, out of entering your suffering and challenging God Almighty to have or to give or to withhold mercy. There will be two of us at the mercy seat: *my Lord, and I!*[213]

Just as Baldwin redefines redemption through the love of another—and not just God—so gospel music embraces and works through a suffering that is particular, not just theological. "Our history," the narrator of *Just Above* concludes, "is each other. . . . Perhaps that is what the gospel singer is singing."[214]

By using the spiritual heritage of gospel music, Baldwin redefines the boundaries of the secular and the sacrilegious. In both *Beale Street* and *Just Above*, Baldwin invokes gospel music to signal and define a sexual love that retains a spiritual purity. In *Beale Street*, Tish explicitly refers to the gospel song, "Steal Away." By noting how "I was in his hands, he called me by the thunder at my ear. I was in his hands: I was being changed," Tish recasts the gospel lyrics, "My Lord, He calls me, He calls me by thunder / The trumpet sound within my soul."[215] In *If Beale Street*, Baldwin uses the references to gospel songs to bridge the gap between the sacred and the secular, the body and the spirit. Thus, as they make love, Tish recalls how "[a] singing began in me and his body became sacred—his buttocks, as they quivered and rose and fell . . . brought me to another place."[216]

In *Just Above*, Baldwin again uses gospel song as an expression of sexual love. In his last novel, however, gospel music becomes a way of sanctifying love between men: a medium that facilitates otherwise prohibited relationships. Like Reid-Pharr, I remain unconvinced that Baldwin "was trying to demonstrate that a homosexual might add some new element to the traditional practice of gospel singing."[217] Rather, Baldwin implies that gospel music encourages a breaking down of walls and barriers, whether musically (between blues and church music) or sexually. When Arthur and Crunch play music together, the songs become a vicarious experience of spiritual sexual fulfillment:

> He [Arthur] paused again . . . trusting every second of this unprecedented darkness, knowing Crunch and he were moving together, here, now, in the song, to some new place; they had never sung together like this before, his voice in Crunch's sound, Crunch's sound filling his voice.[218]

The language is strongly evocative both of religious conversion ("some new place") and of sexual intimacy: a medium that allows the boys to enter and fill one another. As Arthur and Crunch sing gospel music, it becomes a way of expressing the spirituality of their desire for one another, exemplified by Baldwin's nuancing of traditional songs: "*somebody touched me . . . it must have been the hand of the Lord!*"[219]

By framing same-sex relationships through gospel music, Baldwin attempts both to redefine the boundaries of sacrilegiousness and to insist on the purity of all love. As Hall, the narrator of *Just Above*, records, for Arthur and Jimmy music became a way of placing and defining their love. Music "became for them, then, theirs, a sacrament, a stone marking a moment on their road: the point of no return, when they confessed to each other, astounded, terrified, but having no choice, in the hearing of men, and in the sight of God." As Hall marvels at the depth of love between Jimmy and Arthur, he is struck at how "sacrilegious" his brother's love is; and yet, he is also struck by Arthur's response, "which seemed to ring out over those apocalyptic streets."[220]

Love, then, aided and nurtured through gospel music, becomes the bedrock of Baldwin's new spirituality. Irrespective of class, gender, or sexuality, love becomes, for Baldwin, a redemptive act. In *Just Above*, this is explicitly illustrated through Arthur's relationship with Crunch:

> And yet, he knows that, when he was happy with Crunch, he was neither guilty nor ashamed. He had felt a purity, a shining joy, as though he had been, astoundingly, miraculously blessed, and had feared neither Satan, man, nor God. He had not doubted for a moment that all love was holy.[221]

In Baldwin's writing, spiritual love becomes a cornerstone. With a quiet radicalism, Baldwin's characterization of spirituality includes sexual love, whether queer, straight, or bisexual, in his vision and depiction of the disinherited. For it is "love," Baldwin concludes, "which is salvation."[222]

{ Chapter 4 }

"I Am a Stranger Everywhere":
Travel and Transnational Tensions in Baldwin's Work

> I don't believe in nations anymore. Those passports, those borders
> are as outworn and useless as war.
>
> —"CONVERSATION: IDA LEWIS AND JAMES BALDWIN"

> You can't be an expatriate anymore because America is all over
> the world.
>
> —JOE WALKER, "EXCLUSIVE INTERVIEW WITH JAMES BALDWIN"

The issuance of a James Baldwin stamp in 2004 by the US Postal Service seemed to give the writer—despite his peripatetic life—some sense of finally coming home. Baldwin's place in the critical history of American literature, though now more secure, has been precarious. For many critics, Baldwin's refusal to be pinned down as essayist or novelist, religious writer or critic of the church, black or gay has contributed to his uncertain place in American and African American literature. Like David in *Giovanni's Room* who is "too various to be trusted," Baldwin has arguably received less than his fair share of recognition precisely because his work crosses so many boundaries, disciplines, and genres.[1]

Together with the publication of the Library of America volumes of Baldwin's early novels and selected essays, the stamp is a small nod toward the recognition of the achievements of this prolific and enigmatic writer. And though there are few monuments, plaques, or parks named after him, the stamp is a fitting tribute for a writer so closely associated with travel; a writer who refused to be contained by the geographical, cultural, and sexual boundaries of the United States. The stamp is a useful reminder of Baldwin's impact, not just across northern America, but across the globe. As a self-confessed "trans-Atlantic commuter" who traveled to Africa, Europe, and the Middle East, Baldwin lived (and died) in France, also spending an interrupted decade in Turkey.

Despite Baldwin's itinerant life shuttling between Europe and the United States, his work does not fit easily into theories of the Black Atlantic or in wider discussions of the diaspora. Baldwin's writing in fact draws attention to the difficulties, both material and aesthetic, that face the black American writer in Europe, the African in Europe, the North African in Paris, and the African American in Africa. Baldwin's writing about exile is less concerned with a dialogic encounter between Europe and America, or Africa and the United States, but rather about using exile to gain perspective and insight into the pressing material difficulties facing black Americans in the United States. Few of Baldwin's works in fact focus on the countries where he lived and wrote, although many of his most insightful works were written outside of the United States. During the ten intermittent years that he spent in Turkey Baldwin finished or wrote a number of works—including *Another Country*, *The Fire Next Time*, *Blues for Mister Charlie*, *Going to Meet the Man*, *Tell Me How Long the Train's Been Gone*, *One Day When I Was Lost*, and *No Name in the Street*. Baldwin also directed a critically acclaimed production of the Canadian playwright John Herbert's *Fortune and Men's Eyes* (1964) in Turkey, a success that American critics knew little about.[2]

Baldwin's reflections on his stay in Turkey suggest that it afforded him a vantage point and critical distance to analyze the United States. "During my stay in Istanbul," Baldwin told Ida Lewis, "I learned a lot about dealing with people who are neither Western nor Eastern." For Baldwin, Turkey's liminal position between East and West gave him a new perspective. Living among people "whom nobody cares about," Baldwin stated, "You learn about the brutality and the power of the Western world."[3] Baldwin's recollection of living in Istanbul echoes the black American writer Willard Motley, author of *Knock on Any Door* (1947), who sought exile in Mexico during the 1950s and 1960s. For Motley, like Baldwin, "you never realize how psychologically sick the US is from this point of view until you live in a foreign country."[4] Unlike Motley, whose insightful and barbed writing on US racism and imperialism were frequently turned down by cautious publishers, Baldwin's own work flourished during his first decade and a half abroad. Like Motley, Baldwin repeatedly points out that geographical distance from North America enabled him to write more acutely about his birthplace. "One sees [one's country] better from a distance," Baldwin stated in Sedat Pakay's 1970 film *From Another Place*, "from another place, another country."[5]

In *James Baldwin's Turkish Decade*, Zaborowska breaks new ground by focusing on Baldwin's life and work away from American and European soil, maintaining that Baldwin's ten years in Turkey contribute toward the developing field of transnational African American studies, an area that has grown and expanded since Paul Gilroy's established theories of Black Atlantic cultures. As Zaborowska points out, critics "have paid scant attention to how he [Baldwin] was received and seen abroad and by non-Americans," arguing that his decade in Turkey added "an increasingly transnational perspective" to his fiction and nonfiction.[6] Zaborowska's biography encourages a reading of Baldwin's work from an international—rather than a North American— critical perspective and highlights how his "awareness of the imperial presence of the United States in the world and of global racism increased and sharpened while he was living in Turkey."[7] Baldwin would write of his sojourn in Turkey as an experience where "the whole somber question of America's role in the world today stared at me in a new and inescapable way."[8] At the same time, Baldwin did not produce a sustained fictional or nonfictional piece of writing about Turkey, a country that looms in the background of his writing from the 1960s and *James Baldwin's Turkish Decade* exaggerates as much as it updates the contribution of his transnational production in the growing field of transatlantic studies. Baldwin's spell in Turkey almost certainly afforded him a sense of anonymity and relative peace away from New York, but this relative calm did not produce significant works about his adopted country, nor did he deliver commissioned articles to the *New Yorker* about his trips to Israel and countries in Africa.[9] Similarly, though Baldwin was quite vocal about the plight of the Algerians in France, this was another theme that he did not develop into a major novel or essay at the time—even though the Algerian war was front-page international news during the mid-1950s, a period Baldwin witnessed from inside France.[10] As James Campbell notes, Baldwin "seems never to have considered settling down to write something . . . about the colonial eruption which, at first glance, it would seem should have inspired him." The war in Algeria, Baldwin wrote to Philip Rahv—in one of only several mentions—"was dreadful (but interesting)."[11]

Baldwin matured as a writer in Europe, but his observations about France and later Turkey are unremarkable aside from the paucity of references to the recovering postwar European political landscape. Baldwin's move to Paris in 1948 rather heightened his perception of his native America, just as his visits to African countries later galvanized his most penetrating writing about the United States. Although critics frequently refer to Baldwin as a transatlantic writer, his work is in fact animated by a determination to pick apart and make sense of postwar American identity—what he termed "a profound and dangerous . . . mystery" in *No Name*—rather than by embracing the cultural ebb and flow of black transnationalism.[12] As I hope to make clear, Baldwin's writing highlights the ways in which his constant traveling was profoundly disorientating; that his writing calls attention to his physical displacement, or dis-position, as much as it is a celebration of cosmopolitan exile.

In a 1961 letter to his agent Robert P. Mills, Baldwin describes the United States as "intolerable" and "menacing," noting the "incessant strain and terror" of living in a racially segregated and sexually intolerant society. Baldwin writes in the same letter that he is reconciled "to being a transatlantic commuter," but his conclusion that "I am stranger everywhere" is an important rejoinder to the frequently celebratory tone of much scholarship on transnationalism and transatlantic studies.[13]

When Baldwin turns his attention away from the United States—as he does in his writings about Africans and Algerians in Paris—he frequently illuminates his views on the state of the American nation. His early essays, as Cheryl Wall observes, deploy what she terms a "strategic American exceptionalism"; an insistence on the United States as "profoundly and stubbornly unique," but a position that highlights "the presence of black people and the challenge that their presence poses to Americans' sense of the nation and of themselves."[14] Baldwin's cosmopolitan outlook reaches beyond the United States as he becomes increasingly attuned to the internationalism of the black experience. At the same time, his critical gaze remains focused on the United States, acknowledging that "if he has been preparing himself for anything in Europe, he been preparing himself—for America."

In what follows, I trace Baldwin's writing on and about exile from the United States, beginning with a reading of the author's relationship to and discussion of Paris, a key city in the history of transatlantic black culture. While Baldwin's insistence on linguistic and cultural differences between Africans and black Americans seems to put him at odds with theorists of the Black Atlantic such as Paul Gilroy, his work in fact enriches an understanding of the challenges and potential of transatlantic collaboration, something that is illuminated by charting his shifting views on the continent of Africa. Thus, Baldwin's varied travel (and residence) abroad sharpens his observation of the society and culture in which he reached maturity.

Baldwin and Paris

In *No Name in the Street* (1972), James Baldwin recollects the moment that propelled him to leave the sanctity of Paris in order to participate in the civil rights movement. In the fall of 1956 Baldwin covered the first International Congress of Black Writers and Artists at the Sorbonne. "One bright afternoon," Baldwin recalls, he was "meandering up the Boulevard St. Germain, on the way to lunch," accompanied by Richard Wright and other unnamed companions.[15] The leisurely stroll is ruptured by the image of Dorothy Counts "on every newspaper kiosk." The sight of the fifteen-year-old African American student who was "reviled and spat upon by the mob" as she made her way to school in Charlotte, North Carolina, convinced Baldwin that he "could . . . no longer sit around in Paris discussing the Algerian and the black American problem. Everybody else was paying their dues, and it was time I went home and paid mine."[16]

Baldwin is in fact wrong about the dates, though for more pertinent reasons than a lapse in memory: the Congress of Black Writers and Artists took place nearly a year before the photograph of Counts was taken, suggesting the ways in which he would ultimately rewrite—or reenvision—his reasons for leaving Paris for the South of the United States in 1957.[17] Baldwin's first account of the Congress, "Princes and Powers," published in 1957, describes a very different scene from his recollections in *No Name*. Here, the "newspaper vendors seemed cheerful; so did the people who bought the newspapers."[18] Baldwin's incorrect memory of the simultaneity of encountering the Counts photograph and the 1956 Congress, however, says much about the writer's relationship to Paris. Baldwin recalls seeing Counts's photograph in a "tree-shaded boulevard," in Paris, a safe and genteel environment, far removed from the "strange fruit" on the poplar trees that Billie Holiday evoked so disturbingly or Baldwin's description in "Nobody Knows My Name" of the red soil of Georgia, stained "from the blood that had dripped down from these trees."[19] Baldwin's description of "meandering" in Paris and his acknowledgment that he also "dawdled" in Europe is in sharp contrast to the urgency of the civil rights movement, where, as he recalled in *No Name*, he was "wearily, marching, marching," along with Martin Luther King Jr.[20] If Baldwin positions himself as reporter and even flâneur at the start of *No Name*, the remaining sections of this long essay seek to show that he marched purposely as a civil rights activist. *No Name* is, in this sense, a carefully constructed rejoinder to mounting criticism that Baldwin was passé, that he had lost his way as a writer.

Baldwin would claim with a disingenuous flourish that he came to Paris by accident. "My journey, or my flight," he recalled in *No Name*, "had not been *to* Paris, but simply *away* from America. . . . I ended up in Paris almost literally by closing my eyes and putting my finger on a map."[21] Baldwin's qualification (*"almost* literally") suggests that he may have peeped when placing his finger on the map. He was no doubt aware of Richard Wright's voyage to Paris in 1947, one year before Baldwin set sail for France. Given the long history of "Black Paris," it is likely that Baldwin would also have associated the French capital at least in part with its black American visitors, among them Countee Cullen, Langston Hughes, and Jessie Fauset. By 1972, Baldwin's description of closing his eyes and placing his finger on the map suggests an acknowledgment that he had become blind to the struggles of the civil rights movement while in France, where his eyes would be reopened by the photograph of Counts, or by the collision of events that image represented for Baldwin.

Baldwin's recollection of waking from his Paris reverie may be inaccurate, but it illustrates the writer's complicated relationship to the French capital in what I term his "Paris essays": "Encounter on the Seine" (1950), "Equal in Paris" (1955), and "Princes and Powers" (1957). Like Richard Wright's oeuvre, few of Baldwin's fictional works are set in Paris, with the exception of his second novel. Here I explore the relationship of *Giovanni's Room* (1956) to wider discussions about black transnationalism and Baldwin's uneasy relationship, not only with Richard Wright and Chester Himes but also with African and black Francophone writers in Paris. Unlike Wright, who played a key role in the 1956 conference, Baldwin was present as a skeptical reporter. In contrast to Paul Gilroy's later call for an understanding of the Black Atlantic as a "single, complex unit of analysis," Baldwin repeatedly questions the unity of black transnational culture.[22] Tellingly, Baldwin's decision to head to the American South, into the heat and heart of the civil rights movement, is precipitated precisely at the moment when the architects of the 1956 Congress—Richard Wright, Leopold Senghor, and Alioune Diop—were attempting to define and develop a black transnational artistic and political community. For Baldwin, it seems, this project was less pressing than the material reality of the burgeoning US civil rights movement. Here I want to trace Baldwin's move from the United States to Paris to show the ways in which he sought exile from the stifling postwar constructions of American identity. My reading of his essays about Paris indicates that Baldwin repeatedly questioned the importance or legitimacy of what is now called transatlantic or transnational collaboration. Rather, he explores how transnational exchange is fraught with difficulties that arise from cultural and linguistic differences, a feature of Baldwin's essays that has arguably obscured his significance as a transatlantic writer. This "transatlantic commuter," who not only lived in Paris and died in the south of France, rarely features in works about black transnational culture. He is, for example, conspicuously absent from Gilroy's *The Black Atlantic*.[23]

My aim here is not to recuperate Baldwin as a key transnational writer but to argue that his writing about Paris nonetheless constitutes a developing and coherent political aesthetic; one that anticipates and feeds into contemporary theories of transnational culture that are attentive to the different structures that make up black internationalism. Baldwin's views on national identity and US imperialism evolved; his later work, in particular, shows that he was keenly attuned to North America's role in a global context, both militarily and culturally. Baldwin's writings about Paris and the transatlantic in the 1950s do not merely trouble the idealistic critical romance of transnational culture. Rather, his work adds to and enriches our understanding of the ways in which, as Brent Hayes Edwards notes, "the cultures of black internationalism . . . are equally 'adversarial' to themselves, highlighting differences and disagreements among black populations on a number of registers."[24]

If Baldwin's essays about black internationalism articulated what we might call a political aesthetic of difference, his fictional writing about Paris seems on the surface to be unconcerned about black transnational culture. In *Giovanni's Room*, set in a white expatriate Paris community, Baldwin seems interested rather in racial homogeneity and sexual difference. And yet as I demonstrate through a close reading of Baldwin's second novel, a work replete with references to the sea, sailors, and nationality, Baldwin was nonetheless

drawn to the ways in which black internationalism challenged the founda-
tions of national identity in France and the United States as white and heterosexual. Like his contemporaries Ralph Ellison and LeRoi Jones (Amiri
Baraka), who were also expatriates in Rome and Puerto Rico, respectively, in
1956, Baldwin was "attempting to define African Americanness not escape
it."[25] In "Stranger in the Village" (1953), Baldwin concluded that "[t]his world
is white no longer, and it will never be white again."[26] Three years later, Baldwin published *Giovanni's Room*, a novel with no black characters. Here, Baldwin undertakes the risky—and shockingly iconoclastic for 1956—strategy of
employing a white middle-class narrator in order to expose the fabrications of
white, North American heterosexual identity.[27]

FROM NEW YORK TO PARIS

Baldwin's decision to leave America for Paris on Armistice Day, 1948, has
become a seminal moment in the writer's literary and political journey. His
move abroad afforded the writer distance from the stifling sexual and racial
discrimination that he explored so powerfully in *Notes of a Native Son* (1955),
from what he later described as "five desperate years in the Village."[28] In
"Notes of a Native Son," Baldwin had recalled the painful experience of being
refused service at a Princeton burger bar, an episode that nearly cost him his
life when he hurled a water mug at the waitress who refused to take his order.[29]

Baldwin would reiterate in an interview that "I didn't *come* to Paris in 1948,
I simply *left* America" and it is important to see his departure from the United
States in the context of an increasingly hostile Cold War climate that drove
hundreds of North American artists to seek creative refuge in other countries.[30] As Rebecca Schreiber has shown in her study of Cold War exiles in
Mexico, the political and cultural climate of the 1940s and 1950s forced large
numbers of US writers, artists, and filmmakers into exile. James A. Dievler
and other cultural critics have pointed out the ways in which "postwar culture fed the development of rigid identity categories in the postwar period,"
illustrated by mainstream discussions in existentialism and psychoanalysis
about "the self," "identity," and "alienation."[31] For Baldwin, as illustrated by
his writing during and about the late 1940s and early 1950s, these rigid identity categories were not only stifling but dangerous, particularly in the ways
that mainstream culture created and perpetuated myths about what it meant
to be American—a construction that inevitably meant male, white, and heterosexual. The increasing rigidity of sexual and racial categories in postwar
New York led Baldwin to note in his 1985 essay "Freaks and the American
Ideal of Manhood" (also published as "Here Be Dragons") that "on every
street corner, I was called a faggot" but also that the New York homosexual
subculture could not contain or reflect his experience.[32] "The queer—not yet
gay—world," Baldwin writes, "was an even more intimidating area of this hall

of mirrors."[33] Although Baldwin acknowledges that he was "in the hall and present at this company," he recalls that "the mirrors threw back only brief and distorted fragments of myself," an echo, perhaps, of the mirror shattered by the mug in the Princeton diner.[34] Finally, as Baldwin recalled in an interview, he had to leave America: "I no longer felt I knew who I really was, whether I was really black or really white, really male or really female, really talented or a fraud, really strong or merely stubborn. I had become a crazy oddball. I had to get my head together to survive and my only hope of doing that was to leave America."[35]

Importantly, exile afforded Baldwin the opportunity to reflect on what he had left behind. It is unlikely that Baldwin would have written his bold essay about masculinity and homosexuality, "Preservation of Innocence" (1949), if he had remained in America—and it is less likely that it would have been published. According to James Campbell, the editors of *Partisan Review*, who were only too happy to republish "Everybody's Protest Novel," a critique of Wright and protest fiction, would not touch "Preservation" "with a ten-foot pole."[36]

Paris Essays

"Someone, some day," Baldwin writes in his essay, "Alas, Poor Richard," "should do a study in depth of the role of the American Negro in the mind and life of Europe, and the extraordinary perils, different from those of America but no less grave, which the American Negro encounters in the Old World."[37] Baldwin's essays about the French capital do not constitute an in-depth study and yet "Encounter on the Seine" from *Notes of a Native Son*, "Equal in Paris" also from *Notes*, and "Princes and Powers" from *Nobody Knows My Name* puncture and call into question the myth of Paris as, in Wright's words, the "city of refuge."[38]

In 1955 *Commentary* published "Equal in Paris," an essay in which Baldwin recalls his early years in the French capital, a period when he "floated, so to speak, on a sea of acquaintances," adding that he "knew almost no one."[39] Baldwin's oceanic metaphor calls attention to Gilroy's focus on the ship as a vessel of intercultural exchange: "the circulation of ideas and activists as well as the movements of key cultural and political artefacts."[40] Baldwin, however, seems to have remained detached from any single cultural or intellectual community in Paris. Baldwin's essays about Paris focus rather on the lack of community among African Americans and black Francophone writers and students, what he describes in "Encounter on the Seine" as the black American's "deliberate isolation."[41] As I discussed in chapter 1, Baldwin's relationship with Wright was strained, if not tense. Unlike Wright, who was on the editorial board of *Présence Africaine* and actively involved in Sartre's Rassemblement Democratique Révolutionnaire, Baldwin kept his distance from established intellectual or artistic communities.[42] Although he is often associated with Himes and Wright, as Kevin Bell astutely points out, this triumvirate never formed "an ideological or creative unit" and yet are frequently "viewed within a certain unitary fusion."[43]

Baldwin's Paris essays focus on the difficulties of developing black transnational culture, anticipating Edwards's observation that the "cultures of black internationalism are formed only within . . . 'paradoxes.'"[44] In *The Practice of Diaspora*, Edwards expands on Gilroy's call in *The Black Atlantic* to consider the Atlantic as "one single, complex unit of analysis," arguing rather that "black modern expression takes form not as a single thread, but through the often uneasy encounters of peoples of African descent with each other."[45] In Baldwin's "Paris Essays," in particular, it is precisely these "uneasy encounters" between African Americans and other people of African descent that characterize his writing on transnational culture. Baldwin's writing on Paris counters the suggestion that the French capital is a site of community and cultural exchange. In "Encounter on the Seine," Baldwin makes it clear that African Americans abroad may share the common experience of exile, but they share little else; a point that he outlined in his resistance to Wright's Franco-American Fellowship Club. For Baldwin, it is only the dwindling black American musicians and singers in Paris who "are able to maintain a useful and unquestioning comradeship with other Negroes."[46] Baldwin's writing underscores his view that exile does not necessarily foster community; black Americans who have fled the ghettos of the United States, Baldwin points out, do not necessarily want to live together.

In "Encounter" Baldwin emphasizes the importance of understanding his American identity, which was the only way that he can "hope to make articulate to himself or to others the uniqueness of his experience."[47] And yet there is a high price to pay for becoming American. It is only when he is wrongly imprisoned for theft, an episode that Baldwin recounts in "Equal in Paris," that the French authorities see him as American rather than as a "despised black man."[48] As Baldwin later wrote in "The Discovery of What It Means to Be an American" (1959), he left America "to prevent myself from becoming *merely* a Negro; or, even, merely a Negro writer."[49] In "Equal in Paris," Baldwin suggests that becoming American is not just an acquisition, but a painful transformation, giving weight to Cheryl Wall's point that the writer "was committed to defining what it means to be an American, but he was equally committed to figuring out what his personal responsibility as an American was."[50] In an ironic twist, it is only when he is incarcerated—at "a lower point than any I could ever in my life have imagined"—that Baldwin is liberated from racial interpellation.[51]

Baldwin's attention to what he calls the "uniqueness" of the black American's experience is significant, showing his reluctance to consider the possibilities of wider black transnational exchanges. His discussion of the nameless Africans in "Encounter," who are not distinguished by gender, class, or nationality, makes no mention of the long established history of African students in the French capital, where he himself had lived since 1948. More surprising, however, he also makes no reference to Alioune Diop's famous quarterly, *Présence Africaine*, founded a year before Baldwin arrived in Paris. During his early years in Paris, Baldwin may, of course, have struggled to read the articles in *Présence Africaine*, which were not published in English until 1955. At the same time, it is almost certain Baldwin would have known of the journal, which became the preeminent forum for the cultural and political struggles of pan-Africanism and Negritude. Early issues of *Présence Africaine* contained articles by French intellectuals (Sartre, Albert Camus) but also, on Wright's recommendation, works by Gwendolyn Brooks, Horace Cayton, and E. Franklin Frazier.[52] Baldwin's silence on the journal, then, is perhaps a tacit acknowledgment that his ideas about nationalism and transnationalism diverged from those of his peers.

Baldwin wrote of wanting to "articulate" his experience as a writer in Paris, but his audience was clearly not his transatlantic colleagues in Paris. In contrast to the cultural and political exchange signaled by *Présence Africaine*'s inclusion of African American writers, Baldwin writes rather of the cultural and linguistic obstacles in "Encounter": "They face each other, the Negro and the African, over a gulf of three hundred years—an alienation too vast to be conquered in an evening's good will, too heavy and too double-edged ever to be trapped in speech."[53] Baldwin's choice of the words "alienation" and the colonially inflected "conquered" set the African and the African American at odds, rather than positing transcultural interaction. This depiction echoes back to the start of *Giovanni's Room* and David's musings on his conquering ancestors. For Baldwin, the African and African American do not share a common language and are unable to communicate, a state that he underlines with a later comment that "we almost needed a dictionary to talk."[54]

Baldwin's repeated references to translation in relation to diasporic encounters in Paris anticipate Edwards's argument that "the cultures of black internationalism can be seen only *in translation*."[55] Like Baldwin before him, Edwards bursts the bubble of romantic intercultural exchange; both writers recognize that there can be positive exchanges from the diverse population of the diaspora, but both point to the challenges of dialogue, underscoring cultural and linguistic obstacles. In "Princes and Powers," Baldwin writes of a black transnational culture "which has produced so many different subhistories, problems, traditions, possibilities, aspirations, assumptions, languages, hybrids," what Edwards calls "unavoidable misapprehensions and misreadings, persistent blindness and solipsisms, self-defeating and abortive collaborations, a failure to translate even a basic grammar of blackness."[56]

Unlike the American participants at the 1956 Congress—among them Richard Wright, Mercer Cook, and John A. Davis—Baldwin was present as a reporter for *Encounter* (or, as he added, for the CIA).[57] Baldwin's role is significant, illustrating his position as Western observer, not participant in a conference aimed at unifying people of African descent.[58] The Nigerian poet, M. Lasebikan, who speaks an "extremely strange language," Baldwin writes, was "dressed in a most arresting costume," noting that "he was wearing a very subdued but very ornately figured silk robe, which looked Chinese, and he wore a red velvet toque, a sign, someone told me that he was a Mohammedan."[59] Baldwin's attempts to describe Lasebikan's national dress, which are conflated here as oriental, foreign, echo his own earlier discomfort in "Stranger in the Village," where the local Swiss see him as "a living wonder."[60] Like the villagers, Baldwin's views are based on hearsay: Baldwin wrongly assumes Lasebikan is Muslim because "someone told" him. His own description of Lasebikan outlines what he calls "that gulf which yawns between the American Negro and all other men of color." Observing the participants at the conference, Baldwin writes that it was "quite unbelievable for a moment that the five men standing with Wright (and Wright and myself) were defined, and had been brought together in this courtyard by our relation to the African continent."[61]

Despite his initial distance from the speakers at the conference, he is attracted to Senghor's theories on the harmony in African culture between life and art. Nevertheless, echoing his earlier comment in "Encounter" concerning the gulf between the African and African American, Baldwin believes that "Senghor's thought had come into my mind translated."[62] Baldwin questions Senghor's claim that the heritage of the African American was straightforwardly African. Senghor's conclusion that Richard Wright's *Black Boy* (1945) illustrates the latter's African roots, Baldwin argues, overlooks the specific culture and heritage of his Mississippi upbringing. To view *Black Boy* as a great African autobiography, Baldwin writes, is not to restore Wright's African heritage: "rather [it] seemed to be taking away his identity."[63]

In "Princes and Powers" Baldwin repeatedly observes how identities are forged in specific historical conditions, illustrated by his probing question, "[f]or what, beyond the fact that all black men at one time or another left Africa, or have remained there, do they really have in common?"[64] At one point, he concedes that people of black descent did have something in common—their "precarious . . . unutterably painful relation to the white world—but once again Baldwin points to the inexpressibility of such a condition."[65] Eight years later, Baldwin revised his view that oppression was enough to unify disparate cultures of the diaspora. Eight years after the 1956 conference, he noted that he not only "profoundly distrust[ed]" negritude but again argued that "oppressions do not necessarily unify so many millions of people all over the world":

> Well, how in the world is this going to connect to so many different experiences? To be born in Jamaica, Barbados, or Portugal, or New York, or to be black, wouldn't seem to me to be enough . . . and the situation of the man in Jamaica is not the situation of the man in Harlem at all.[66]

In "Princes and Powers," Baldwin is careful to distinguish between the colonial experiences of Africans who wish to overthrow European white rule and the complicated relationship between black Americans and white authority in the United States: "It had never been our interest to overthrow" the dominant white power, Baldwin writes. Rather, "[i]t had been necessary to make the machinery work for our benefit and the possibility of its doing so had been . . . built in."[67] Here as elsewhere in his writing, Baldwin is much more concerned with redefining what it means to be American, than with discarding American identity: he aims not to "overthrow" the concept of a US national identity but to overhaul it.[68] As I show in the following section, Baldwin would challenge the prevailing constructs of postwar American identity most effectively through his character David, the white middle-class protagonist of *Giovanni's Room*.

PARIS FICTIONS

Little of Baldwin's fictional writing focuses on Paris and his literary reputation in France began Rosa Bobia points out, "in slow motion," hampered by the late translation of *Go Tell It on the Mountain* in 1957.[69] When Baldwin arrived in Paris in 1948, he was unknown in the literary and intellectual circles and was writing under the shadow of Richard Wright and, later, Chester Himes. In one of the earliest articles on Baldwin in France, Jacques Howlett, writing for *Présence Africaine* in 1952, criticized the writer for discussing race in universal terms. Anticipating later criticism of Baldwin by some ten years, Howlett concluded by stating that Baldwin, "although a Black American, is not qualified to discuss racism in the United States."[70] Howlett's criticism of Baldwin troubles the romance of the writer's transnational position. While Baldwin maintains that distance from North America enables him to see racial politics with added clarity, Howlett suggests that the writer is cushioned from the harsh realities of the US civil rights movement. Howlett's early article set the tone for Baldwin's uneasy relationship with black Francophone writers. Although *Giovanni's Room*, published in France in 1958 as *L'Ami de Giovanni*, was favorably received, it was not viewed as a work of political importance. Although Baldwin's literary reputation in France fared better than that of Ralph Ellison, who was published by a small French publisher, it would not be until Wright's death in 1960 and, in particular, after the publication of

The Fire Next Time—that "a political Baldwin emerged."[71] Baldwin's visit to
the American South three years before Wright's death—and his accounts of
the trip—illustrate the ways in which he had become politicized. In France,
however, Baldwin's isolation from the communities of black transnational
writers meant that he would emerge as "political" only when his essays on the
US civil rights movement began to circulate in Paris.

In Baldwin's fictional worlds, characters of different nationalities, often in
cameo roles, rub shoulders with the American protagonists in ways that
highlight the injustices of American life but also lay bare the fictions of national identity. In his short story, "This Morning, This Evening, So Soon,"
there is the southern African American narrator, his Swedish wife, their son
who has never been to the United States, and Vidal—a French film director
who was imprisoned in Germany during the war and who has a daughter in
England. There are unnamed Algerians and the Tunisian prizefighter, Boona,
as well as a coterie of young African American students who meet the narrator in a Spanish discothèque that is frequented by Swedes, Greeks, and Span-
iards.[72] In *Giovanni's Room*, set in Paris with forays into North America and
the south of France, Baldwin's characters are an assembly of displaced, sometimes spectral, figures. Giovanni, who has left his Italian village in the south,
is an economic migrant who stands in sharp contrast to the wealthy Belgian-
born American businessman, Jacques. Many of Baldwin's protagonists, like
the author, are frequent travelers in search of a sense of home, characters who
confuse the physical displacement of exile with an interiority of belonging.
David, in Baldwin's second novel, who has come to "find himself," has never
settled, growing up in Brooklyn, San Francisco, Seattle, and New York. Although Paris gives David the illusion of freedom ("with no-one to watch, no
penalties attached"), the novel begins, as it ends, with David alone. For David
has "run so far, so hard, across the ocean even," only to find himself once
again confronted with himself.[73] As Baldwin suggests in *Giovanni's Room*,
freedom is a precarious condition that constantly threatens to slip into isolation. In *Just Above My Head*, Julia also travels to make sense of herself. Yet,
her experiences in Africa do not connect her with her ancestors but with her
more immediate past. Travel, Baldwin suggests poignantly through the
image of the dead Hall Montana, alone in a London pub, comes at great cost
and with great isolation. "Exile," as Edward Said has written, "is one of the
saddest fates."[74]

Baldwin, does, however, suggest the ways in which exile and travel can
have an enabling, even healing effect, a point that he suggests through two
characters, both of whom are actors. In *Tell Me How Long the Train's Been
Gone*, Leo reluctantly accepts a life with his compatriots, whom he describes
as "the emptiest and most unattractive people in the world."[75] Leo is resigned
to acting out his life at home, acknowledging that he "was part of this people,
no matter how bitterly I judged them" and that he "would never be able to

leave this country."[76] Leo, though an actor, is trapped, pinned down by the expectations of white audiences and theater, forced to play "waiters, butlers, porters, clowns." Leo voices Baldwin's earlier concerns that he would be forced into writing diminishing versions of his first novel or be trapped as a Negro—or Negro writer.[77] If Baldwin suggests that Leo is stranded in the mire of racial expectation, then this is sharply contrasted by his portrayal of Eric, the white southern actor in *Another Country* who is first described in an Edenic garden in the south of France with his homophonically suggestive lover, Yves. Baldwin would tell interviewers about his life in France that "I am *not* in exile and I am *not* in paradise. It rains down here, too."[78] However, the novel's opening scene of bucolic sensuality suggests a haven from the harsh metropolis of Manhattan. Crucially, Eric and Yves are, "for the other, the dwelling place that each had despaired of finding," suggesting connections between longing and belonging in the interior landscapes of love, not just physical countries.[79]

As I noted in the introduction, Eric functions as a catalyst or conduit for the main characters in *Another Country*: he sleeps with men and women, black and white, American and European, connecting Baldwin's cast of disparate characters. Importantly, Baldwin describes how Eric's nationality is indeterminate: he "did not look American, exactly; they [people in the bar] were wondering how to place him."[80] Eric, unlike Leo (or Rufus in *Another Country*), occupies an enabling—albeit privileged—position. As an actor, and particularly as a white actor, Eric functions as Baldwin's ideal, one who cannot be placed—not just in terms of nationality but also in terms of sexuality and masculinity. And yet, if Eric suggests an idealized identity that is unfettered by nationality, sexuality, and gender, then Baldwin also suggests that this is a privilege founded on whiteness.

For Cyraina Johnson-Roullier, *Giovanni's Room* is "modern" insofar as it focuses on Baldwin's "newfound understanding of 'American-ness,'" a feature of the novel that I explored in chapter 1.[81] Baldwin is at pains to point out that David, the narrator of *Giovanni's Room*, is tall, blonde, and middle-class, further describing him as "a great American football player" and as "American as pork and beans."[82] During the course of the novel, David's white, heterosexual masculinity unravels as he spends time in Paris, suggesting the ways in which Baldwin dismantled and called into question the propaganda of postwar American national identity. Home, whiteness, nationality, and sexuality are not only inextricably entwined but are dangerous and compelling conditions in *Giovanni's Room* and Baldwin's essays. As the anthropologist Donald Carter writes, "[n]either home nor the elsewhere are definitive positions at rest or can be easily fixed in time and space."[83] Baldwin asserts in his essay "Encounter" that the American search for identity is a "dangerous voyage," one in which white and black Americans will be "in the same boat."[84] If the seafaring images invoke the Middle Passage and transnational exchange,

Baldwin's insistence that the passengers are both black and white complicates such a reading. Baldwin's project is not about separatism but how to recast American, not just African American identity. If postwar American identity is exported as a white, heterosexual construct, *Giovanni's Room* interpolates this fiction through the figure of David.

In "Encounter" Baldwin writes that meeting Africans in Paris "causes the Negro to recognize that he is a hybrid," a position that he expressed rhetorically in *Notes of a Native Son*.[85] In "Many Thousands Gone," one of many instances where the pronoun is ambiguous, Baldwin writes: "*We* do not know what to do with *him* in life; if *he* breaks our sociological and sentimental image of *him we* are panic-stricken and *we* feel *ourselves* betrayed" (emphasis added).[86] As I discussed earlier in the book, writers such as Langston Hughes argued that Baldwin's views were bastardized; they were, the older writer claimed, "half-American, half-Afro-American, incompletely fused."[87] As I illustrate through a reading of *Giovanni's Room*, a "white" novel written by a black American author, it is precisely this indeterminate space that enables Baldwin to reconfigure American national identity.

Giovanni's Room differs from the clutch of modernist novels by African American writers who also focus on flight from the United States to Europe. As Brent Hayes Edwards has noted in his masterful examination of 1920s and 1930s transnational culture, a number of key black American novels from this period use European settings as sites of revelation, illustrating the intercultural ebb and flow of the United States and Europe. As Edwards observes, Berlin is an important setting in James Weldon Johnson's *The Autobiography of an Ex-Colored Man* (1912); Jessie Fauset's novel *Plum Bun* (1929) ends in Paris; Claude McKay's *Banjo* (1929) is set in Marseille; and the most important scenes of Nella Larsen's *Quicksand* (1928) are set in Copenhagen. Paris, as Edwards convincingly argues, is frequently represented as "a special space for black transnational interaction, exchange, and dialogue"; and yet in *Giovanni's Room* there is no discussion or clear allusion to black characters, let alone a transnational community.[88] Unlike *Banjo*, which explores the transnationality of black culture in France, Baldwin's Paris in *Giovanni's Room* is rather the site of the white expatriate community; a place where the black American or African is invisible.[89] *Giovanni's Room*, in other words, seems to follow as much in the tradition of white modernist writing, such as Hemingway's *The Sun Also Rises* (1926), as in the black transnational works that Edwards examines.

Baldwin's focus on a white expatriate community in Paris seems removed from McKay's figuration of black internationalism. And yet *Giovanni's Room* is characterized not only by the theme of flight but also by numerous references to sailing and water, images that draw attention to Gilroy's mapping of Atlantic culture. Baldwin's concern, though, is not so much with connecting black national cultures but with destabilizing—or unanchoring—white

American identity. *Giovanni's Room*, in other words, is not a departure from Baldwin's works that focus on black American culture but a space from which he explores the complex traffic of whiteness, nationality, and belonging.

From the start of the novel, where David considers his ancestors who "conquered a continent . . . until they came to an ocean which faced away from Europe into a darker past," Baldwin punctuates *Giovanni's Room* with over twenty references to the sea or more generally to water.[90] As Magdalena Zaborowska has shown, Baldwin's body of work merits a closer examination in his "use of the motifs of departure, passage, arrival, acculturation, and the ways in which he shows them embroiled with representations and articulations of racialized identities."[91] Although Baldwin is circumnavigated in *The Black Atlantic*, I want to suggest that the repeated oceanic descriptions in *Giovanni's Room* call attention to Gilroy's persuasive argument that sailing enables the "moving to and fro between nations," what he describes as "crossing borders in modern machines that were themselves micro-systems of linguistic and political hybridity."[92] As I will argue, two of the pivotal moments of the novel that resonate with what Gilroy calls the "discursive slippage or connotative resonance between 'race,' ethnicity, and nation" occur with sailors, where, I suggest, we can also add "sexuality" to Gilroy's list. Sailors and sailing, in *Giovanni's Room*, are suggestive of what the narrator of "This Morning" describes as being "floated into danger."[93]

Baldwin's descriptions of the sea, like David, are "too various to be trusted" to one single meaning.[94] David's first sexual encounter with a boy begins with swimming in the sea and is enacted in the shower, creating an image of purity that is in sharp contrast to the "contempt and self-contempt" of Jacques and Guillaume that "bubbled upward out of them like a fountain of black water."[95] In one of the most troubling moments of the book, Giovanni dismisses women as "like water," claiming that they are treacherous and shallow.[96] Yet, it should be noted that the book as a whole makes use of more complex and nuanced water imagery. When David first sees Giovanni, it "was as though his station [the bar] was a promontory and we were the sea," anticipating his later description of how life in their shared room "seemed to be occurring underwater," adding that "it is certain that I underwent a sea-change there."[97] David describes his attraction to Giovanni through water imagery, noting how "I felt myself flow toward him, as a river rushes when the ice breaks up."[98] In the novel, water represents not only the literal Atlantic Ocean, as in David's reference to "when I took the boat for France," but also a liminal space between lands.[99] Here, the sea functions not only as the site of voyage or exchange but a place of continuous displacement, even sociality itself, something which is both terrifying and liberating.

If water at times suggests the unknown, then it is figured explicitly in David's desire to keep his American heterosexual masculinity *anchored*, a word that Baldwin uses. In one scene with Giovanni, David "ached abruptly, intolerably . . . to go home."[100] Home, David makes clear, is not his dwelling in Paris but "home across the ocean, to things and people I knew and understood. . . . I saw myself, sharply, as a wanderer, an adventurer, rocking through the world, unanchored."[101] David's language at once invokes the rhetoric of pioneers, an echo of the novel's beginning where his "ancestors conquered a continent," and yet his reference to being "unanchored" harks back to his reasons for marrying Hella: to give himself "something to be moored to."[102] Baldwin's choice of the word "moored" suggests, too, the absent North Africans (the Moors), missing from David's narrative but hinted at through the spectral figure of the homeless man who is "very black and alone, walking along the river," a reminder of Judith Butler's point that "the derealization of the 'Other' means that it is neither alive nor dead, but indeterminably spectral."[103] David becomes "unanchored" like Baldwin's text, which is un-Moored in its conspicuous absence of black characters. Baldwin, in other words, generates a "discursive slippage" between home and ideas of national rootedness, heterosexuality, and whiteness. For David to be unanchored from his nation and from Hella, Baldwin suggests, is for him to shade into blackness, suggested by the homeless man who embodies this link between lack of domestic anchoring and blackness, and further suggested by the oblique reference (or notable absence) of the Moors, whose expulsion from Spain underscores the link between blackness and national homelessness.

Baldwin's image of David being "unanchored" with reference to his American and heterosexual identity is further explored through his encounters with a sailor. If Gilroy limns out the ship as both the literal and figurative vessel of transnational culture, Baldwin's invocation of the sailor queers Gilroy's reading of the significance of "Marcus Garvey, George Padmore, Claude McKay, and Langston Hughes with ships and sailors"; what Graham Robb, in reference to morally autonomous sites, such as ships, workhouses, and prisons calls "submersion."[104] In *Giovanni's Room*, Baldwin draws more specifically on chartered literary works that align sailing with "submersive" sexual encounters, most famously in Herman Melville's novella, *Billy Budd* (1924). Here Melville draws attention to the ways in which ships are cut off from the gaze of societal sexual mores, illustrated by Claggart's conflicted attraction to the eponymous Billy, and more contemporaneously with *Giovanni's Room*, where Ginsberg's narrator in *Howl* (1956), invokes the transnationality and sexual freedom of sailors "who blew and were blown by those human seraphim, the sailors, caresses of Atlantic and Caribbean love."[105]

In a revealing scene in *Giovanni's Room*, David gazes at a sailor who is "dressed all in white . . . wishing I were he."[106] The sailor's whiteness is reinforced, not only by his uniform, but by his blonde hair—and this moment of recognition—where David sees the man as a younger, more beautiful version of himself, invokes both nostalgia for home and desire. Although Baldwin does not say where the sailor is from, and despite his peripatetic vocation,

David states that "[h]e made me think of home—perhaps home is not a place but simply an irrevocable condition."[107] If home is not a place, but rather a condition, it is the sailor "who wore his masculinity as unequivocally as he wore his skin" who most acutely reflects this. Untroubled by the questions of masculinity and nationality that preoccupy the narrator, the sailor is in the perpetual present, someone without a past or ties to the present, without "any antecedents, any connections at all."[108] The sailor, whose ship is both a domestic space and a vessel for constant motion, is nonetheless at home in his masculinity and whiteness. That he becomes an object of desire for David suggests, in Baldwin's description of their physical likeness, that his narrator both wants him and wants to be him.

David's gaze shifts from recognition to sexual desire, which the sailor instantly recognizes. In another moment, David realizes that the sailor's response, which is already "lewd and knowing" will "erupt into speech," "some brutal variation of *Look, baby. I know you*."[109] This moment of recognition, which forces David to consider how his body has betrayed his queer desire, is couched in a language recognizable to readers of passing narratives, where the boundaries between concealment and revelation are always precarious. David's anticipation that the sailor will *know* him, in other words, strongly echoes the concerns of the eponymous Ex-Colored Man who watches the woman he has fallen for "to see if she was scrutinizing me, to see if she was looking for anything in me which made me different from the other men she knew."[110] Although Hella suspects David's desire for other men, it is only when she finds him in a gay bar, drinking with a sailor that she knows for sure. She leaves David with the parting words that she would like to drink "all the way to Paris and all the way across that criminal ocean."[111] In Baldwin's second novel, it is tempting to read his own attempts to critique what Gilroy calls "narrow nationalism," not only through sailing, but cruising.[112] In *Giovanni's Room*, the sailor represents, not just the trade of cultural production and exchange aligned with theories of transnationalism, but gay trade, a vernacular term associated with travel and casual sex.[113] If American trade in postwar Europe is associated with the Marshall Plan, where the United States invested in war-torn Europe, Baldwin explores another side of the American identity, one constituted through other kinds of trade. In *Giovanni's Room*, Baldwin exposes the degree to which "narrow nationalism" is linked with compulsory heterosexuality by reminding readers that American national identity is structured around sexual, not just cultural and racial, differences.

I want to return to *No Name in the Street*, an essay that not only reflects on Baldwin's literal journeys (written in New York, San Francisco, Hollywood, London, and St. Paul de Vence between 1967 and 1971) but which also reveals his developing views on America, Paris, and transnationalism before charting the author's complicated relationship to the African continent. Contrary to the critical consensus that Baldwin had lost his way as a writer by the early

1970s, *No Name* shows the extent to which he continued to evolve as an astute analyst of the United States' role in international politics. I want to suggest that *No Name* marks a turning point in Baldwin's nonfiction writing, where his preoccupations shift from a discovery of what it means to be an American to something approaching what Gilroy defines as the "desire to transcend both the structures of the nation state and the constraints of ethnicity and national particularity."[114]

If Baldwin's "Paris Essays" and *Notes of a Native Son* can be characterized by his attempts to articulate an experience that is both American and African American, then there is a notable shift in rhetoric in his later work. The "we" Baldwin used in *Notes*, which infuriated and bemused Langston Hughes and other critics, is angrily called into question as Baldwin recalls castigating an old friend. While speaking of the United States' involvement in Vietnam, Baldwin's friend ventures to explain "what I think we're trying to do there." Baldwin narrates his response: "*We?*," I cried, "what motherfucking *we*?"[115] Thus, he violently questions and uproots the pronoun that he had used so interchangeably in his Paris days. For Baldwin, the question of Vietnam, symptomatic of North American's imperialism and thirst for global dominance, not only forces him to reconsider his articulation of national identity but also revises his earlier position in "Princes and Powers." If he had initially claimed that the only thing people of color had in common was "their precarious, their *unutterably* painful relation to the white world" (emphasis added), then his later work suggests that this relation can—and must—be uttered and articulated. Baldwin tells his friend that "Americans had no business in Vietnam; and that black people certainly had no business there, aiding the slave master to enslave yet more millions of dark people."[116]

By the time Baldwin published *No Name*, he had spent an intermittent decade not only in Europe and the United States but also in Turkey, as Magdalena Zaborowska has documented. As she persuasively argues, Baldwin's position at the crossroads of Europe and Asia attuned his thinking, not just to Paris or New York, but to the global ramifications of power. In *No Name*, Baldwin's rhetoric certainly shifts beyond Europe and North America. Gone are the wistful meditations in "Stranger in the Village" to the Swiss illiterati in Loèche-Les-Bains who are related in ways that he is not to "Dante, Shakespeare, Michelangelo, Aeschylus, Da Vinci, Rembrandt and Racine."[117] In an echo of Fanon, Trotsky, and Amílcar Cabral—as well as the internationalism of the Black Panther Party that he supports in *No Name*—Baldwin writes of how

> the cultural pretensions of history are revealed as nothing less than a mask
> for power, and thus it happens that, in order to be rid of Shell, Texaco,
> Coca-Cola, the Sixth Fleet, and the friendly American soldier whose mission it is to protect these investments, one finally throws Balzac and

Shakespeare—and Faulkner and Camus—out with them. Later, of course,
one may welcome them back, but on one's own terms, and, absolutely, on
one's own land.[118]

Baldwin's writing here, echoing his comments on US involvement in Vietnam, displays a keen awareness of the ways in which imperialism and global-
ization are inextricably bound. In "The Discovery," he wrote that Paris
enabled him to feel as "American as any Texas GI," which now shifts from an
invocation of the soldier as a symbol of American nationalism to an awareness of the imperial structures of global power.[119]

As Bill Lyne has persuasively argued through a reading of Baldwin's radical
trajectory, No Name "is the book where Baldwin finally and fully allies himself
with this version of what will come to be called 'Third World Marxism.'"[120]
Lyne rightly points to Baldwin's support of the Black Panthers in his book, to
which it would be useful to add the ways in which both writer and Party, at
least in international outlook, "evolved from self-described 'Black Nationalists'
to 'revolutionary nationalists,' 'internationalists,' and finally to 'revolutionary
intercommunalists' between 1966 and 1972."[121] Similarly, we might consider
Baldwin's praise of Malcolm X in the context of the latter's pronouncement
that "the struggle of Vietnam is the struggle of the whole Third World: the
struggle against colonialism, neo-colonialism, and imperialism."[122]

In No Name, Baldwin revisits his earlier reasons for his "flight" to Paris, a
place which had afforded him a space "where my risks would be more personal," "leaving me completely alone."[123] If Baldwin's move to Paris was connected to what Gilroy calls "the association of self-exploration with the
explorations of new territories," then in No Name he reconsiders what Gilroy
also refers to as "the cultural differences that exist both between and within
groups that get called races."[124] Casting his eye over his years in Paris, Baldwin looks back at the colonial history of France, noting how the "French were
still hopelessly slugging it out in Indo China when I first arrived in France,
and I was living in Paris when Dien Bien Phu fell."[125] In No Name, Baldwin
seems more attuned to parallels between colonialism and racial discrimination in the United States, such as the link he makes in No Name between
ghetto "anti-poverty" programs in North America and "foreign aid" in developing countries.[126] Not only is No Name his first extended account of the
treatment of Algerians in Paris but also his writing now connects the experiences of racial discrimination: "It was strange to find oneself, in another language, in another country, listening to the same old song and hearing oneself
condemned in the same old way."[127] In sharp contrast to his earlier distinctions between colonialism and the legacy of slavery, Baldwin writes how
"[t]he Algerian and I were both, alike, victims of this history, and I was still a
part of Africa, even though I had been carried out of it nearly four hundred
years before."[128]

Paris remains a crucial site in Baldwin's development, from his prophetic title, "Princes and Powers," to his journey, straight from the French capital to the American South in 1957 that he recalled in *No Name*. Visiting the South for the first time and pointing out that he "had come South from Paris," Baldwin recalls that he was "not in my territory now."[129] Although he does not make it clear whether he means Paris or New York, this slippage draws attention to his developing views on nationalism and exile, heightened through his experience of living in France and his drive "to find a resting place, reconciliation, in the land where I was born."[130] Baldwin had initially found himself a stranger in a European village; but in the South he would become a stranger in his own land, displaced in a "territory [that is] absolutely hostile and strange," where he felt "exactly like a foreigner."[131]

Baldwin's meditation on the Algerians in Paris earlier in *No Name* strongly echoes his own experiences in the South. The North Africans, Baldwin writes, "though they spoke French, and had been, in a sense, produced by France, they were not at home in Paris, no more at home than I, though for a different reason," a comment strongly evocative of his first trip to the American South.[132] Tellingly, as he surveys the legacy of slavery and the visible "secret" of miscegenation, he sees not only "[g]irls the color of honey," but eyes "brown like the Arab's, but the description could also refer to the Algerians in France."[133] Paris, in other words, becomes not a city for Baldwin but an irrevocable condition that refracted and distilled his writing. A city, where, as Baldwin wrote in *No Name*, "[n]ow though I was a stranger, I was home."[134]

Baldwin and Africa

Baldwin's nose, like the North-seeking needle on a compass, is forever pointed toward his adopted fatherland, Europe . . .

—ELDRIDGE CLEAVER, *SOUL ON ICE*

If Baldwin felt a sense of belonging in Paris, his writings on Africa suggest a more troubled and complicated relationship to the continent, which in turn sheds light on his shifting views about transnational collaboration. Focusing additionally on Baldwin's uneasy relationship with the continent of his forebears adds much to this debate, highlighting the ways in which his views vacillated from the 1950s to the 1980s. While a handful of critics claim to have unearthed something approaching Baldwin's Africanicity, his views on Africa are in fact consistently complicated, characterized by reservations about cultural and linguistic difference. True to form, Baldwin's views on Africa are seldom romantic, quashing notions of transhistorical connections between African Americans and their forebears in the continent of Africa. At the same time, a detailed examination of these shifting views suggests that Baldwin was close to revising his earlier reservations about cultural and linguistic interchange between Africans and black Americans, views that say much about his ongoing project to flesh out the elusive state of what it means to be American.

In an intriguing interview with Harold Isaacs, presented at the Third Annual Conference of African culture in 1960, the author recalls how his first thoughts of Africa were inextricably linked to his stepfather. "I don't know when Africa came in first," Baldwin told Isaacs, adding "[i]t *must* have been from my father":

> Somehow my first association with Africa comes through him. I compared the people in my father's church to African savages. This was because of my relation to my father . . . I was ten or twelve. The church and my father were synonymous. Music and dancing, again sweat, out of the jungle. It was contemptible because it appeared to be savage. But this was also my image of my father. I guess I was hipped on being American and things they did seemed so common, so vulgar.[135]

Baldwin's early associations with Africa are not in the context of a longed-for motherland but through his stepfather and his church. By connecting Africa with his stepfather, Baldwin illustrates not only his uneasy relationship with David Baldwin but also hints at his complicated relationship with Africa, illustrated by his striking use of the words "contemptible," "savage," and "vulgar."

Baldwin's troubled relationship with his stepfather, David, had already been well documented by the time Isaac's paper was published in 1960. In "Notes of a Native Son," the title essay of his first collection, Baldwin recalled how he "had got on badly" with the man he called his father, noting how the elder Baldwin disapproved of his desire to become a writer. David Baldwin "looked to me," the young writer recalled, "like pictures I had seen of African tribal chieftains: he really should have been naked, with warpaint on and barbaric mementos standing among spears."[136] Baldwin's discussions of Africa elsewhere in *Notes of a Native Son*, like those of his stepfather, are characterized by uncertainty, stereotype, and unease.

Baldwin's links between his stepfather and Africa gain further significance in "Autobiographical Notes," the opening essay of *Notes of a Native Son*. For Baldwin "the most crucial time in my own development came when I was forced to recognize that I was a kind of bastard of the West," a statement that surely refers back to his own illegitimacy.[137] Born James Jones, Baldwin never knew the identity of his biological father, and this question of lineage haunts his fiction and nonfiction—not least in the title of his first collection of essays, *Notes of a Native Son*. In the interview with Isaacs, Baldwin refers once again to his stepfather, noting that "[m]y father thought of himself as a king . . . and he would have said something like we were descended from kings in Africa," a comment that would have sidelined the young James Baldwin.[138] Again, in his first novel, *Go Tell It on the Mountain* (titled "In My Father's House" in an early version), the protagonist's stepfather, Gabriel, envisages "a royal line," with John on the outside as the bastard stepson.[139] In "Notes of a Native Son," Baldwin had recounted his painful and embittered relationship with his stepfather whose patrimony was "bitterness," which "now was mine."[140]

According to James Campbell, "Baldwin never came to a coherent or thought-out position on the Afro-American's predicament *vis-à-vis* his ancient African cousins," adding that "it is impossible to discern a meaningful pattern."[141] Campbell is right to suggest that Baldwin's views of Africa vacillated over the years and that it can be difficult to make sense of the writer's conclusions.[142] In sharp contrast to African American writers who dream of a connection with the motherland, Baldwin's at times acerbic comments suggest removal and distance, echoing his strained relationship with his stepfather.

During speeches, Baldwin at times invoked his African past for rhetorical effect, claiming he hailed from Sierra Leone; yet he also scolded black American students at Bowling Green State University for claiming to be African.[143] Some of his comments on Africa dance between astringency and belligerence. Recollecting his years in Paris in the conversation with Harold Isaacs, Baldwin recalled how he was both "frightened" and "disgusted" by his encounters with Africans in Paris.[144] Not surprising, some African critics, including the Nigerian writers Femi Ojo-Ade and Ezenwa-Ohaeto, have accused Baldwin respectively of evincing "his superior attitude towards Africans" and of demonstrating an "inability to grasp the predicament of the African."[145] Baldwin himself would confess to Sol Stein that his writing "suffered from a certain . . . condescension I've got in me towards Africans," and he would write in *No Name* that "it is hard to speak of Africa except as a cradle and a potential."[146] At the same time, Baldwin was a member of the little known American Society for African Culture (AMSAC) and clearly supported the move toward African independence.[147]

Baldwin was by no means the only African American writer to express ambivalence or uncertainty about the continent, what Ojo-Ade has called the "love-hate relationship" between "Blacks from Africa and those in the United States."[148] In "Heritage," one of the most well-known African American meditations on Africa, the Harlem Renaissance poet Countee Cullen (Baldwin's former teacher) asks "[w]hat is Africa to me . . . ?," where the pagan beat of the poet's imagined Africa troubles the narrator, setting the tone for a number of African American writers.[149] In Ralph Ellison's interview with Harold Isaacs, the author of *Invisible Man* expresses his interest in African art but makes it clear that "I have great difficulty associating myself with Africa."[150] While Richard Wright's relationship with Africa is complex, he made no secret of his suspicion of Marcus Garvey in *Lawd Today!* (1963). For the Nigerian writer Chimalum Nwankwo, Wright's account of his travels in Ghana, *Black Power* (1954), is little more than "an obscene travelogue," a book that is replete with stereotypes about savagery and barbarism.[151] As Ewa Barbara Luczak points out, a number of African American writers "began to treat Europe as a gateway to Africa," including William Gardner Smith's travels in Ghana from France, Julian Mayfield's political exile in Ghana, and Maya Angelou's move from New York to Cairo.[152] For some writers, like William Melvin Kelley (who lived in Rome in 1965 then Paris in 1966), their visits to Africa had a profound effect on their relationship to the continent. Kelley's 1963 view that "the Negro was so completely cut loose from Africa that next to nothing is left of it in his culture" would be revised five years later. By 1968 he declared that "our oral tradition remained alive, and with it, Africa in the United States."[153] As we will see, Baldwin's views on Africa changed, too; but he would remain cautious about the continent, shaking hands with but never quite embracing the continent of his ancestors.

As a follow-up to the 1956 Congress of Black Writers and Artists, John A. Davis edited *Africa Seen by American Negroes*—first as a special issue of *Présence Africaine* in 1958 and then republished in the United States in 1963 as a substantial book by a range of African American scholars, including Mercer Cook, E. Franklin Frazier, W. E. B. Du Bois, and Ulysses Lee. Although the aim of the book was to further understanding between Africans and black Americans, the central problem, as Rayford W. Logan notes, is one of information and access to facts. "Few Americans or any 'race,'" Logan writes, "know enough about Africa to have an informed view of it."[154] For St. Clair Drake in another essay in this volume, "many African societies and cultures . . . are often viewed with contempt, and sometimes with fascinated horror, by the people of the Western World, including the black masses of the United States."[155]

Baldwin, Wright, and Ellison did not necessarily set the tone for black American and African relationships, but all three were conspicuous absentees from "The Negro Writer and His Roots," a 1959 New York conference organized by AMSAC, a US-based offshoot of the Société Africaine Conference, run from Paris.[156] Although the 1959 conference was attended by writers, including Langston Hughes, Julian Mayfield, and Lorraine Hansberry, there was little consensus as delegates debated questions of nationalism and assimilation. Significantly, there were no African writers present and, for Horace Cayton, echoing Baldwin's views, there was a "sentimental interest in Africa," and scant attention to the black American's relationship to colonial power.[157]

Baldwin's writings on Africa fit into the wider sense of unease felt by a number of African American writers toward the continent. Africa continues to trouble and preoccupy him long after his famous essay, "Princes and Powers," and beyond his first visit to Africa in 1962. Notwithstanding the momentary oscillations that do occur, a complete reading of his work reveals a coherent—if surprising—picture. Beginning with a discussion of Baldwin and the church, I trace Baldwin's views on Africa through a reading of his criticism of colonial powers through to his fictional and nonfictional descriptions of Africa, including one of his last published essays—a commentary on African art.

The Church, the Father, and Africa

> When I joined the church at fourteen . . . I imagined myself as an
> African boy, dancing as I might have danced thousands of years ago.[158]

In "Notes of a Native Son" Baldwin describes a pivotal moment where his stepfather challenges him with the question "You'd rather write than preach, wouldn't you?"[159] Baldwin's reply was that he wished to write and yet his early writing is filled with his life as a preacher and his years in the church where his stepfather looms. Baldwin's decision to write—rather than to preach the Word—is reminiscent of Derrida's claim that "writing is parricidal," where writing undermines the spoken authority of the father/king who cannot write, particularly when we recall the title of Baldwin's early story about his stepfather, "The Death of the Prophet."

And yet Baldwin's decision to write, and not to preach, had not been his first act of defiance. By moving from a Baptist (his stepfather's tradition) to a Pentecostal church at the age of fourteen, Baldwin entered a less mainstream Protestant tradition. Historically, as I have traced elsewhere, the formal birth of Pentecostalism is marked by the Azusa Street revivals of 1906, an event that precipitated the formation of the Holiness church.[160] As I noted in chapter 3, Pentecostalism, according to writers such as Zora Neale Hurston and James Tinney, in its attempts to define a more authentic religion has been traced to much older African traditions. I am not concerned here with the contested links of Pentecostalism to African forms of worship, but I want to explore the ways in which Baldwin's early writing hints at a relationship between ecstatic worship in the Holiness movement and West African religious practices. For a handful of critics, Baldwin's first novel has direct parallels or overt connections to African cultural practices.[161] For Ernest Champion, Baldwin's first novel "can be seen as the fulfillment of what began in [Chinua Achebe's] *Things Fall Apart*" (1958); whereas, for Babacar M'Baye *Go Tell It on the Mountain* "reflects distinctive African retentions that affirm his reverence for his African heritage."[162] This idea of Baldwin's "reverence for his African heritage" simplifies his cautious and occasionally caustic views on the continent, but both Champion and M'Baye are right to emphasize the links between possession, the "shout," and the ring dance in Holiness and West African religious practices.[163]

Critics have long been divided about the degree to which African cultural heritage survived the Middle Passage and slavery. Therefore, it is difficult to argue against (or, conversely, find convincing evidence to prove) the idea that *Go Tell It on the Mountain*, as M'Baye does, "reflects cultural patterns that have parallels in Africa."[164] Similarly, it is unlikely that Carolyn Holmes's claim that "Baldwin's search for his identity could very well have been the same search for unity that his ancient ancestors in the Nile Valley had struggled to attain thousands of years ago" would have had enthralled him.[165] Even so, Holmes's bid to uncover the connections between Baldwin and Zora Neale Hurston through an Afro-centric reading of *Their Eyes Were Watching God* (1937) and *The Fire Next Time* is of interest. For Holmes, "Baldwin's cosmology had a deeper structure [than critics supposed] and possibly an Ancient Kemetic source." For both writers, their "early connections with the church were natural (or perhaps unnatural) outgrowths of their lost African ancestral heritage."[166]

This emphasis on the connections between Baldwin and Hurston is I think productive, not least because the latter was one of the earliest writers to comment on the Sanctified church. Unlike Holmes, I am not concerned with proving, once and for all, the African heritage of the two writers. Instead I want to offer another reading of Baldwin's short story "The Outing" alongside a brief interpretation of *Jonah's Gourd Vine* in order to illustrate how both writers probe the links between the Christian church and African worship.

As I explored in the previous chapter, "The Outing" is in many ways a short version or prelude to Baldwin's first novel. During the service on board the boat, David and Johnnie enter the blissful throes of the saints while Elisha is in agony on the threshing floor. Baldwin describes it

> as though their youth, barely begun, were already put away; and the animal, so vividly restless and undiscovered, so tense with power, ready to spring had been already stalked and trapped and offered, a perpetual blood sacrifice, on the altar of the Lord. Yet their bodies continued to change and grow, preparing them, mysteriously, and with ferocious speed, for manhood. No matter how careful their movements, these movements suggested, with a distinctness dreadful for the redeemed to see, the pagan lusting beneath the blood-washed robes.[167]

In contrast to the Saints who long to soar "far past the sordid persistence of the flesh," Baldwin emphasizes the irrepressible body beneath the veneer of the holy robes. By describing the boys' lust as "pagan," and by drawing attention both to the "bestial sobs" and "the music [which] grew more savage," Baldwin implicitly links the boys to a pre-Christian era, tacitly suggesting that the African roots of Pentecostalism have burst through.[168]

Baldwin's muted reference to Pentecostalism's pre-Christian origins is strongly reminiscent of the work of Zora Neale Hurston, whose repeated insistence that the "Negro is not a Christian really" echoes Baldwin's claim that the "essential religion of Black people comes out of something which is not Europe."[169] In her novel *Jonah's Gourd Vine*, Hurston depicts a service among African American workers that transmutes into a pre-Christian cele-bration. As the workers discard the instruments of the white folks (guitar and fiddle), they clap, invoking the "voice of Kata-Kumba, the great drum," so that "the shore of Africa receded."[170] Similarly, Hurston's preacher protagonist, John Pearson, fails to recognize the division between spirit and flesh. When he preaches, Hurston draws explicitly on his African heritage, writing that he "rolled his African drum up to the altar, and called his Congo gods by Chris-tian names," reciting his "Pagan poesy."[171]

Hurston's explicit references to Pentecostalism's African heritage illumi-nate Baldwin's attempts to collapse the divisions between body and flesh. In *Go Tell It on the Mountain*, John's conversion is described explicitly as a "pos-session," an experience, as Joseph A. Brown has noted, that "is traceable through all African-based cultures in the Americas."[172] Crucially, Baldwin frames the moment of conversion with a language of physicality and desire. At the very moment when John is in agony on the threshing floor, he experi-ences a terrible desire for Elisha, rather than a surrendering unto the Lord. This contradiction is central to Baldwin's exploration of the relationship be-tween sexual and religious communion, where the church becomes not just a site of sexual prohibition, but a place that mediates sexual encounters.[173]

My aim here is not to over-sexualize the African American concept of "soul," a point that Amitai Avi-Ram has warned against, but to stress that the Puritan strictures of Pentecostalism are not as straightforward as they appear.[174] Critics such as Avi-Ram and Michael Dyson have made the point that African Amer-ican religious beliefs do not always reflect the Western dualism of body and soul.[175] Rather than polarizing the body and the spirit, Avi-Ram notes that "one tends to find a smooth continuity between body and soul," a point echoed by Michael Ventura who notes that black culture has "transcended the split be-tween mind and body inherited from Descartes and certain forms of Christian theology."[176] In the case of Pentecostalism, a religion that some scholars argue most closely retains its African heritage, there is not only less of a division be-tween the spirit and the flesh, but more specifically, an acceptance between Africanisms and homosexuality.[177] Despite Baldwin's tentative articulation of a pre-Christian sensibility in "The Outing," his subsequent essays questioned any straightforward relationship between the African American and African.

Africa and Beyond

Baldwin's comments on Africa prior to visiting the continent suggest a certain degree of apprehension in a prose that is already wistful for a connection that he knows he will not find. In a letter to his agent Robert P. Mills, he writes cryptically that "[m]y bones know, somehow, something of what waits for me in Africa" but elsewhere that "I have a gloomy feeling that I won't find any answers in Africa, only more questions."[178] Asked in 1961 why he had not been to Africa, Baldwin replied that once he had visited the continent he would "not be able to dream anymore."[179] In an interview with Ida Lewis he claimed that he "didn't dare go to Africa" when he was first supposed to.[180] His reluctance to visit Africa may have been connected to his mistrust of black Americans who had started to identify with African culture, a theme he would return to on many occasions. David Leeming notes that Baldwin was "frankly skeptical of the interest among American blacks at the time in their African 'homeland,'" which is corroborated by the author in a letter to Mills, where he observes that "Africa has been black a long time but American Negroes did not identify themselves with Africa until Africa became identified with power."[181]

According to William Shawn, the former editor of the New Yorker, Baldwin suggested writing several articles for the magazine about a proposed trip to Africa in late 1959 or early 1960. "We gave him an advance," Shawn recalls, "and then we didn't hear from him again. For years."[182] Baldwin visited several African countries for the first time in July 1962. Accompanied by his sister Gloria, he spent time in Sierra Leone, Guinea, Monrovia, and the Ivory Coast. Although there are no detailed accounts of his first trip, most biographers agree with Fern Eckman's conclusion that "Baldwin had no sense of homecoming in Africa." Besides, any notion of homecoming would no doubt have been tarnished by problems with visas that Baldwin encountered on his entry into Dakar.[183]

David Leeming recalls that Baldwin took copious notes on his trip but was uncomfortable in his role as reporter, which he acknowledged to Mills, noting that he could not employ "journalistic skill[s]" and that he could "deal with it only in an extremely, even dangerously personal way."[184] In interviews and biographical accounts of his first trip to African countries, Baldwin struggled to articulate his thoughts. Leeming recalls that Baldwin was struck by "the sheer beauty of the landscape, the farms, the people," although these were things that "really attracted him but which he was unable to pursue in any depth."[185] After an enjoyable start to the trip in Sierra Leone—where his sister Gloria would meet her future husband, Frank Karefa-Smart—Baldwin realized that he did not want to write the articles on Africa for the New Yorker and he handed William Shawn, instead, a long essay on America, "A Letter from a Region in My Mind." In interviews Baldwin talked of writing a book on Africa—but not for a long time—and instead wrote what would become The Fire Next Time, his most incendiary engagement with the state of the American nation.[186]

Baldwin's second trip to Africa, a brief visit to Kenya to celebrate the country's independence, gives some indication of his growing awareness of, and commitment to, the anti-colonial movements in Africa. Again, though, Baldwin's stance is hard to gauge. Much later the critic Ezenwa-Ohaeto picked up the difficulty of reading Baldwin's views on the continent of Africa. In *The Devil Finds Work*, Baldwin was "aware of the economic and political dimensions to the suffering of the Africans"; he had started, Ezenwa-Ohaeto observes, to "become sensitive to the African reality." And yet despite his claim that Baldwin became more attuned to the reality of Africa, Ezenwa-Ohaeto maintains that the writer "does consider them [Africans] inferior to him."[187]

Ezenwa-Ohaeto does not mention Baldwin's participation in Kenya's independence celebrations nor his participation in a forum sponsored by the Liberation Committee for Africa, published in 1961 as *Nationalism, Colonialism and the United States: One Minute to Twelve*. Baldwin's essay, though hardly his most fluent, attempts to map out the connections between nationalism and colonialism, turning back, once again, to the United States: "The only hope this country has is to turn overnight into a revolutionary country, and I say revolutionary in the most serious sense of that word."[188]

Published a year before *Another Country*, Baldwin's appeal to radicalism seems out of place. After all, this is a writer who would become ignored and dismissed by a generation of younger writers, including Amiri Baraka and Eldridge Cleaver. In *Soul on Ice*, Cleaver takes Baldwin to task for his "antipathy toward the black race" in "Princes and Powers."[189] According to Cleaver, Baldwin "the reluctant black" expressed "revulsion" at the Africans at the 1956 conference through "the perfumed smoke screen of his prose." For Cleaver, Baldwin's homosexuality means that he can, in fact, never be "truly black," connecting the latter's sexuality with a "racial death-wish." And, in a comment that must have infuriated Baldwin, Cleaver concludes that the writer echoes "the black bourgeoisie who have completely rejected their African heritage."[190]

Despite criticism by Cleaver and other younger writers, Baldwin refused to embrace what he saw as the fashion of African culture. In an interview with Eve Auchincloss and Nancy Lynch in 1969, he dismissed neo-Africans as "romantic American Negroes who think they can identify with the African struggle, without having the least idea what it's about."[191] Although Baldwin would on occasion invoke his African heritage, he would more frequently admonish younger African Americans who referred to themselves as "we Africans."[192]

In Baldwin's last novel, *Just Above My Head*, published at the end of the 1970s but set in the turbulent decade before, Baldwin briefly discusses his character Julia's visit to the West African city of Abidjan, where she lived for two years. As Andrew Shin and Barbara Judson astutely point out, "Julia's trip to Africa offers a kind of secular redemption for the religious hypocrisy that she unwittingly contributed to as a child."[193] In Africa she meets a *"really* black" man who is old enough to be her father, the only male who "understood something" about her.[194] And yet, as Shin and Judson note, Baldwin suggests that "pan-Africanism is not really a viable solution for the problems of American blacks."[195] "A black girl in Africa," Julia concludes, "who wasn't *born* in Africa . . . is a very strange creature for herself, and for everyone who meets her."[196] In *Just Above My Head*, echoing his comments in the Paris essays, Baldwin refuses to romanticize relationships between Africans and black Americans. For Baldwin, like Edwards, "black modern expression takes form not as a single thread, but through the often uneasy encounters of peoples of African descent with each other."[197]

I want to conclude by suggesting that Baldwin's opinions on Africa shifted in the late 1970s and that by his death in 1987 there was a notable if not fully articulated change in his views. As Eleanor Traylor persuasively argues, Baldwin's participation in the 1980 African Literature Association marked a turnaround in his otherwise shifting responses to Africa. In his encounter with the Nigerian writer Chinua Achebe, Baldwin, it seems, found kinship and companionship, despite the cultural and geographical differences. Commenting on Achebe's *Things Fall Apart*, Baldwin stated that "I recognized everybody in it. And that book was about my father."[198] For Traylor, Achebe's recollection of first reading Baldwin points to a mutual recognition that exceeds the parameters of postcolonial or postmodern theorization. "When Achebe looks into the mirror of *Go Tell It on the Mountain*," Traylor writes, "[h]e sees neither 'self' nor 'other;' he sees 'kin,' or to borrow Alice Walker's much later term, he seems a 'familiar.'"[199]

Although the Baldwin-Achebe encounter was a profound event, it seems to me that Baldwin's ideas of Africa had already started to shift by the late 1970s. In an interview with *Africa: International Business, Economic and Political Magazine* in 1978, he began to articulate the need and desire for a dialogic encounter between black Americans and Africans, engaging with what he termed their "cultural interdependence."[200] Here Baldwin explicitly reworked his earlier notion that the "only thing that really unites all black men everywhere is, as far as I can tell, the fact that white men are on their necks."[201] In the *Africa* interview Baldwin pointedly discussed a relationship that is "much deeper than the common experience of colonialism or neo-colonialism," what he later termed "cultural interplay." Noting how his nephew had found his visit to Africa "tremendously liberating,"[202] Baldwin spoke of his hope for more cultural interaction between the United States and Africa for the younger generation. And as he stated in a later interview with Jordan Elgrably and George Plimpton, "If I were twenty-four now, I don't know . . . where I would go . . . I don't know if I would go to France, I might go to Africa."[203]

In the Elgrably and Plimpton interview, Baldwin seems to revise his strident earlier views about the gulf separating Africans and African Americans. In "Stranger in the Village," Baldwin seemed almost envious that "the most illiterate among them [the villagers] is related, in a way that I am not, to

Dante, Shakespeare . . . Chartres."[204] In *No Name*, far from looking wistfully at European culture, Baldwin wrote that "the South African coal miner, or the African digging for roots . . . have no reason to bow down before Shakespeare, or Descartes . . . or the Cathedral at Chartres."[205] In the Elgrably-Plimpton interview, this position is again stated more clearly: "Europe is no longer a frame of reference, a standard bearer, the classic model for literature and for civilization. . . . When I was a kid, the world was white . . . and now it's struggling to *remain* white—a very different thing."[206]

Baldwin's comments here and elsewhere in the last decade or so of his life suggest the ways in which his aesthetic and political outlook had shifted to include a broader, transcultural perspective. As Baldwin stated in the late 1970s, "America is vast by itself, and yet the sense is that one no longer wishes to be isolated on the American continent," adding that "we have to know what is going on in Africa and Africa has to know what is going on in Black America."[207]

Baldwin's reference to what he later called "cultural interdependence" is illustrated in an interview that was published in the year of his death, appearing in *Perspectives: Angles on African Art*. Baldwin was one of a number of writers and artists asked to select objects from the exhibition of African art that ran from 1987 to 1988 and to be interviewed by Michael John Weber. A large photograph of a regal-looking Baldwin wearing a corduroy jacket and an African-inspired bangle begins his section, where the text is placed alongside photographs of African sculpture. The interview responses (the questions are not shown) are frequently cryptic as Baldwin comments on his selected objects. "I feel reconciled to myself and my past," Baldwin states, "I come more directly from this than from Rembrandt." In sharp contrast to his criticism of negritude or "authentic blackness," Baldwin claims that "[i]t says something to me because I am black."[208]

During the interview there are two notable, recurring themes. The first is Baldwin's recognition of kinship with the African art. Commenting on a woman with a Luba staff, Baldwin states that "I recognize the women; I met them in Harlem."[209] And yet even as he approaches some sense of cultural interdependence, he struggles, like Julia in *Just Above My Head*, to articulate his connection to the art of Africa, illustrating what Traylor calls an "emergent language . . . situated in that in-between space of becoming."[210] You "cannot *hear* another language, unless you've heard it already," claims Julia in the novel.[211] "It's hard to describe these things in a Western language," Baldwin himself states at one point, later adding, "I can't go there. I'm not equipped at all to discuss that." Pressed by the interviewer to comment further on a piece, Baldwin states simply, "I recognize it. I don't know how I recognize it. I don't know how to put it to you." During the interview Baldwin seems worn out, exhausted by his attempts to translate his experience: "I'm not sure I can articulate it," he adds at one point, adding "I'm also very weary, weary, weary of trying to deal with this."[212] These late reflections do not resolve the questions about Africa that he asked himself throughout his lifetime. It is clear, however, that Baldwin was increasingly open to the idea of a transcultural— or, to use his term, interdependent—relationship between the African and the African American. For Traylor, both Achebe and Baldwin "own a language that, as profound as it is playful, will dare to strip away the mask of the *egwugwu*; look the ancestor right straight in the eye; face alone *ogbuagali-odu*."[213] For Baldwin, reflecting on a Yoruba mask, "[i]t's not a Western face. One could say an African face, but it's something deeper than that. I can't find the word for it. *Africa*, for lack of a better term."[214]

Afterword

As I explored in the last chapter, Baldwin's work is preoccupied with the themes of home, exile, and belonging. The titles of his work testify to this pre-occupation: "Stranger in the Village," *Giovanni's Room*, *Another Country*, and *No Name in the Street*. There is a bitter irony that Baldwin, one of the twentieth century's most insightful writers on the theme of home, has found his own work, at least until recently, rootless and misplaced. As Consuela Francis has observed, Baldwin's reception "has been equal parts critical devotion and critical neglect."[1] As I have shown throughout this book, there are a number of reasons why this has been the case. Critics have been unsure about where to place Baldwin; unwilling or unable to acknowledge how his work crosses multiple disciplines, genres, and boundaries. Frequently, critics seem intent on assigning him to one or another place or category: he is either an essayist or a novelist, an artist or a spokesman. His early novels showed promise, many critics contend, but his later works became unwieldy and unfocused. As Lawrie Balfour has noted, Baldwin's *oeuvre* is frequently divided into "political" or "non-political" categories, just as critics often view him as either a religious writer or a fierce critic of the church.[2] Historically, critics have also been troubled by Baldwin's sexuality, either sidelining his queer writing or treating his sexuality and African American identity as separate categories.

In the last few years, Baldwin has started to find a home in the academy. Cultural studies, black queer studies, and interdisciplinarity in scholarship have all played a part in resuscitating critical writing on Baldwin. Much recent criticism on the author is insightful and mindful of his divisive critical history, reminding readers that his work should not be placed in one or another camp, whether homosexual, black, and so on. While this shift has opened up a broader discussion of the author's work, there is also a danger that some criticism veers toward a dissipated picture of Baldwin as a writer who is "post-categorical" and without any cohesion. This is a tendency the author himself was only too aware of: "It is a curious way to find your identity," Baldwin told Margaret Mead, "labeling yourself by labeling all the things that you're not."[3]

Over the last few years there have been a handful of conferences held on Baldwin's life and work in Washington, DC, London, Suffolk (Boston), New York City, and Montpellier, France, as well as a steady trickle of articles and several newly edited collections; notably the publication of previously uncollected reviews and articles, *The Cross of Redemption* (2010), and the launch of the journal, the *James Baldwin Review* in 2014.[4] In November 2011, Baldwin was the forty-forth inductee to the American Poets' Corner, where he joined eminent writers including Emerson and one of Baldwin's personal favorites, Henry James. Yet, it still seems that Baldwin does not share the steadfast reputation of his peers, notably Richard Wright and Ralph Ellison. His papers at the Schomburg Center for Research in Black Culture, though of interest, are scant in comparison to those of Wright or Ellison, and his letters remain unpublished.

While his work has not enjoyed the sustained critical attention lavished on some of his peers, Baldwin continues to be invoked in high-profile magazine articles such as Colm Tóibín's *New York Review of Books* article, which compared Barack Obama to Baldwin.[5] Baldwin's appeal, it seems, continues to extend beyond the academy. The novelist Randall Kenan's book *The Fire This Time*, written to celebrate the forty-fifth anniversary of Baldwin's *The Fire Next Time*, follows in the elder author's footsteps, asking how far African Americans have come after Hurricane Katrina. Writing in a blend of autobiography and social commentary, Kenan reminds us of what Baldwin might have made of the world around him since 1987. More recently, Herb Boyd's biography of Baldwin and Harlem, again written for a general readership, suggests the writer's appeal beyond undergraduate and graduate students, which is further illustrated by Jewelle Gomez's play about Baldwin, *Waiting for Giovanni*, which premiered at the New Conservatory Theater in San Francisco in 2011, along with a production of *The Amen Corner* at the National Theatre in London (2013). In 2014, Columbia University hosted a series of cultural events, "The Year of James Baldwin" in New York City to celebrate and commemorate Baldwin's ninetieth anniversary, highlighting continuing interest in the writer from outside and within the academy.

As I have suggested during this book, however, the very reasons for Baldwin's continuing appeal—in particular his involvement in the civil rights movement and his capacity to write popular as well as polemical works—have also contributed to his uncertain place in American literature. What is more, though often seen as the eloquent voice of black rage during the civil rights movement, Baldwin was also vulnerable to charges that he was out of touch; that his life in exile dulled the sharpness of his social and political observations. His geographical distance from the United States has also contributed to a view of the writer as an isolated individual, when in fact he was

a frequent collaborator on projects, as well as maintaining enduring friendships with artists including Maya Angelou, Nina Simone, Miles Davis, and
Sydney Poitier, in addition to maintaining old friendships with folk including
Beauford Delaney and Lucien Happersberger. Critics have frequently suggested, too, that he spent too much time during the 1960s on the rostrum
when he should have been at his desk. Again, though a successful writer in a
number of genres, there are frequent suggestions that Baldwin should have
focused on only one genre—critics most often mention the essay form—after
the mid-1960s.

One of Baldwin's enduring traits seems to have been his willingness to
revel in the role of maverick and disturber of the peace, as illustrated by repeated jabs at the FBI's director, J. Edgar Hoover. Amid the cacophony of
charges that he was too old, out of touch, or an ailing novelist, Baldwin repeatedly refused to be pinned down or to be held to account. In order to facili-
tate change, Baldwin declared to the poet Nikki Giovanni, "[w]e have to make
our own definitions and begin to rule the world that way."[6] Baldwin's repeated
insistence on self-definition and his suspicion of what is now termed identity
politics serve as an important rejoinder to theory's attempts at fixity. Baldwin's refusal to view identity or history as fixed serves as a pertinent reminder
that his own work was continuously evolving, highlighting the need to read it
in the context(s) of the four decades in which his writing emerged.

My aim has not been to celebrate or romanticize Baldwin's paradoxes or
inconsistencies but to argue that much of his seemingly contradictory work
begins to cohere when read in the context of the material reality out of which
he lived and wrote from the 1940s to the 1980s. As Cheryl Wall has noted in
relation to his essays, which I would extend to much of his work, in Baldwin's
writing "the larger the topic, the more the questions open out to other questions."[7] One of the most striking features of Baldwin's work is his ability to
demonstrate integrity and commitment while at the same time insisting on
the right to oscillate, prevaricate, and think through philosophical questions
with the reader. In *No Name in the Street*, for example, he ponders the term
"Afro-American," which he picks apart as "a wedding . . . of two confusions,
an arbitrary linking of two undefined and currently undefinable proper
nouns." Even as Baldwin struggles to find a language for the peculiar condition he describes—"These questions—they are too vague for questions, this
excitement, this discomfort"—he brings the reader with him on his urgent
moral, philosophical, and intellectual enquiries, which are not about rhetoric,
but about the dangerous and compelling condition of twentieth-century life
in America, the continent of Africa, and beyond.[8]

Baldwin began writing in a postwar left-wing intellectual milieu and
ended, in another country, when Ronald Reagan was in office. By paying close
attention to these cultural and political shifts, Baldwin's work, I have suggested, begins to cohere. Baldwin's life and career on the Left during the 1940s

and his repeated defiance of McCarthy do much to illuminate discussions of politics and literature during this period. His FBI files, too—by turns voluminous, chilling, and on occasion incomprehensible—again add much to an understanding of the relationship between the Bureau and the role of writers, particularly black American authors. Prophetic, brilliant, and at times exasperating, the work of all those strangers called James Baldwin repeatedly calls attention to the ways in which Western powers continued to create fictions and fabrications, an exemplification of what he called the West's "striking addiction to irreality."[9] "[T]he air of this time and place is so heavy with rhetoric, so thick with soothing lies," Baldwin wrote in 1962—in a rhetoric that has lost none of its relevance—"that one must really do great violence to language, one must somehow disrupt the comforting beat, in order to be heard."[10] Baldwin's multifaceted brilliance, his deep sense of political, moral, and cultural responsibility, as well as his refusal to suffer fools or identity politics gladly, make him a writer worthy of far more attention within the academy. This critical lacuna requires an important intervention, one that I hope this book begins by disrupting the comforting critical beat and by grappling with the life and work of an artist as complex as the multitudes we call Jimmy Baldwin.

{ NOTES }

Introduction

1. Colm Tóibín, "The Last Witness," *London Review of Books* 23, no. 18 (September 20, 2001): 15.

2. Brian Norman, *The American Protest Essay and National Belonging: Addressing Division* (Albany: SUNY Press, 2007), 88.

3. Fern Marja Eckman, *The Furious Passage of James Baldwin* (New York: M. Evans & Co., 1966), 160; Magdalena Zaborowska, *James Baldwin's Turkish Decade: Erotics of Exile* (Durham: Duke University Press, 2009), 91.

4. Zaborowska, *James Baldwin's Turkish Decade*, 93.

5. Nat Hentoff, "'It's Terrifying,' James Baldwin: The Price of Fame," in *Conversations with James Baldwin*, ed. Fred L. Standley and Louis H. Pratt (Jackson: University of Mississippi Press, 1989), 34; James Baldwin, *Another Country* [1962] (London: Penguin, 1990), 18.

6. Augusta Strong, Review of *Another Country*, by James Baldwin, *Freedomways* (Fall 1962): 501. See also Stanley Edgar Hyman, "No Country for Young Men," the *New Leader* (June 25, 1962): 22, 23, who found the novel "weak and unconvincing," 32.

7. Irving Howe, "Black Boys and Native Sons," in *Selected Writings, 1950–1990* (San Diego: Harcourt Brace Jovanovich Publishers, 1990), 135.

8. Mike Thelwell, "*Another Country*: Baldwin's New York Novel," in *The Black American Writer*, vol. 1: *Fiction*, ed. C. W. E. Bigsby (Baltimore, MD: Penguin Books, 1969), 182; Norman Podhoretz, "In Defense of a Maltreated Best Seller," *Show* 2, no. 10 (October 1962): 91.

9. Podhoretz, "In Defense of a Maltreated Best Seller," 91.

10. Thelwell, "*Another Country*," 189.

11. Ibid., 188.

12. James Baldwin, "As Much Truth as One Can Bear," *New York Times Book Review* (January 14, 1962), 38; reprinted in James Baldwin, *The Cross of Redemption: Uncollected Writings*, ed. and introd. Randall Kenan (New York: Pantheon Books, 2010), 28–34.

13. John Hall, "James Baldwin Interviewed," in *Conversations with James Baldwin*, 104.

14. Cited by Laura Quinn, "'What Is Going on Here?' Baldwin's *Another Country*," in *Gay and Lesbian Literature since the War: History and Memory*, ed. Sonya L. Jones (London and New York: Harrington Press, 1998), 51.

15. Hyman, "No Country for Young Men," 22, 23. Hyman writes that "[s]ince *Giovanni's Room* was distinguished by the delicacy and taste of its erotic scenes, I can only conclude that Baldwin has changed his ways in order to achieve a best-seller," 23.

16. Eldridge Cleaver, *Soul on Ice*, introd. Maxwell Geismar (New York: Ramparts, 1968), 107.

17. James Baldwin, "Alas, Poor Richard," in *Collected Essays*, ed. Toni Morrison (New York: The Library of America, 1998), 251.

18. Cited by Rosa Bobia, *The Critical Reception of James Baldwin in France* (New York: Peter Lang, 1997), 37.

19. Paul Goodman, "Not Enough of a World to Grow In," *New York Times Book Review* (June 24, 1962): 5.

20. LeRoi Jones [Amiri Baraka], "Brief Reflections on Two Hotshots," in *Home: Social Essays*, 1966; reprint, with a preface by LeRoi Jones (Hopewell, NJ: Ecco Press, 1998), 119.

21. William A. Cohen, "Liberalism, Libido, Liberation: Baldwin's *Another Country*," in *The Queer Sixties*, ed. Patricia Juliana Smith (New York: Routledge, 1999), 216.

22. Cleaver, *Soul on Ice*, 109; Goodman, "Not Enough," 5.

23. In sharp contrast, Edward Margolies complained that "Baldwin's anger somewhat shrouds his art," in a discussion of the novel in "The Negro Church: James Baldwin and the Christian Vision," in *James Baldwin: Modern Critical Views*, ed. Harold Bloom (Philadelphia: Chelsea House Publishers, 1986), 73. See also Lorelei Cederstrom, "Love, Race and Sex in the Novels of James Baldwin," *Mosaic* 17, no. 2 (Spring 1984): 179, who writes that Baldwin "presents a fully-developed picture of black rage and the societal elements which have worked to produce that rage."

24. See Rebecca Aanerud, "Now More Than Ever: James Baldwin and the Critique of White Liberalism," in *James Baldwin Now*, ed. Dwight A. McBride (New York: New York University Press, 1999), 56–74, esp. 57–58; see Thelwell, *"Another Country*," 188.

25. Baldwin, "In Search of a Majority," in *Collected Essays*, 220. This essay was adapted from a 1960 speech.

26. William Cohen convincingly works out the date of 1956 by working out in Book 2, ch. 1, that Yves, who is twenty-one, had been five during the German occupation of 1940 (n. 219). The year 1956 was, of course, the publication year of Baldwin's second novel, *Giovanni's Room*, and Baldwin may be linking his homosexual character Yves to his later bold novel about homosexual love.

27. Lorelei Cederstrom, "Love, Race and Sex," 181.

28. See Robert J. Corber, *Homosexuality in Cold War America: Resistance and the Crisis of Masculinity* (Durham: Duke University Press, 1997), esp. 168.

29. Cohen, "Liberalism, Libido, Liberation," 202.

30. Baldwin, "The Fire Next Time," in *Collected Essays*, 347.

31. Baldwin, *Another Country*, 340.

32. Baldwin, "No Name in the Street," in *Collected Essays*, 363.

33. Yvonne Neverson, "The Artist Has Always Been a Disturber of the Peace," in *Conversations with James Baldwin*, 171.

34. Margaret Mead and James Baldwin, *A Rap on Race* (New York: Dell, 1971), 136.

35. Baldwin, "Autobiographical Notes," in *Collected Essays*, 8.

36. David A. Gerstner, *Queer Pollen: White Seduction, Black Male Homosexuality and the Cinematic* (Champaign University of Illinois Press, 2011), 73.

37. Robert Reid-Pharr, *Black Gay Man* (New York: New York University Press, 2001), 92; Gerstner, *Queer Pollen*, 130.

38. Baldwin, "In Search of a Majority," in *Collected Essays*, 220.

39. Baldwin, "Autobiographical Notes," in *Collected Essays*, 9.

40. Baldwin, "The Price of the Ticket," in *Collected Essays*, 834. See Lawrie Balfour, *The Evidence of Things Not Said: James Baldwin and the Promise of American Democracy* (Ithaca: Cornell University Press, 2011), who argues that "[d]espite Baldwin's declaration that 'all theories are suspect,' his essays speak directly to the concerns of political theory," 20.

41. See Dwight A. McBride, "Introduction: New Approaches to Baldwin," in *James Baldwin Now*, where he rightly observes that the emergence of cultural studies has finally equipped critics to see the author in his varied complexity.

42. Cora Kaplan and Bill Schwarz, "Introduction," in *James Baldwin: America and Beyond*, ed. Cora Kaplan and Bill Schwarz (Ann Arbor: University of Michigan Press, 2011), 3.

43. In "Cabin Fever," *New York Times* (October 22, 2006), Henry Louis Gates Jr., for example, develops the oft-cited essay/fiction split in Baldwin's work by writing that "[t]he paradox of Baldwin's career is that he wrote essays with all of the lyricism and subtlety of a great novelist; yet he approached the craft of the novel with an essayistic didacticism," http://www.nytimes.com/2006/10/22/books/review/Gates.t.html.

44. Miller, *A Criminal Power*, 12.

45. Baldwin, "Everybody's Protest Novel," in *Collected Essays*, 17.

46. In recent years, a number of scholars have encouraged a more holistic critical framework for viewing race and sexuality. Pioneering scholars include Robert Reid-Pharr, Dwight McBride, Marlon Ross, E. Patrick Johnson, and Mae G. Henderson.

47. For readings that stress the complexity of Baldwin's views on homosexuality and masculinity, see Douglas Taylor, "Three Lean Cats in a Hall of Mirrors: James Baldwin, Norman Mailer and Eldridge Cleaver on Race and Masculinity," *Texas Studies in Literature and Language* 52, no. 1 (Spring 2010): 70–101. In a reading of "The Black Boy Looks at the White Boy," Taylor argues that Baldwin's essay "ultimately, fails to disentangle itself from the masculinist premises it attempts to critique," 80. See Miko Tuhkanen, "James Baldwin on the American Express and the Queer Underground," *English Language Notes* 45, no. 2 (Fall/Winter 2007): 123–31, who is attuned to Baldwin's contradictory portraits of homosexuality in his fiction.

48. James Baldwin, *Giovanni's Room* [1956] (London: Penguin, 1990), 41.

49. For a useful reading of sexual disgust, see Jonathan Dollimore's essay, "Sexual Disgust," in *Sex, Literature and Censorship* (Cambridge: Polity, 2001), 46–69, which includes a brief discussion of *Giovanni's Room*.

50. See Guy Mark Foster, "African American Literature and Queer Studies: The Conundrum of James Baldwin," in *Companion to African American Literature*, ed. Gene A. Jarett (Hoboken, NJ: Wiley-Blackwell, 2010), 393–408, who maps out the relationship between Queer Studies and African American Literature through a reading of Baldwin. Foster is alert to the ways in which Baldwin's writing has been claimed and misrepresented by white and black queer critics alike. He points out, for example, Baldwin's references to his heterosexual white women, referring to queer readings that efface such details (399).

51. David Ikard, *Breaking the Silence: Toward a Black Male Feminist Criticism* (Baton Rouge: Louisiana State University Press, 2007), 52.

52. James Baldwin and Nikki Giovanni, *A Dialogue*, foreword by Ida Lewis, afterword by Orde Coombs (London: Michael Joseph, 1975), 42, 48.

53. Baldwin and Giovanni, *A Dialogue*, 47, 52.

54. Ibid., 52.

55. Ibid., 55.

56. Balfour, *The Evidence of Things Not Said*, 55.

57. See Rolland Murray, *Our Living Manhood: Literature, Black Power, and Masculine Ideology* (Philadelphia: University of Pennsylvania Press, 2007), who comes down hard on Baldwin's *If Beale Street Could Talk*, describing it as "utterly phallic and patriarchal," adding that "Baldwin, who had once mapped the restrictive logic of patriarchal social arrangements, rewrites patriarchy as a source of security, stability, and continuity," 32.

58. There have been several high-profile international conferences on Baldwin in the last decade, including: Howard University (2000), Queen Mary, University of London (2007), Suffolk University, Boston (2009), New York University (2011), and Montpellier, France (2014). Recent notable publications include: Lynn Orilla Scott's *James Baldwin's Later Fiction: Witness to the Journey* (2002); Scott's co-edited volume with Lovalerie King, *James Baldwin and Toni Morrison: Comparative Critical and Theoretical Essays* (2006); Magdalena Zaborowka's *James Baldwin's Turkish Decade: Erotics of Exile* (2009); my own edited volume *A Historical Guide to James Baldwin* (2009); Cora Kaplan and Bill Schwarz's edited volume, *James Baldwin: America and Beyond* (2011); and D. Quentin Miller's *A Criminal Power: James Baldwin and the Law* (2012).

59. George Shulman, *American Prophecy: Race and Redemption in American Political Culture* (Minneapolis: University of Minnesota Press, 2008), 90.

60. Marlon B. Ross, "Some Glances at the Black Fag: Race, Same-Sex Desire, and Cultural Belonging," in *The Black Studies Reader*, ed. Jacqueline Bobo, Cynthia Hudley, and Claudine Michel (New York: Routledge, 2004), 159.

61. See Robert Corber, "Everybody Knew His Name: Reassessing James Baldwin," *College Literature* 42, no. 1 (2001): 166–75. For Corber, the term "queer" "acknowledges, as Baldwin himself did, the limitations of identity categories without discarding them altogether," 168–69.

62. Here my approach dovetails with Roderick Ferguson's theory of "queer of color," which works "to debunk the idea that race, class, gender and sexuality are discreet formations, apparently insulated from one another." See *Aberrations in Black: Toward a Queer of Color Critique* (Minneapolis: University of Minnesota Press, 2004), 4.

63. Robert Reid-Pharr, *Once You Go Black: Choice, Desire, and the Black American Intellectual* (New York: New York University Press, 2007), 100.

64. Quincy Troupe, "Last Testament: An Interview with James Baldwin," in *Conversations with James Baldwin*, 284.

Chapter 1

1. James Baldwin, "Introduction: The Price of the Ticket," in *The Price of the Ticket: Collected Nonfiction, 1948–1985* (New York: St. Martin's/Marek, 1985), ix. Surprisingly, Baldwin does not mention the support of Bucklin Moon, the influential associate editor at Doubleday. According to Lawrence P. Jackson in *The Indignant Generation: A Narrative History of African American Writers and Critics, 1934–1960* (Princeton and Oxford: Princeton University Press, 2010), 261, Moon "befriended him [Baldwin] and took him seriously." If this is so, then Baldwin pulled no punches in his 1949 review of Moon's *The High Cost of Prejudice*, describing the "easy generalization," "muted tone," and "earnestness" that abound in the book. James Baldwin, Review of Vishnu V. Oak et al., in *The Cross of*

Redemption: Uncollected Writings, ed. and introd. Randall Kenan (New York: Pantheon Books, 2010), 269. An earlier version of this section appeared in *English Literary History* 78, no. 4 (2011): 833–62. Reprinted with permission by Johns Hopkins University Press.

2. Baldwin published a total of twenty pieces up until 1949 including short stories. I have not included "Everybody's Protest Novel," "Preservation of Innocence," and "Journey to Atlanta" as book reviews.

3. Baldwin, "Introduction: The Price of the Ticket," xiii.

4. Ibid.

5. According to Jackson in *The Indignant Generation,* 261, Baldwin "had attended League of American Writers lectures and workshops as a teenager."

6. Alan M. Wald, *The New York Intellectuals: The Rise and Decline of the Anti-Stalinist Left from the 1930s to the 1980s* (Chapel Hill: University of North Carolina Press, 1987), 14.

7. Jackson, *The Indignant Generation,* 361.

8. See Bill Lyne, "God's Black Revolutionary Mouth: James Baldwin's Black Radicalism," *Science and Society* 74 (January 2010): 12–36. Lyne seeks to recoup the radicalism of Baldwin's work through an insightful reading of "The Fire Next Time," but he does not focus on his early associations with the Left. See also Roderick A. Ferguson, "The Parvenu Baldwin and the Other Side of Redemption: Modernity, Race, Sexuality, and the Cold War," in *James Baldwin Now,* ed. Dwight A. McBride (London and New York: New York University Press, 1999), 233–61. Ferguson performs astute readings of "Everybody's Protest Novel" and "Preservation of Innocence" in relation to Baldwin and the avant-garde.

9. David Estes, "An Interview with James Baldwin," in *Conversations with James Baldwin,* ed. Fred L. Standley and Louis H. Pratt (Jackson: University of Mississippi Press, 1989), 276. Baldwin's comment does, however, resonate with Edwin Seaver's comments in 1944: " 'An astonishing number of the manuscripts' addressed racial injustice, 'what we call the 'Negro Problem' " (cited by Jackson, *The Indignant Generation,* 178).

10. Baldwin, "Autobiographical Notes," in *Collected Essays,* ed. Toni Morrison (New York: The Library of America 1998), 5.

11. Mary McCarthy, "Baldwin," in *James Baldwin: The Legacy,* ed. Quincy Troupe (New York: Simon & Schuster, 1989), 48. See Jackson, *The Indignant Generation,* 265, for a brief but convincing analysis of McCarthy's "patronizing snobbery." Jackson makes the point that "[h]er suggestion that Baldwin had some expert facility that enabled him to evaluate art without a flawed racial consciousness is . . . disingenuous."

12. Baldwin, "Introduction: The Price of the Ticket," xii.

13. Baldwin also discusses Worth in his 1960 essay "The New Lost Generation," originally published in *Esquire* (July 1961) and reprinted in *The Price of the Ticket,* 305–13. Worth appears on the 1930 Federal Census (New York City, Brooklyn Borough) as an eight-year-old but thereafter is something of a mystery. There are no records of his death in the Social Security Death Index and the Commissioner's Office, City of NY, confirmed that his name does not appear in records of deaths reported between 1946 and 1947, and there is no record of his death in the records of the Office of Chief Medical Examiner.

14. Baldwin, "Introduction: The Price of the Ticket," xii.

15. Baldwin, "No Name in the Street," in *Collected Essays,* 370.

16. See, for example, Richard Parish, "How Jim Crow Is Building a Tension That Will Explode in Race Riots," *Challenge* 1, no. 5 (October 1943): 2, 6. See also Robin Myers, "Socialists Expose Sham Old Party Race Pranks," *Challenge* 2, no. 3 (October 1944): 1, 8.

17. For a useful selection of *Challenge!* (the periodical of the Young People's Socialist League), see *Challenge! YPSL*, Volumes 1–4: 1943–46, introd. Milton Cantor (Westport, CT: Greenwood Press, 1970). This is a useful resource for scholars wishing to see the kinds of articles that Baldwin would have been reading and contains a useful overview of the periodical and YPSL.

18. Stan Weir, "Meetings with James Baldwin," *Against the Current* 18 (January–February 1989): 36.

19. Ibid.

20. See Gary Edward Holcomb, *Codename Sasha: Queer Black Marxism and the Harlem Renaissance* (Gainesville: University Press of Florida, 2007).

21. I am indebted to Alan Wald for pointing out the ambiguity of Baldwin's claims and clarifying that Baldwin could have been a member of one of two Trotskyite groups.

22. James Campbell, *Talking at the Gates: A Life of James Baldwin* (Boston: Faber and Faber, 1991), 40.

23. Geraldine Murphy, "Subversive Anti-Stalinism: Race and Sexuality in the Early Essays of James Baldwin," *English Literary History* 63(1996): 1024.

24. In *James Baldwin: Artist on Fire* (London: Penguin, 1990), 52, W. J. Weatherby notes that Baldwin's early commissions for the *Nation* and the *New Leader* were inextricably linked to his socialist connections—and, in particular, to his Young People's Socialist League membership.

25. Ferguson, "The Parvenu Baldwin and the Other Side of Redemption," 243.

26. David Leeming, *James Baldwin: A Biography* (New York: Alfred A. Knopf, 1994), 44.

27. Ibid., 7. See *James Baldwin and Sol Stein, Native Sons* ed. Sol Stein (New York: Ballantine Books, 2004), where Stein documents his editorship of Baldwin's first nonfiction book.

28. Neil Jumonville, ed., "Partisan Review Editorial Statement" (1934), in *The New York Intellectuals Reader* (New York: Routledge, 2007), 56.

29. Ibid., 55.

30. Wald, *The New York Intellectuals*, 11.

31. Ibid., 74.

32. Harvey Teres, *Renewing the Left: Politics, Imagination and the New York Intellectuals* (New York: Oxford University Press, 1996), 46.

33. The first English edition was published in 1925.

34. Wald, *The New York Intellectuals*, 92.

35. Leon Trotsky, *Literature and Revolution*, ed. William Keach, trans. Rose Strunksy (Chicago: Haymarket Books, 2005), 144.

36. Ibid., 185, 64.

37. This was a view also shared by the likes of Arthur P. Davis, who would state in the mid-1940s that "a thesis is one thing, a good novel another." Quoted in Jackson, *The Indignant Generation*, 233.

38. Wald, *The New York Intellectuals*, 142.

39. Baldwin, "As Much Truth as One Can Bear," *The New York Times Book Review* (January 14 1962): 1; reprinted in Baldwin, *The Cross of Redemption*, 28–34.

40. Houston A. Baker Jr., *Modernism and the Harlem Renaissance* (Chicago: University of Chicago Press, 1987); James de Jongh, *Vicious Modernism: Black Harlem and the Literary Imagination* (Cambridge: Cambridge University Press, 1990).

41. Jackson, *The Indignant Generation*, 178, 217.

42. Ibid., 241.

43. Horace Porter, *Stealing the Fire: The Art and Protest of James Baldwin* (Middletown, CT: Wesleyan University Press, 1989), 126; T. E. Cassidy, "The Long Struggle," *Commonweal* 58 (May 22 1953): 186.

44. Porter, *Stealing the Fire*, 126.

45. Robert J. Corber, *Homosexuality in Cold War America: Resistance and the Crisis of Masculinity* (Durham: Duke University Press, 1997), 161.

46. Ibid.

47. Cyraina Johnson-Roullier, "(An)Other Modernism: James Baldwin, *Giovanni's Room*, and the Rhetoric of Flight," *Modern Fiction Studies* 45, no. 4 (Winter 1999): 934.

48. See Teres, *Renewing the Left*, esp. 106–8, for a discussion of the revival of Henry James's reputation.

49. Teres, *Renewing the Left*, 109.

50. Wald, *The New York Intellectuals*, 218.

51. For nuanced and convincing readings of Henry James and homosexuality, see Hugh Stevens, *Henry James and Sexuality* (Cambridge: Cambridge University Press, 1998).

52. Teres, *Renewing the Left*, 85.

53. Dwight Macdonald, "The Soviet Cinema, 1930–1938," *Partisan Review* 5, no. 2 (July 1938): 37–50; and Clement Greenberg, "Avant-garde and Kitsch," *Partisan Review* 6, no. 6 (Fall 1939): 34–49.

54. Teres, *Renewing the Left*, 95, 79.

55. Wald, *The New York Intellectuals*, 162.

56. Ibid., 222.

57. Ibid.

58. Nathan Abrams, foreword by Edward N. Luttwak, *Commentary Magazine, 1945–59* (Portland: Valentine Mitchell, 2007), 63; Teres, *Renewing the Left*, 215.

59. Herb Boyd, *Baldwin's Harlem: A Biography of James Baldwin* (New York: Atria Books, 2008), 104.

60. No declared author, "What Do Negroes Expect of Jews?," *Amsterdam News* (February 27 1960): 4.

61. For a brief but useful account of the Baldwin–Katz debate, see Eric J. Sundquist, *Strangers in the Land: Blacks, Jews, Post-Holocaust America* (Cambridge, MA: Harvard University Press, 2005), 402–3. For the exchange between Baldwin and Katz, see "An Open Letter to James Baldwin," *Midstream* 17 (April 1971): 3–5; and Baldwin's response, "Of Angela Davis and 'The Jewish Housewife Headed for Dachau': An Exchange," *Midstream* 17, no. 6 (June/July 1971): 3–10.

62. See Sundquist, *Strangers in the Land*, 403.

63. Baldwin, "The Fire Next Time," in *Collected Essays*, 308.

64. Ruth R. Wisse, "The New York (Jewish) Intellectuals," *Commentary* 84, no. 5 (1987): 29.

65. Ibid., 34.

66. Abrams, *Commentary Magazine*, 47.

67. Ibid., 73, 75.

68. Ibid., 61.

69. Baldwin, "The Harlem Ghetto," in *Collected Essays*, 49.

70. Ibid., 50.

71. Ibid., 53, 50.

72. Cited by Sundquist, *Strangers in the Land*, 2. While there are many books on the relationship between black Americans and Jews in the United States—including Nat Hentoff, ed., *Black Anti-Semitism and Jewish Racism* (New York: Richard W. Baron, 1969); Murray Friedman, *What Went Wrong? The Creation and Collapse of the Black-Jewish Alliance* (New York: Free Press, 1995); and Maurianne Adams and John Bracey, eds., *Strangers and Neighbors: Relations between Blacks and Jews in the United States* (Amherst: University of Massachusetts Press, 2000)—Sundquist's tome has emerged as the definitive book.

73. Sundquist, *Strangers in the Land*, 17.

74. Harold Orlansky, "A Note on Anti-Semitism among Negroes," *Politics* 2 (August 1945): 250.

75. Baldwin, "The Harlem Ghetto," in *Collected Essays*, 50; Orlansky, "A Note on Anti-Semitism," 251. See Baldwin, "The Fire Next Time," in *Collected Essays*, where he recalls how "the Jewish boys in high school were troubling because I could find no point of connection between them and the Jewish pawnbrokers and landlords and grocery-store owners in Harlem." He goes on to write that "I knew that these people were Jews—God knows I was told it often enough—but I thought of them only as white," 308.

76. Kenneth B. Clark, "Candor about Negro-Jewish Relations: A Social Scientist Charts a Complex Social Problem," *Commentary* 1, no. 4 (1946): 8.

77. Ibid., 10.

78. Christopher Phelps, ed. and introd., *Race and Revolution* by Max Shachtman (London: Verso, 2003), xliii.

79. Phelps, "Introduction," *Race and Revolution*, lxiii.

80. Shachtman, *Race and Revolution*, 3, 4.

81. Ibid., 63.

82. See ibid., 78–79.

83. Ibid., 72.

84. Ibid., 72, 72–73.

85. Ibid., 73.

86. Anatole Broyard's 1948 essay, "A Portrait of the Hipster," could also be considered the first essay of note by an African American writer to appear in *Partisan Review* after Sterling Brown was published there in 1936. Broyard, however, did not announce his racial identity. See Henry Louis Gates Jr., "The Passing of Anatole Broyard," in *Thirteen Ways of Looking at a Black Man* (New York: Random House, 1997), 180–214.

87. Teres, *Renewing the Left*, 213.

88. Ibid., 210.

89. Ibid., 205.

90. Alexander Bloom, *Prodigal Sons: The New York Intellectuals and Their World* (New York: Oxford University Press, 1986), 432 n. 47.

91. Ibid.

92. Arnold Rampersad, *Ralph Ellison: A Biography* (New York: Alfred A. Knopf, 2007), 402.

93. Baldwin, "Smaller Than Life," the *Nation* 165, no. 3 (July 19 1947): 78; reprinted in Baldwin, *Collected Essays*, 577–78.

94. Ibid.

95. Ibid.

96. Baldwin, "History as Nightmare," Review of *Lonely Crusade*, by Chester Himes. the *New Leader* 30, no. 25 (October 25 1947): 11; reprinted in Baldwin, *Collected Essays*, 579–81.

97. Ibid.

98. Baldwin, "History as Nightmare," 15.

99. Ibid., 11.

100. Ibid.

101. Jackson, *The Indignant Generation*, 38.

102. Ibid., 314.

103. Baldwin, "Everybody's Protest Novel," in *Collected Essays*, 13; Baldwin, "History as Nightmare," 11.

104. Jackson, *The Indignant Generation*, 8.

105. Baldwin, "The Image of the Negro," *Commentary* 5, no. 4 (April 1948): 378; reprinted in Baldwin, *Collected Essays*, 582–87.

106. Ibid.

107. Ibid.

108. See Brandon Gordon, "Physical Sympathy: Hip and Sentimentalism in James Baldwin's *Another Country*," *Modern Fiction Studies* 57, no. 1 (Spring 2011): 75–95, who offers an insightful rereading of Baldwin's critique of sentimentalism. Gordon argues that "despite his condemnation of sentimentalism as disingenuous and kitschy emotion, Baldwin is fascinated by the significance of genuine emotion and sensation," 79.

109. See Andreas Huyssen, *After the Great Divide: Modernism, Mass Culture, Post-modernism* (Bloomington: Indiana University Press, 1986), who traces the nineteenth-century concept that "mass culture is somehow associated with women" (47).

110. Baldwin, "The Image of the Negro," 378.

111. Teres, *Renewing the Left*, 25.

112. Baldwin, "The Image of the Negro," 380.

113. Teres, *Renewing the Left*, 50.

114. Baldwin, "Everybody's Protest Novel," in *Collected Essays*, 15.

115. Wald, *The New York Intellectuals*, 219.

116. Baldwin, "Too Late, Too Late," *Commentary* 7 (January 1949): 96; reprinted in James Baldwin, *The Cross of Redemption*, 267–72.

117. Ibid.

118. Baldwin, "Too Late, Too Late," 98.

119. In *Commentary* 9 (March 1950): 257–61, the title is "The Death of the Prophet." In *The Cross of Redemption*, the story's title is "The Death of a Prophet."

120. Murphy, "Subversive Anti-Stalinism:" 1025.

121. Baldwin, "Change Within a Channel," the *New Leader* 31, no. 17 (April 24 1948): 11; reprinted in *The Cross of Redemption*, 257–58; Baldwin, "Modern Rover Boys," the *New Leader* 31, no. 33 (August 14, 1948): 12; reprinted in *The Cross of Redemption*, 259–60.

122. Baldwin, "Maxim Gorky as Artist," the *Nation*, 164 (April 12, 1947): 428; reprinted in *The Cross of Redemption*, 239–41.

123. Ibid.

124. Ibid.

125. Baldwin, "Battle Hymn," the *New Leader* 30, no. 29 (November 29, 1947): 10; reprinted in *The Cross of Redemption*, 242–44.

126. Ibid.

127. Interview with George Solomos in London, July 14, 2008.

128. See, for example, *The Price of the Ticket*, where it erroneously states that "Everybody's Protest Novel" was "[o]riginally published in *Partisan Review*, June 1949," 27.

129. Francis Stonor Saunders, *Who Paid the Piper? The CIA and the Cultural Cold War* (London: Granta, 2000), 70.

130. Murphy, "Subversive Anti-Stalinism," 1034.

131. See Jackson, *The Indignant Generation*, 408–9.

132. Baldwin, "Preservation of Innocence," in *Collected Essays*, 600; "Everybody's Protest Novel," in *Collected Essays*, 16.

133. See Jackson, *The Indignant Generation*, who makes the link between Edmund Wilson's review of the Modern Library edition of *Uncle Tom's Cabin* in the *New Yorker* (November 27, 1948, 126–33)—which argued for the literary merit of *Uncle Tom's Cabin*—and Baldwin's refutation of this assertion. Jackson suggests that Baldwin is responding directly to Wilson's article, although the latter does not mention Wilson by name, 283.

134. See Adam Lively, *Masks: Blackness, Race and the Imagination* (London: Vintage, 1999), 87.

135. Baldwin, "Everybody's Protest Novel," in *Collected Essays*, 17.

136. Ibid.

137. For a useful discussion of "the difference between revolutionary anti-Stalinism and anticommunism," see Wald, *The New York Intellectuals*, esp. 271. For a persuasive account of former radicals' involvement in the Cultural Cold War, see *Who Paid the Piper*.

138. Baldwin, "Envoi," *A Quarter-Century of Un-Americana, 1938–1963: A Tragi-Comical Memorabilia of HUAC*, ed. Charlotte Pomerantz (New York: Marzani & Munsell Publishers, 1963), 127; reprinted in *The Cross of Redemption*, 222–23. Baldwin, "No Name in the Street," in *Collected Essays*, 372.

139. Baldwin, "No Name in the Street," in *Collected Essays*, 459.

140. Lawrie Balfour, *The Evidence of Things Not Said: James Baldwin and the Promise of American Democracy* (Ithaca: Cornell University Press, 2001), 138.

141. James Baldwin, "Staggerlee Wonders," *Jimmy's Blues: Selected Poems* (London: Michael Joseph, 1983), 7.

142. James Campbell, *Exiled in Paris: Richard Wright, James Baldwin, Samuel Beckett, and Others on the Left Bank* (New York: Scribner, 1995), 92.

143. Baldwin, "No Name in the Street," in *Collected Essays*, 383; for an excellent account of the CIA's involvement with left-wing journals, see Saunders, *Who Paid the Piper?*, esp., 184–89, on *Encounter*.

144. Campbell, *Exiled in Paris*, 91; Baldwin, "The Fire Next Time," in *Collected Essays*, 371.

145. John A. Noakes, "Racializing Subversion: The FBI and the Depiction of Race in Early Cold War Movies," *Ethnic and Racial Studies* 26, no. 4 (July 2003): 728–29.

146. Kenneth O'Reilly, "Racial Integration: The Battle General Eisenhower Chose Not to Fight," *Journal of Blacks in Higher Education* no. 18 (Winter 1997–98): 112. See also Thomas Borstelmann's *The Cold War and the Color Line: American Race Relations in the Global Arena* (Cambridge, MA: Harvard University Press, 2001), esp., 86–110.

147. Andrew Ross, *No Respect: Intellectuals and Popular Culture* (New York: Rout-ledge, 1989), 45; James F. Davis, *Who Is Black? One Nation's Definition* (University Park: Pennsylvania State University Press, 1991), 56.

148. Davis, *Who Is Black?*, 17.

149. Mary Dudziak, *Cold War and Civil Rights*, 111. White Citizens' Councils were formed in 1954. See A. Robert Lee, *Multicultural American Literature: Comparative Black, Latino/a and Asian American Fictions* (Edinburgh: Edinburgh University Press, 2003), who notes that "to many [the White Citizens' Councils were] simply the Klan and its sympathizers under another name, and given to camouflaging its ideology under the mantle of state rights," 252.

150. "Southern Declaration on Integration," *New York Times* (March 12 1956); reprinted in Anthony Cooper, ed., *The Black Experience, 1865–1978* (Dartford: Greenwich University Press, 1995), 239–40.

151. Davis, *Who Is Black?*, 17.

152. Campbell, *Exiled in Paris*, 208.

153. Leerom Medovoi, "Reading the Blackboard: Youth, Masculinity, and Racial Cross-Identification," in *Race and the Subject of Masculinities*, ed. Harry Stecopoulos and Michael Uebel (Durham: Duke University Press, 1997), 145.

154. Ibid.

155. Benjamin Muse, *Ten Years of Prelude: The Story of Integration since the Supreme Court's 1954 Decision* (Beaconsfield: Darwen Finlayson, 1964), 45. Muse also mentions the revival of the film *Birth of a Nation* after 1954, which had not circulated widely since the 1930s, 41.

156. Quoted by Stephen J. Whitfield, *The Culture of the Cold War*, 2nd ed. (Baltimore MD: Johns Hopkins University Press), 21.

157. Muse, *Ten Years of Prelude*, 39. See also Numan V. Bartley, *The Rise of Massive Resistance: Race and Politics in the South During the 1950s* (Baton Rouge: Louisiana State University Press, 1969), esp. 185–87.

158. O'Reilly, "Racial Integration," 114. For a brief but useful account of Paul Robeson and communism, see Tom Engelhardt, *The End of Victory Culture: Cold War America and the Disillusioning of a Generation* (Amherst: University of Massachusetts Press, 1995), 127. See Whitfield, *The Culture of the Cold War*, who points out that *I Was a Communist for the FBI* "shows the [Communist] Party taking credit for race riots in Harlem and Detroit in 1942," 21.

159. Quoted by Borstelmann, *The Cold War and the Color Line*, 89. In *Go Tell It on the Mountain* there is a brief description of a castrated African American veteran.

160. Jackson, *The Indignant Generation*, 7. Jackson also claims that around the time of *Brown v. Board*, "most of the major publishing houses enlisted the work of at least one black novelist, dealers in words who lifted their pens in the struggle of art and life, but who also served notice to the new American racial liberalism," 7.

161. John S. Lash, "On Negro Literature," *Phylon* 6, no. 3 (1945): 240–47; and "What Is 'Negro Literature'"? *College English* 1, no. 9 (1947): 37–42.

162. Jackson, *The Indignant Generation*, 319.

163. Baldwin, Review of Vishnu V. Oak et al., in *The Cross of Redemption*, 270.

164. Jackson, *The Indignant Generation*, 7.

165. Richard Wright, "The Literature of the Negro in the United States," in *White Man, Listen!* (Westport, CT: Greenwood Press, 1957), 148.

166. Wright, "The Literature of the Negro in the United States," 149. There are, of course, antecedents to these debates: in their introduction to their 1941 co-edited anthology, *The Negro Caravan: Writings by American Negroes*, introd. Julius Lester (1941) (New York: Arno Press and the *New York Times*, 1970), 7, Sterling A. Brown, Arthur P. Davis and Ulysses Lee made explicit their rejection of the term "Negro literature," a term, the editors argued, that placed black literature "in an alcove apart." Central to the editors' introduction is the imperative that African American writers must dilute and even write out any traces of black culture and language, what they term the "structural peculiarity" of black American writing.

167. Jackson, *The Indignant Generation*, 272.

168. Other "raceless" novels by black American writers include Zora Neale Hurston's *Seraph on the Sewanee* (1948); William Gardner Smith's *Anger at Innocence* (1950); Chester Himes's *Cast the First Stone* (1952); and Richard Wright's *Savage Holiday* (1954). See Jackson, *The Indignant Generation*, 272.

169. Jordan Elgrably and George Plimpton, "The Art of Fiction 1984: James Baldwin," in *Conversations with James Baldwin*, 239.

170. Arnold Rampersad, *The Life of Langston Hughes*, vol. 1 (New York: Oxford University Press, 1988), 335.

171. Addison Gayle Jr., "The Function of Black Literature at the Present Time," in *The Black Aesthetic*, ed. Addison Gayle Jr. (New York: Doubleday and Company, 1971), 389, 390.

172. Jackson, *The Indignant Generation*, 391, 409.

173. Baldwin, "Many Thousands Gone," in *Collected Essays*, 20 (emphasis added).

174. See also Morris Dickstein, *Gates of Eden: American Culture in the Sixties* (New York: Basic Books, 1977), where he notes that "Baldwin's 'we' sometimes wobbles in the early essays, acting out his predicament by assuming now a white, now a black face," 173.

175. Leeming, *James Baldwin: A Biography*, 101.

176. Robert Bone, *The Negro Novel in America* (1958; rev. ed. New Haven, CT: Yale University Press, 1965), 218, 226.

177. Ibid., 226.

178. Ibid., 249–50.

179. Ibid., 3, 250.

180. Ibid., 168, 248. Also see Jackson, *The Indignant Generation*, who notes Richard Gibson's critique of Bone's book: "[H]is freehanded distributions of merits and demerits to Negro writers is a wild distortion of literary criticism," 474.

181. Bone, *The Negro Novel in America*, 248.

182. Ibid., 248, 4.

183. Ibid., 247. See also Rosemary Jackson, *Fantasy: the Literature of Subversion* (London and New York: Routledge, 1995), who notes that "'fantasy' is etymologically rooted in the Greek word *phantasikos* meaning 'to make visible,'" 13.

184. Elaine K. Ginsberg, "Introduction," in *Passing and the Fictions of Identity*, ed. Elaine K. Ginsberg (Durham: Duke University Press, 1996), 8.

185. James Baldwin, *Giovanni's Room* [1956] (London: Penguin, 1990), 12, 13, 14; Robert Reid-Pharr, *Black Gay Man* (New York: New York University Press, 2001), 125. For critics who have interpreted "encoded" black characters, see Donald H. Mengay, "The Failed

Copy: *Giovanni's Room* and the (Re) Contextualisation of Difference," *Genders* 17 (1993): 60. See also Porter, *Stealing the Fire*, esp., 141–52.

186. Charles Rolo, "Other Voices, Other Rooms," *Atlantic Monthly* 198, no. 6 (December 1956): 98.

187. Robert J. Corber, *Homosexuality in Cold War America: Resistance and the Crisis of Masculinity* (Durham: Duke University Press, 1997), 1. Although Fiedler and other left-wing critics denied the legitimacy of a homosexual identity, see Donald Webster Corey, *The Homosexual in America: A Subjective Approach* (New York: Greenberg, 1951). Corey argued that homosexuals experienced discrimination comparable to ethnic minorities.

188. Leslie Fiedler, "A Homosexual Dilemma," the *New Leader* 39, no. 10 (1956): 17.

189. Leslie Fielder, "Come Back to the Raft Ag'in, Huck Honey!" in *The Collected Essays of Leslie Fiedler*, vol. 1 (New York: Stein and Day, 1971), 142–51; Robyn Wiegman, "Fiedler and Sons," in *Race and the Subject of Masculinities*, 50.

190. Corber, *Homosexuality in Cold War America*, 137.

191. Weatherby, *James Baldwin: Artist on Fire*, 119.

192. Gore Vidal, Preface to *The City and the Pillar* [1949] (reprint, with a new preface by Gore Vidal, London: Abacus, 1994), 3.

193. See James Baldwin, "Preservation of Innocence," *Zero* 1 (Summer 1949): 14–15, where Baldwin challenges the naturalness of gender and sexual identities. Reprinted in *Collected Essays*, 594–600.

194. John D'Emilio and Estelle B. Freedman, *Intimate Matters: A History of Sexuality in America* (New York: Harper & Row, 1988), 260.

195. Alfred Kinsey, *Sexual Behavior in the Human Male* (Philadelphia: W. B. Saunders Company, 1948).

196. Ibid., 610.

197. John D'Emilio, *Sexual Politics, Sexual Communities: The Making of a Homosexual Minority in the United States, 1940–70* (Chicago: University of Chicago Press, 1983), 35.

198. Kinsey, *Sexual Behavior*, 637.

199. See, for example, D'Emilio, *Sexual Politics*, esp. 49–50.

200. Robert J. Corber, *In the Name of National Security: Hitchcock, Homophobia, and the Political Construction of Gender in Postwar America* (Durham: Duke University Press, 1993), 8.

201. Ibid., 61; see also Harry M. Benshoff, *Monsters in the Closet: Homosexuality and the Horror Film* (Manchester: Manchester University Press, 1997), who cites an article from the gentleman's magazine, *Sir!* (March 1958). The author warns that "Not All Homos Are Easy to Spot," and informs the reader that although 15–20% of men are homosexual, less than 4% are "effeminate," 131–32.

202. Corber, *In the Name of National Security*, 62–63.

203. Ibid., 8.

204. Elaine Tyler May, *Homeward Bound: American Families in the Cold War Era* (New York: Basic Books, 1988), 95; see also David Savran, *Communists, Cowboys and Queers: The Politics of Masculinity in the Work of Arthur Miller and Tennessee Williams* (Minneapolis: University of Minnesota Press, 1992), who notes the "intense level of surveillance posted over the circulation of sexuality in and around the nuclear family facilitated an unprecedented level of social control," 9.

205. George Chauncey, *Gay New York: The Making of the Gay Underworld, 1890–1940* (London: Flamingo, 1995), 4.

206. Corber, *In the Name of National Security*, 19, 19–20; Vidal, *The City and the Pillar*, 148, 149.

207. Baldwin, *Giovanni's Room*, 31. There are a number of instances in the novel where David is conscious that his actions will betray his sexuality. See, for example, his cruising of a sailor: "We came abreast and, as though he had seen some all-revealing panic in my eyes, he gave me a look contemptuously lewd and knowing. . . . And in another second . . . I was certain that there would erupt into speech . . . some brutal variation of *Look, baby. I know you,*" 88.

208. Fiedler, "A Homosexual Dilemma," 16.

209. See also Leslie Fiedler, *The Return of the Vanishing American* (London: Jonathan Cape, 1968), where he writes: "[O]ne suspects Baldwin's Giovanni of being a Negro disguised as a European, and the book consequently of being a disguised Southern," 20.

210. Sigmund Freud, *On Metapsychology*, vol. 11, trans. James Strachey (1915) (London: Penguin, 1984), 195; Frantz Fanon, *Black Skins, White Masks*, trans. Charles Lam Markmann (1952) (London: Pluto Press, 1986), 115.

Chapter 2

1. http://www.fbi.gov/. Since 2009, the FBI website has changed and it has become increasingly aimed at high school students. There is now (July 2, 2012) a "Fun and Games" section tab, alongside the "Most Wanted" tab.

2. There are a number of useful works on Malcolm X's FBI file, including *Malcolm X: The FBI Files*, by Wayne Taylor. The wonderwheel.net website (http://wonderwheel.net/work/foia/) has useful annotations to navigate the large number of files; see David Gallen, ed., *Malcolm X: The FBI File*, introd. Spike Lee with commentary by Claybourne Carson (New York: Carroll & Graf, 1992). More recently, Manning Marable's *Malcolm X: A Life of Reinvention* (New York: Allen Lane, 2011) contains numerous key references to the FBI's surveillance of Malcolm X from 1950 until his death in 1965. For more on MLK and the FBI, see David J. Garrow, *Bearing the Cross: Martin Luther King, Jr., and the Southern Christian Leadership Conference* (New York: Harper Perennial Modern Classics, 2004).

3. Baldwin's FBI files can be requested under the US Freedom of Information Act by writing to the Bureau. For a sample letter, see https://www.muckrock.com/foi/united-states-of-america-10/fbi-files-on-james-baldwin-9724/. Unlike the file of many authors, including Richard Wright, Baldwin's are not available online. Baldwin's FBI files are paginated but are not chronological. The files are delivered in three parts: Part 1: 1–559; Part 2: 560–943; Part 3: 944–1,884. The FBI's pagination will be referenced parenthetically.

4. Natalie Robins, *Alien Ink: The FBI's War on the Freedom of Expression* (New Brunswick, NJ: Rutgers University Press, 1992), 50.

5. For a study that focuses on the FBI's harassment of musicians, see John Potash, *The FBI War on Tupac Shakur and Black Leaders: US Intelligence's Murderous Targeting of Tupac, MLK, Malcolm, Panthers, Hendrix, Rappers & Linked Ethnic Leftists*, 5th ed., foreword by Pam Africa with Mumia Abu-Jamal, afterword by Fred Hampton Jr. (New York:

Progressive Left Press, 2010). Potash argues that "evidence supports that US Intelligence murderously targeted political and cultural leftist leaders, including Malcolm X, Martin Luther King, Black Panthers, Jimi Hendrix, Bob Marley and activist rappers," 1. There is a brief discussion of Richard Wright (177) but no mention of Baldwin.

6. Potash, *The FBI War on Tupac Shakur and Black Leaders*, 28.

7. Eve Auchincloss and Nancy Lynch, "Disturber of the Peace: James Baldwin—An Interview," in *Conversations with James Baldwin*, ed. Fred L. Standley and Louis H. Pratt (Jackson: University Press of Mississippi, 1989), 171.

8. James Campbell, *Talking at the Gates: A Life of James Baldwin* (London and Boston: Faber and Faber, 1991); David Leeming, *James Baldwin: A Biography* (New York: Alfred A. Knopf, 1994). See also Campbell, "'I Heard It Through the Grapevine': James Baldwin and the FBI," in *Syncopations: Beats, New Yorkers, and Writers in the Dark* (Berkeley: University of California Press, 2008), 78–81, in which he details how Baldwin's FBI files were fully declassified in 1998.

9. Gary Edward Holcomb, *Code Name Sasha: Queer Black Marxism and the Harlem Renaissance* (Gainesville: University Press of Florida, 2007), 30.

10. William B. Maxwell, "African-American Modernism and State Surveillance," in *A Companion to African American Literature*, ed. Gene Jarrett (Oxford: Blackwell, 2010), 255.

11. Baldwin, "Princes and Powers," in *Collected Essays*, ed. Toni Morrison (New York: The Library of America, 1998), 161. See Kevin Gaines, "Exile and the Private Life: James Baldwin, George Lamming, and the First World Congress of Negro Writers and Artists," in *James Baldwin: American and Beyond*, ed. Cora Kaplan and Bill Schwarz (Ann Arbor: University of Michigan Press, 2011), who provides a deft reading of this phrase in relation to the Jamesian notion of the interior life, 177–78. See also William B. Maxwell, "Total Literary Awareness: Why Cold War Hooverism Pre-Read Afro-Modernity Writing," in *American Literature and Culture in an Age of Cold War: A Critical Reassessment*, ed. Steven Belletto and Daniel Grausam (Iowa City: University of Iowa Press, 2012), 20–21, where Maxwell documents Hoover's support of McCarthy, noting Ellen Schrecker's conclusion that McCarthyism should really be termed "Hooverism."

12. Noam Chomsky, "Introduction," in Nelson Blackstock, *COINTELPRO: The FBI's Secret War on Political Freedom* (1975; New York: Pathfinder, 1988), 12.

13. Robins, *Alien Ink*, 17.

14. Campbell, "I Heard It Through the Grapevine," 100; Maxwell, "Total Literary Awareness," 22.

15. Robins, *Alien Ink*, 17.

16. Blackstock, *COINTELPRO*, 198.

17. Baldwin originally took the surname of his mother, Emma Berdis Jones as his father's identity was unknown. He changed his surname after his mother married David Baldwin in 1927.

18. See Campbell, "I Heard It Through the Grapevine," 78.

19. Robins, *Alien Ink*, 228.

20. Kenneth O'Reilly, *"Racial Matters": The FBI's Secret File on Black America, 1960–1972* (New York: Free Press, 1989), 355.

21. Blackstock, *COINTELPRO*, 17.

22. John A. Noakes, "Racializing Subversion: The FBI and the Depiction of Race in Early Cold War Movies," *Ethnic and Racial Studies* 26, no. 4 (July 2003): 731.

23. Robins, *Alien Ink*, 282.

24. Blackstock, *COINTELPRO*, 92.

25. Kenneth O'Reilly, *Black Americans: The FBI Files*, ed. David Gallen (New York: Caroll & Graf Publishers, 1994), 14.

26. Robins, *Alien Ink*, 346.

27. Ibid., 320.

28. O'Reilly, *Black Americans*, 48–50.

29. Marable, *Malcolm X*, 479.

30. Chomsky, "Introduction," 18, 19.

31. Baldwin, "The Devil Finds Work," in *Collected Essays*, 547.

32. Ibid., 544.

33. Campbell, *Talking at the Gates*, 167.

34. Unlike Baldwin's file, Richard Wright's is available on the FBI's website at http://www.fbi/gov. Baldwin is mentioned in Wright's file, section 1b. (There is no pagination in the online version, but it is on p. 49 of the hard copy.)

35. Layhmond Robinson, "Robert Kennedy Consults Negroes Here about North," *New York Times* (May 25, 1963): 1.

36. Arthur M. Schlesinger Jr., *Robert Kennedy and His Times* (New York: Ballantine Books, 1978), 331.

37. Campbell, *Talking at the Gates*, 169.

38. See, for example, "Conversation: Ida Lewis and James Baldwin," in *Conversations with James Baldwin*, 92.

39. Harold Cruse, *The Crisis of the Negro Intellectual: A Historical Analysis of the Failure of Black Leadership* (1967; reprint with a foreword by Bazel E. Allen and Ernest J. Wilson III, New York: Quill, 1984), 194; Cruse also notes Norman Podhoretz's failed attempts to get Baldwin "off that personal kick and make him talk about solutions and programs," 194.

40. Campbell, *Talking at the Gates*, 172.

41. Baldwin, "The Fire Next Time," in *Collected Essays*, 293–94; Campbell, "I Heard It Through the Grapevine," 77.

42. In a further twist, the FBI sent letters to prominent individuals and radical publications to smear George Weissman, a SWP leader and managing editor of the *Militant* in 1964. Weissman was falsely accused of stealing funds from the Committee and the FBI sent letters to Baldwin, Harold Cruse, and LeRoi Jones. See Blackstock, *COINTELPRO*, 105. For a brief but useful overview of the Committee to Aid the Monroe Defendants (CAMD), see Ward Churchill and Jim Vander Wall, *The COINTELPRO Papers: Documents from the FBI's Secret Wars Against Dissent in the United States* (1990; Cambridge, MA: South End Press, 2002), 51–52. The authors note that "[o]ne of the first 'tasks' undertaken through COINTELPRO-SWP was to attempt to abort the judicial process in the case of the so-called Monroe defendants."

43. Campbell, "I Heard It Through the Grapevine," 86–87.

44. See ibid., 87.

45. Ibid., 100.

46. Robins, *Alien Ink*, 143.

47. Ibid., 175.

48. James Baldwin, *Just Above My Head* [1979] (London: Penguin, 1994), 350. In *Just Above My Head*, the narrator, Hall, talks about "some hitherto unpublished FBI report" with the implication that the Bureau was closely monitoring the South, 414.

49. Robins, *Alien Ink*, 347.

50. See Robert J. Corber, *Homosexuality in Cold War America: Resistance and the Crisis of Masculinity* (Durham: Duke University Press, 1997). Corber points out that many homosexual men and women were targeted as security risks on account of their sexuality during the height of the Cold War.

51. Ibid.

52. Lawrence Amey, Timothy L. Hall, et al. *Censorship*, vol. 1 (Englewood Cliffs, NJ: Salem Press, 1997), 59.

53. It is, of course, easier for the contemporary reader to make these links after the pioneering work of scholars such as Michael Lynch and Clarence Hardy. See the following chapter.

54. William H. Epstein, "Counter-Intelligence: Cold War Criticism and Eighteenth-Century Studies," *English Literary History* 57, no. 1 (1990): 260; Maxwell, "African American Modernism and State Surveillance," 260.

55. Robins, *Alien Ink*, 67.

56. *The People of the State of California Plaintiff v. Lawrence Ferlinghetti* (1958). Available: http://mason.gmu.edu/~kthomps4/363-s02/horn-howl.htm.

57. See Bill Morgan and Nancy J. Peters, eds., *Howl on Trial: The Battle for Free Expression* (San Francisco: City Lights Books, 2006).

58. Robins, *Alien Ink*, 76.

59. Ibid., 293–94, 294.

60. Ibid., 78.

61. There are many examples, but see, in particular, 218.

62. Maurice Wallace, "'I'm Not Entirely What I Look Like': Richard Wright, James Baldwin, and the Hegemony of Vision; or, Jimmy's FBEye Blues," in *James Baldwin Now*, ed. Dwight A. McBride (New York: New York University Press, 1999), 298.

63. This article is from the August 18, 1969, edition of the Istanbul daily newspaper *Milliyet* (FBI Files, 933).

64. Robins, *Alien Ink*, 18.

65. See Gérard Genette, *Palimpsests: Literature in the Second Degree*, trans. Channa Newman and Claude Doubinsky, foreword by Gerald Prince (Lincoln: University of Nebraska Press, 1997).

66. Blackstock, *COINTELPRO*, 78. According to Blackstock, there are more COINTELPRO files on Clifton DeBerry than anyone else, 73.

67. Marable, *Malcolm X*, 139–40.

68. Wallace, "I'm Not Entirely What I Look Like," 300.

69. See, for example, Joseph J. Firebaugh, "The Vocabulary of 'Time' Magazine," *American Speech* 15, no. 3 (October 1940): 232–42.

70. Maxwell, "African American Modernism and State Surveillance," 255.

71. See, for example, Firebaugh, "The Vocabulary of 'Time' Magazine," 232–42.

72. Among numerous references to Baldwin as an inspiration to gay writers (both black and white), see Joseph Beam, ed., *In the Life: A Gay Black Anthology* (Boston: Alyson Publications, 1986), 90, 95, 231; Barbara Smith, "We Must Always Bury Our Dead Twice:

A Tribute to James Baldwin," in *The Truth That Never Hurts: Writings on Race, Gender, and Freedom* (New Brunswick, NJ: Rutgers University Press, 1998), 75–80.

73. Joseph Beam, "Not a Bad Legacy Brother," in *Brother to Brother: New Writings by Black Gay Men*, ed. Essex Hemphill (Boston: Alyson Publications, 1991). 185.

74. E. Patrick Johnson and Mae G. Henderson, *Black Queer Studies: A Critical Anthology* (Durham: Duke University Press, 2005), 6.

75. David Bergman, "The Agony of Gay Black Literature," in *Gaiety Transfigured: Gay Self-Representations in American Literature* (Madison: University of Wisconsin Press, 1991), 165.

76. Richard Goldstein, "Go the Way Your Blood Beats: An Interview with James Baldwin," *Village Voice* 26 (June 1984): 13. A number of critical works have focused on *Giovanni's Room* as an important gay text: Claude J. Summers, "'Looking at the Naked Sun': James Baldwin's *Giovanni's Room*," in *Gay Fictions: Wilde to Stonewall* (New York: Continuum, 1990), 172–94; Marlon B. Ross, "White Fantasies of Desire: Baldwin and the Racial Identities of Sexuality," in *James Baldwin Now*, 13–55; Kemp Williams, "The Metaphorical Construction of Sexuality in *Giovanni's Room*," in *Literature and Homosexuality*, ed. Michael Meyer (Amsterdam: Rodopi, 2000), 23–33.

77. Goldstein, "Go the Way Your Blood Beats," 13.

78. James Mossman, "Race, Hate, Sex, and Colour: A Conversation with James Baldwin and Colin MacInnes," in *Conversations with James Baldwin*, 54.

79. Goldstein, "Go the Way Your Blood Beats," 13.

80. Leeming, *James Baldwin*, 359; cited by Auchincloss and Lynch, "Disturber of the Peace," in *Conversations with James Baldwin*, 80. Baldwin's negative statements are even more surprising given the prevalence of AIDS in the black community; see Phillip Brian Harper, "Eloquence and Epitaph: Black Nationalism and the Homophobic Impulse in Responses to the Death of Max Robinson," in *The Lesbian and Gay Studies Reader*, ed. Henry Abelove, Michèle Aina Barale, and David M. Halperin (New York: Routledge, 1993), where Harper notes that, although African Americans account for less than 6% of the US population, 23% of reported cases of AIDS were African American, 159.

81. It should be noted that Baldwin was also against all forms of exhibition; see Fern Marja Eckman, *The Furious Passage of James Baldwin* (London: Michael Joseph, 1966), where Baldwin states, "I loathe parades. . . . The whole *parade* idea—there's something in me that profoundly disapproves of it," 215. For a further example, see Mossman, "Race, Hate, Sex, and Colour," in *Conversations with James Baldwin*, where Baldwin describes the public intimacy of interracial couples as "a kind of desperate advertising," 49.

82. Donald Gibson, "James Baldwin: The Political Anatomy of Space," in *James Baldwin: A Critical Evaluation*, ed. Therman B. O'Daniel (Washington, DC: Howard University Press, 1977), 9.

83. Emmanuel Nelson, "The Novels of James Baldwin," 13; see also Carolyn Sylvander, *James Baldwin* (New York: Frederick Ungar Publishing, 1980), who notes that David is "a negative and confusing embodiment of the homosexual experience," 51.

84. See Samuel R. Delany and Joseph Beam, "Samuel Delany: The Possibility of Possibilities," in *In the Life*, 185–208, esp. 196.

85. Goldstein, "Go the Way Your Blood Beats," 14.

86. Baldwin, "The Male Prison," in *Collected Essays*, 231.

87. Goldstein, "Go the Way Your Blood Beats," 13.

88. Jerome de Romanet, "Revisiting *Madeleine* and 'The Outing': James Baldwin's Revisions of Gide's Sexual Politics," *Melus* 22, no. 1 (Spring 1997): 8.

89. Emmanuel Nelson, "Critical Deviance: Homophobia and the Reception of James Baldwin's Fiction," *Journal of American Culture* 14(1991): 91.

90. Henry Louis Gates Jr., "The Black Man's Burden," in *Fear of a Queer Planet: Queer Politics and Social Theory,* ed. Michael Warner (Minneapolis: University of Minnesota Press, 1993), 234.

91. Cheryl Clarke, "The Failure to Transform: Homophobia in the Black Community," in *Home Girls: A Black Feminist Anthology,* ed. Barbara Smith (1983; reprint, New Brunswick, NJ: Rutgers University Press, 2000), 198; see also bell hooks, "Homophobia in Black Communities," in *The Greatest Taboo: Homosexuality in Black Communities,* ed. Delroy Constantine-Simms (New York: Alyson Books, 2001), 67–73.

92. This account was reprinted as "A Fly in Buttermilk," in *Nobody Knows My Name: More Notes of a Native Son.*

93. Leeming, *James Baldwin,* 175.

94. Campbell, *Talking At the Gates,* 125.

95. Campbell, "I Heard It Through the Grapevine," 92.

96. Auchincloss and Lynch, "Disturber of the Peace," in *Conversations with James Baldwin,* 81.

97. Morris Dickstein, *Gates of Eden: American Culture in the Sixties* (New York: Basic Books, 1977), 168.

98. "Races: Freedom—Now," *Time* 81, no. 20 (May 17 1963): 26; see also Jean François Gounard, *The Racial Problem in the Works of Richard Wright and James Baldwin,* trans. Joseph J. Rodgers Jr., foreword by Jean F. Béranger (Westport, CT: Greenwood Press, 1992), who notes that Baldwin's upbringing gave him "an unpredictable temperament. It made him a sensitive and nervous person. Thus the slightest event could have surprising effects on him," 149–50; see also Calvin C. Hernton, *White Papers for White Americans* (New York: Doubleday, 1966), who writes that it "is immensely revealing that the first Negro to get his face on a full page of the very feminine *Harper's Bazaar* (April 1963) is James Baldwin," 120.

99. See Stanley Crouch, "Chitlins at the Waldorf: The Work of Albert Murray," in *Notes of a Hanging Judge: Essays and Reviews, 1979–1989* (New York: Oxford University Press, 1990), 113; Hernton, *White Papers,* 119.

100. For an insightful discussion of the term "queen," see Lee Edelman, "The Part for the (W)hole: Baldwin, Homophobia and the Fantasmatics of 'Race,'" in *Homographies: Essays in Gay Literary and Cultural Theory* (New York: Routledge, 1994), esp. 42–44.

101. Campbell, "I Heard It Through the Grapevine," 91.

102. Ibid., 92.

103. Erika Doss, "Imaging the Panthers: Representing Black Power and Masculinity, 1960s–1990s," *Prospects* 23 (1998): 486.

104. Doss, "Imaging the Panthers," 488.

105. Eldridge Cleaver, "The Death of Martin Luther King," in *Post-Prison Writings and Speeches,* ed. and introd. Robert Scheer (New York: Random House, 1969), 73.

106. Cleaver, "Psychology: The New Black Bible," in *Post-Prison Writings,* 18; Cleaver argues that Fanon's book "legitimize[s] the revolutionary impulse to violence," 20.

107. Doss, "Imaging the Panthers:" 478.

108. Eldridge Cleaver, *Soul on Ice*, introd. Maxwell Geismar (New York: Ramparts, 1968), 106.

109. Clarke, "The Failure to Transform," 191.

110. King's chief-of-staff, Bayard Rustin, was dismissed under the guise of his left-wing commitments but mainly on account of his homosexuality. See W. J. Weatherby, *James Baldwin: Artist on Fire* (London: Michael Joseph, 1990), 143; see also Reginald Lockett, "Die Black Pervert," in *Black Fire: An Anthology of Afro-American Writing*, ed. LeRoi Jones and Larry Neal (New York: William Morrow & Co., 1968), 354.

111. Michelle Wallace, *Black Macho and the Myth of the Superwoman* (1978; reprint with a new introduction by Wallace, New York: Dial Press, 1990), 37.

112. See Harper, "Eloquence and Epitaph," esp. 165–66.

113. Clarke, "The Failure to Transform," 191.

114. See Cleaver, "Stanford Speech," in *Post-Prison Writings*, 125, who notes that at thirty-eight, he was the oldest Panther; see also James Baldwin, "An Open Letter to My Sister, Miss Angela Davis," *New York Review of Books* 15, no. 2 (January 7, 1971), where he acknowledges George Jackson's dismissal of his generation, 15.

115. Henry Louis Gates Jr., "The Welcome Table," in *Lure and Loathing: Essays on Race, Identity, and the Ambivalence of Assimilation*, ed. and introd. Gerald Early (New York: Allen Lane, 1993), 153.

116. Wallace, *Black Macho*, 59.

117. For a useful overview of how the Black Panthers wrested power from the no longer ascendant Nation of Islam, see Cleaver, "The Decline of the Black Muslims," in *Post-Prison Writings*, 13–17.

118. Wallace, *Black Macho*, 33.

119. Cleaver, "*Playboy* interview with Nat Hentoff," in *Post-Prison Writings*, 203.

120. Doss, "Imaging the Panthers," 493.

121. Ron Simmons, "Some Thoughts on the Challenges Facing Black Intellectuals," in *Brother to Brother*, 223; see also Marlon Riggs, "Black Macho Revisited: Reflections of a SNAP! Queen," in *Brother to Brother*, esp. 254.

122. Robert Reid-Pharr, "'Tearing the Goat's Flesh': Homosexuality, Abjection and the Production of a Late Twentieth Century Masculinity," *Studies in the Novel* 28, no. 3 (1996): 373–74.

123. Cleaver, *Soul on Ice*, 106.

124. bell hooks, "Reflections on Race and Sex," in *Yearning: Race, Gender and Cultural Politics* (Boston: South End Press, 1990), 58.

125. Doss, "Imaging the Panthers:" 496.

126. See Cleaver, "Stanford Speech," in *Post-Prison Writing*, where he states that black people "have turned away from the bootlicking leadership," 116.

127. LeRoi Jones, "Black Art," in *Black Fire*, 302.

128. Cleaver, *Soul on Ice*, 107.

129. Wallace, *Black Macho*, 68; see Clarke, "The Failure to Transform," who argues that she does not debunk this view of homosexuality, 197; see also Edelman, who notes the pervasiveness in African American literature of the black man who is forced to submit to sex by a white male. Homosexuality, in this context, is depicted as "the conflictual undoing of one man's authority by another," 54.

130. Wallace, *Black Macho*, 68.

131. Cleaver, *Soul on Ice*, 14.

132. Robert Staples, *Black Masculinity: The Black Man's Role in American Society* (San Francisco: Black Scholar, 1982), 2.

133. Cleaver, *Soul on Ice*, 177.

134. Ibid., 206.

135. For an insightful reading of Cleaver's attack on Baldwin, see Stephanie K. Dunning, *Queer in Black and White: Interraciality, Same Sex Desire, and Contemporary African American Culture* (Bloomington: Indiana University Press, 2009). Dunning closely reads Cleaver's "Notes on a Native Son," suggesting the former's desire for Baldwin and his discomfort with interracial sex, rather than just homosexuality. See esp. 47–60.

136. Wallace, *Black Macho*, 31; see Staples who contested the report's findings on matriarchy; see also his article, "The Myth of the Black Matriarchy," *Black Scholar* (January 1970): 8–16.

137. Edelman, "The Part for the (W)hole," 48–49.

138. Kobena Mercer and Isaac Julien, "Race, Sexual Politics and Black Masculinity: A Dossier," in *Male Order: Unwrapping Masculinity*, ed. Rowena Chapman and Jonathan Rutherford (1988; reprint, London: Lawrence & Wishart, 1996), 112; Staples, *Black Masculinity*, 64.

139. Cleaver, *Soul on Ice*, 185; James Baldwin, "The Black Boy Looks at the White Boy," in *Collected Essays*, 269–70.

140. Frantz Fanon, *Black Skins, White Masks*, trans. Charles Lam Markamm, introd. Homi K. Bhabba [1952] (London: Pluto Press, 1986), 170; Baldwin, *Just Above*, 105.

141. Jordan Elgrably and George Plimpton, "The Art of Fiction: James Baldwin 1984," in *Conversations with James Baldwin*, 252.

142. Gates, "The Black Man's Burden," 233.

143. Weatherby, *James Baldwin: Artist on Fire*, 293.

144. Gates, "The Welcome Table," 159.

145. Dwight McBride, "Can the Queen Speak? Racial Essentialism, Sexuality and the Voice of Authority," *Callaloo* 21, no. 2 (1998): 376.

146. Gates, "The Welcome Table," 154.

147. Ibid., 153.

148. See Campbell, *Talking at the Gates*, who notes that "it seems safe to quote Baldwin's remarks on certain events as if they were written at the time," 219.

149. Goldstein, "Go the Way Your Blood Beats," 14.

150. Baldwin, "No Name In the Street," in *Collected Essays*, 357.

151. James Baldwin, "From Dreams of Love to Dreams of Terror," in *Natural Enemies? Youth and the Clash of Generations*, ed. Alexander Klein (Philadelphia: J. B. Lippincott, 1967), 278.

152. Baldwin, "No Name in the Street," in *Collected Essays*, 440.

153. Ibid., 412; Gates, "The Welcome Table," 156. For a useful account of Baldwin's shifting rhetoric, see Rolland Murray, *Our Living Manhood: Literature, Black Power, and Masculine Ideology* (Philadelphia: University of Pennsylvania Press, 2007). Murray notes that "Baldwin's rhetoric crudely echoes the call for autonomous control of black communities issued by Stokely Carmichael and other activists, but neither the subtleties that characterized the ideological distinctions between factions of Black Power nor the explicit strategies for attaining political autonomy appear in Baldwin's response," 28–29.

154. See Campbell, *Talking at the Gates*, who notes that Baldwin "said little that was positive about Malcolm X . . . until after Malcolm was killed," 219.

155. Campbell, *Talking at the Gates*, 219.

156. Baldwin, "No Name in the Street," in *Collected Essays*, 450.

157. See Leeming, *James Baldwin*, 284, 288, 299, 301–3, 306, 313.

158. There are many examples in Baldwin's FBI files, but see 852–54 for a useful overview.

159. See Baldwin's speech in *Speeches from the Soledad Brothers Rally, Central Hall, Westminster* (London: Friends of Soledad, 1974). The meeting was held on April 20, 1971. The speech is reprinted in Baldwin, *The Cross of Redemption: Uncollected Writings*, ed. and introd. Randall Kenan (New York: Pantheon, 2010), 98–102. There is also a rare recording of Baldwin responding to the murder of George Jackson, which can be found at: http://www.freedomarchives.org/struggle_inside_Aug.html.

160. Baldwin, "No Name in the Street," in *Collected Essays*, 381; for his earlier discussion of Western culture, see "Autobiographical Notes," in *Collected Essays*, 7.

161. Baldwin, "No Name in the Street," in *Collected Essays*, 421. See also James Baldwin and Margaret Mead, *A Rap on Race* (New York: Dell, 1971), 64.

162. Stanley Crouch, "The Rage of Race," in *Notes of a Hanging Judge*, 234.

163. See Campbell, *Talking at the Gates*, on Baldwin's romanticization of this period of his life, 247–48.

164. Baldwin, "No Name in the Street," in *Collected Essays*, 362.

165. Ibid., 408.

166. Ibid., 455. Cleaver, "Introduction to the Biography of Huey P. Newton," in *Post-Prison Writing*, 41.

167. Baldwin, "No Name in the Street," in *Collected Essays*, 472. See also "Conversation: Ida Lewis and James Baldwin," [1970] in *Conversations with James Baldwin*, where Baldwin states that with the deaths of Malcolm X and King, "dialogue is gone," 85; see also Cleaver, "Stanford Speech," in *Post-Prison Writing*, where he states that "words are becoming more and more irrelevant," 114.

168. James Baldwin, "Notes for *Blues*," in *Blues for Mister Charlie* [1964] (New York: Vintage Books, 1992), xiv; Calvin C. Hernton, "Dynamite Growing Out of Their Skulls," in *Black Fire*, 101; Cleaver, "The Land Question and Black Liberation," in *Post-Prison Writings*, 72.

169. Crouch, "The Rage of Race," in *Notes of a Hanging Judge*, 234.

170. Baldwin, "No Name in the Street," in *Collected Essays*, 370.

171. Cleaver, *Soul on Ice*, 60; Baldwin, "No Name in the Street," in *Collected Essays*, 412.

172. Baldwin, "No Name in the Street," in *Collected Essays*, 392.

173. Wallace, *Black Macho*, 60, 62.

174. Ibid., 62; for examples of Baldwin's emphasis on black manhood and disagreements with black female radicals, see "Revolutionary Hope: A Conversation between James Baldwin and Audre Lorde," *Essence* 15 (December 1984): 72–74, 129–33; see also James Baldwin and Nikki Giovanni, *A Dialogue*, foreword by Ida Lewis, afterword by Orde Coombs (London: Michael Joseph, 1975), esp. 7, 39–40, 41–42, 45, 49, 52–55.

175. Crouch, "The Rage of Race," in *Notes of a Hanging Judge*, 231.

176. Stanley Crouch, "Meteor in a Black Hat," in *Notes of a Hanging Judge*, 197; Amiri Baraka, "*Jimmy!*—James Arthur Baldwin," in *Eulogies* (New York: Marsilio Publishers, 1996), 96.

177. Hernton, *White Papers*, 131; Philip Roth, "Blues for Mister Charlie," *Modern Critical Views: James Baldwin*, ed. Harold Bloom (Philadelphia: Chelsea House Publishers, 1986), 41.

178. Gates, "The Welcome Table," 158; Baldwin, "No Name in the Street," in *Collected Essays*, 459.

179. Baldwin, "No Name in the Street," in *Collected Essays*, 459.

180. Ibid., 359.

181. Ibid., 398–99, 364.

182. Ibid., 459, 410. For an explanation of this term, which refers to the white search for a contender to beat the first black heavy weight champion, Jack Johnson, see Carlton Moss, "The Great White Hope," in *A Freedomways Reader*, ed. Ernest Kaiser, foreword by James Baldwin (New York: International Publishers, 1977), 50–63. In an intriguing and convincing argument, Walton Muyumba in *The Shadow and Act: Black Intellectual Practice, Jazz Improvisation, and Philosophical Pragmatism* (Chicago: University of Chicago Press, 2009), compares Baldwin's public discourse to that of a boxer; he writes that "Baldwin's essays accentuate a striking style of black intellectual practice: the black intellectual as prizefighter," 94. He goes on to argue that to view "Baldwin as prizefighter helps us to locate both his body (and his criticism) at the center of the discourse that trusses the 'incessant battles for the framing and definition of reality,'" 94.

183. Baldwin, "No Name in the Street," in *Collected Essays*, 427.

184. For example, see James Baldwin, *Tell Me How Long the Train's Been Gone* [1968] (London: Penguin, 1994), where Leo recalls his relationship with a Harlem racketeer, 210; compare this to his recollection in "Freaks and the American Ideal of Manhood," in *Collected Essays*, 819; see also Leeming, *James Baldwin*, 279–80.

185. Baldwin, "No Name in the Street," in *Collected Essays*, 363; Baldwin, *Tell Me How Long the Train's Been Gone*, 382; hereinafter abbreviated as *TMHL*.

186. Eliot Fremont Smith, "Books of the Times: Another Track," *New York Times* (May 31, 1968): 27.

187. David Llorens, "Books Noted," *Negro Digest* (August 1968): 51, 85–86; Isa Kapp, "In Perspective and Anger," the *New Leader* (June 3, 1968): 18–20.

188. Mario Puzo, "His Cardboard Lovers," Review of *TMHL*, *New York Times Book Review* (June 23, 1968): 5.

189. Guy Davenport, "If These Wings Should Fail Me, Lord," *National Review* 20 (July 16, 1968): 701.

190. Granville Hicks, "From Harlem with Hatred," *Saturday Review*, 51, no. 1 (June 1968): 23.

191. Nelson Algren, "Sashaying Around," Review of *TMHL*, *The Critic* (October–November 1968): 86.

192. Irving Howe, "James Baldwin: At Ease in Apocalypse," *Harper's* 237 (September 1968): 95, 96, 100.

193. Stuart Hall, "You a Fat Cow Now," *New Statesman* (June 28 1968): 871.

194. See Campbell, *Talking at the Gates*, where Baldwin notes that Leo was Rufus Scott, but without the suicide, 228.

195. James Giles, "Religious Alienation and 'Homosexual Consciousness' in *City of Night* and *Go Tell It on the Mountain*," *College English* 36 (1974): 378; see also Emmanuel Nelson, "The Novels of James Baldwin: Struggles for Self-Acceptance," *Journal of American Culture* 8, no. 4 (Winter 1985), who suggests that Baldwin tried to appease black militants by his negative portrayals of white homosexuality, 15.

196. See also where Baldwin refers to a "poor white faggot" and "another faggot," 325.

197. See Murray, *Our Living Manhood*, for a useful reading of Baldwin's treatment of radical politics and homosexuality, although Murray overstates the ways that the relationship between Christopher and Leo resolves these tensions. For Murray it "magically resolves the very contradictions that Baldwin experienced in his own relationship with Black Power advocates," 37.

198. Countee Cullen, *The Black Christ and Other Poems* (New York: Harper & Brothers, 1929), 69–110.

199. See "Hubert Fichte Interviews Jean Genet," *Gay Sunshine Interviews*, vol. 1, ed. Winston Leyland (San Francisco: Gay Sunshine Press, 1978), 69.

200. Cited by Edmund White, *Genet: A Biography* (New York: Alfred A. Knopf, 1993), 441. Occasionally Genet did provoke outrage: on one occasion, White notes that Genet "took too many Nembutals and danced in a pink negligée for Hilliard and three other Panthers," 529.

201. See White, *Genet: A Biography*, who notes that Baldwin and Genet often dined alone and frequented the same gay bar in Paris in the early 1950s. In *Giovanni's Room* (London: Penguin, 1990), David describes a man who had won a literary prize based on "half his life in prison," 107. The description of the man who is celebrated for his books based on his life in prison is quite possibly a reference to Genet. Baldwin was also a great admirer of *The Blacks*, 439. For details of their collaboration with the Panthers, see White, *Genet: A Biography*, 544, 563; for details of Genet's input, see ch. 18, esp. 521–46; see also Jean Genet, *May Day Speech*, introd. Allen Ginsberg (San Francisco: City Lights Books, 1970); Jean Genet, *Prisoner of Love*, trans. Barbara Bray, introd. Edmund White (London: Picador, 1989), esp. 41–49, 83–86, 213–20, 258–61.

202. Jean Genet, *Here and Now for Bobby Seale* (New York: Committee to Defend the Panthers, 1970). White notes that Genet contacted a journalist from the widely read magazine *Le Nouvel Observateur* to discuss the plight of the Panthers; the interview was soon translated into English, German, and Italian, 539.

203. See Fichte, "Hubert Fichte Interviews Jean Genet," esp. 93.

204. Ibid.; Cleaver, "The Courage to Kill: Meeting the Panthers," in *Post-Prison Writings*, 23; Cleaver also describes his first meeting with the Panthers as "the most beautiful sight I had ever seen," 29; Jonathan Dollimore, *Sexual Dissidence: Augustine to Wilde, Freud to Foucault* (Oxford: Clarendon Press, 1991), 353. For a brief but useful overview of Genet's "revolutionary erotics," see Pascale Gaitet, "Jean Genet's American Dream: The Black Panthers," *Literature and History* 1, no. 1 (Spring 1992): 48–63.

205. Fichte, "Hubert Fichte Interviews Jean Genet," 80.

206. Genet, *Prisoner of Love*, 126, 260.

207. Ibid., 259.

208. Ibid., 260, 83.

209. Baldwin, "No Name in the Street," in *Collected Essays*, 410.

210. George Jackson, *Soledad Brother: The Prison Letters of George Jackson*, foreword Jonathan Jackson Jr., introd. Jean Genet [1970] (Chicago: Lawrence Hill Books, 1994), 332.

211. See Angela Davis, *An Autobiography* [1974] (London: The Women's Press, 1990). Davis notes that she used part of Baldwin's open letter to her in 1970 to name her anthology *If They Come in the Morning*, 306.

212. See Edmund White's introduction to *Prisoner of Love*, where he notes that "political action filled the void left in his [Genet's] life when he was awakened from his reverie as an artist," ix.

213. See Campbell, *Talking at the Gates*, who cites criticism that Baldwin held a "vague position," in contrast to the Panthers, 219; see also Gates, "The Welcome Table," where he states that "his [Baldwin's] arguments, richly nuanced and self-consciously ambivalent, were far too complex to serve straightforwardly political ends," 150.

214. See Fichte, "Hubert Fichte Interviews Jean Genet," where Genet says, "[p]erhaps I'm a black with white or pink skin, but I'm a black," 75.

215. Cited by White, *Genet: A Biography*, 528. The open letter was published in the *Black Panther* newspaper (August 15, 1970). See Fichte, "Hubert Fichte Interviews Jean Genet," where Genet claims that he told Bobby Seale that if he attacked homosexuals, he would attack black Americans. According to Genet, Newton's letter was published one week later, 93.

216. Fichte, "Hubert Fichte Interviews Jean Genet," 92.

217. Wallace, *Black Macho*, 61–62.

218. Stanley Crouch, "Clichés of Degradation," *Village Voice* (October 29, 1979): 39; cited by Emmanuel Nelson, "Critical Deviance: Homophobia and the Reception of James Baldwin's Fiction," *Journal of American Culture* 14 (1991): 92; James Baldwin, *Just Above*, 471.

Chapter 3

1. David Leeming, *James Baldwin: A Biography* (New York: Alfred A. Knopf, 1994), 387.

2. Jonathan Sheehan, "Enlightenment, Religion, and the Enigma of Secularization: A Review Essay," *American Historical Review* 108, no. 4 (October 2003): 1063. Stanley Macebuh, *James Baldwin: A Critical Study* (New York: Third Press, 1973). Clarence E. Hardy's *James Baldwin's God: Sex, Hope, and Crisis in Black Holiness Culture* (Knoxville: University of Tennessee Press, 2003) is a useful overview of Baldwin's complicated relationship to the black church.

3. Michael Lynch, "A Glimpse of the Hidden God: Dialectical Visions in Baldwin's *Go Tell It on the Mountain*," in *New Essays on* Go Tell It on the Mountain, ed. Trudier Harris (Cambridge: Cambridge University Press, 1996), 32.

4. Melvin Dixon, *Ride Out of the Wilderness: Geography and Identity in Afro-American Literature* (Urbana: University of Illinois Press, 1987), 124; Harold Bloom, "Introduction," in *James Baldwin: Modern Critical Views*, ed. Harold Bloom (Philadelphia: Chelsea House Publishers, 1986), 3.

5. Cornel West, *Prophesy Deliverance!: An Afro-American Revolutionary Christianity* (Philadelphia: Westminster Press, 1982), 85.

6. Dixon, *Ride Out*, 124.

7. Craig Werner, "The Economic Evolution of James Baldwin," in *Critical Essays on James Baldwin*, ed. Fred L. Standley and Nancy V. Burt (Boston: G. K. Hall, 1988), 78.

8. Ibid., 91; Joseph A. Brown, "'I, John Saw the Holy Number': Apocalyptic Visions in *Go Tell It on the Mountain* and *Native Son*," *Religion and Literature* 27 (1995): 61.

9. See George Shulman, *American Prophecy: Race and Redemption in American Political Culture* (Minneapolis: University of Minnesota Press, 2008), who describes Baldwin as "nontheistic because he does not announce God's words or point of view as a messenger, but prophetic," 132. Shulman suggests we might read Baldwin's prophetic writing as secular.

10. Ernest A. Champion, *Mr Baldwin, I Presume: James Baldwin-Chinua Achebe: A Meeting of Minds*, foreword by David Leeming (New York: University Press of America, 1995), 28, 100.

11. James Baldwin and Margaret Mead, *A Rap on Race* (New York: Dell, 1971), 83, 86.

12. James Baldwin, "Introduction: The Price of the Ticket," in *The Price of the Ticket: Collected Nonfiction, 1948–1985* (New York: St. Martin's/Marek, 1985), xvi.

13. Katherine Clay Bassard, *Spiritual Interrogations: Culture, Gender, and Community in Early African American Women's Writing* (Princeton, NJ: Princeton University Press, 1999), 141. Joanna Brook's pathbreaking *American Lazarus: Religion and the Rise of African-American and Native American Literatures* (New York: Oxford University Press, 2003) skillfully charts the importance of religion—but in early American literature.

14. Ibid.

15. James W. Coleman, *Faithful Vision: Treatments of the Sacred, Spiritual, and Supernatural in Twentieth-Century African American Fiction* (Baton Rouge: Louisiana State University Press, 2006), 1.

16. Joanna Brooks, "From Edwards to Baldwin: Heterodoxy, Discontinuity, and New Narratives of American Religious-Literary History," *American Literary History* 22, no. 2 (2010): 447, 448.

17. Clarence E. Hardy, *James Baldwin's God*, 64.

18. Walton Muyumba, *The Shadow and Act: Black Intellectual Practice, Jazz Improvisation, and Philosophical Pragmatism* (Chicago: University of Chicago Press, 2009), 37.

19. See Robert M. Anderson, *Vision of the Disinherited: The Making of American Pentecostalism* (1979; reprint with a new preface by Anderson; Peabody, MA: Hendrickson Publishers, 1992), where the author notes "the paucity and unavailability of source materials" on Pentecostalism, xii. More recently, critics have noted Baldwin's Pentecostal background. See David Hempton, *Evangelical Disenchantment: Nine Portraits of Faith and Doubt* (New Haven: Yale University Press, 2008), who writes that "[a]lthough Baldwin's adolescent flirtation with black Pentecostalism was relatively brief, his working out its effects lasted a lifetime," 167, adding that "what interested him about Christianity were not so much its doctrines and sacred texts, but its fidelity or otherwise to the principles of love that it preached but did not practice," 172.

20. Hardy, *James Baldwin's God*, xi.

21. Ibid., 26.

22. Kalamu ya Salaam, "James Baldwin: Looking Towards the Eighties," in *Conversations with James Baldwin*, ed. Fred L. Standley and Louis H. Pratt (Jackson: University Press of Mississippi, 1989), 182.

23. Cited by Hardy, *James Baldwin's God*, 13.

24. Sondra O'Neale, "Fathers, Gods, and Religion Perceptions of Christianity and Ethnic Faith in James Baldwin," in *Critical Essays on James Baldwin*, ed. Fred L. Standley and Nancy V. Burt (Boston: G. K. Hall, 1988), 126.

25. Cheryl J. Sanders, *Saints in Exile: The Holiness-Pentecostal Experience in African American Religion and Culture* (New York: Oxford University Press, 1996), 49.

26. David Bergman, "The Agony of Gay Black Literature," in *Gaiety Transfigured: Gay Self-Representations in American Literature* (Madison: University of Wisconsin Press, 1991), 163–87. Two exceptions are James S. Tinney, "The Blackness of Pentecostalism," *Spirit* 3, no. 2 (1979), where he notes that "Pentecostalism is an important part of James Baldwin's own past," 28; and also Sanders, *Saints in Exile*, who notes that Baldwin's "relevance to this discussion [Pentecostalism] is his deep rootedness and rejection of the Sanctified Church" (111). In "From Edwards to Baldwin," Joanna Brooks traces

the genealogy of Baldwin's religious education, providing useful information about Rosa Horn.

27. James Campbell, *Talking at the Gates: A Life of James Baldwin* (London: Faber & Faber, 1991), 9, 10.

28. Baldwin, "The Fire Next Time," in *Collected Essays*, ed. Toni Morrison (New York: The Library of America, 1998), 296.

29. Baldwin, "The Fire Next Time," in *Collected Essays*, 301.

30. Baldwin, "To Crush a Serpent," *Playboy* 34 (July 1987): 66–68; reprinted in James Baldwin, *The Cross of Redemption: Uncollected Writings*, ed. and introd. Randall Kenan (New York: Pantheon Books, 2010), 158–65.

31. For a useful account of why most African Americans have historically been Methodist and Baptist, see Joseph. R. Washington, "Methodists and Baptists," in *Black Sects and Cults* (New York: Doubleday, 1972), 36–57; see also D. W. Wills, "Exodus Piety: African American Religion in an Age of Immigration," in *Minority Faiths and the Protestant Mainstream*, ed. Jonathan Sarna (Urbana: University of Illinois Press, 1998), 116–88.

32. Joseph R. Washington, *Black Religion: The Negro and Christianity in the United States* (Boston: Beacon Press, 1964), 163; Sanders, *Saints in Exile,* 96.

33. For a useful account of these terms, see Anderson, *Vision of the Disinherited*, 16–19.

34. E. Franklin Frazier, *The Negro Church in America* (Liverpool: Liverpool University Press, 1964), 61; M. Mark Fischer, "Organized Religion and the Cults," in *African American Religious History: Documentary Witness*, ed. Milton C. Scott (Durham: Duke University Press, 1999), 464–72.

35. Frazier, *The Negro Church*, 61; for a brief mention of Mother Horn, see also Fischer, "Organized Religion and the Cults," 467. See also Fern Marja Eckman, *The Furious Passage of James Baldwin* (London: Michael Joseph, 1968), 70.

36. Frazier, *The Negro Church*, 54; see Langston Hughes, *Tambourines to Glory, Five Plays by Langston Hughes*, ed. and introd. Webster Smalley [1949] (Bloomington: Indiana University Press, 1968); the two main characters, Laura and Essie, start a church explicitly to make money, 191; see also Buddy who states that "[t]his church racket's got show business beat to hell," 210.

37. Washington, *Black Religion*, 115.

38. Zora Neale Hurston, "The Sanctified Church," in *The Sanctified Church*, foreword by Toni Cade Bambara (New York: Marlowe & Co., 1981), 103.

39. Sanders, *Saints in Exile*, 4.

40. Anderson, *Vision of the Disinherited*, 214.

41. See William Wasserstrom, "James Baldwin: Stepping Out of the Promise," in *Black Fiction: New Studies in the Afro-American Novel since 1945*, ed. A. Robert Lee (New York: Barnes and Noble Books, 1980), who states that Baldwin "cast the whole enterprise of expatriation into the discourse of spiritual exercise," 90.

42. Anderson, *Vision of the Disinherited*, 7.

43. Hurston, "The Sanctified Church," 103; Kalamu ya Salaam, "James Baldwin: Looking Towards the Eighties," in *Conversations with James Baldwin*, 182.

44. Sanders, *Saints in Exile*, 137.

45. For a detailed account of the revivals, see Anderson, *Vision of the Disinherited*, 66–71.

46. Hurston, "The Sanctified Church," 105–6.

47. Tinney, "The Blackness of Pentecostalism," 31; see also where he notes that "James Baldwin calls the drum the indispensable element in Pentecostal religion, the same as in African religion," 32.

48. Tinney, "The Blackness of Pentecostalism," 27, 28.

49. Cited by Sanders, *Saints in Exile*, 8.

50. Frazier, *The Negro Church*, 6, 13; Hurston, "Shouting," in *The Sanctified Church*, 91; see also Jon Michael Spenser, "The Ritual of Testifying in the Black Church," in *Celebrations of Identity: Multiple Voices in American Ritual Performance*, ed. Pamela R. Frese, foreword by Emiko Ohnuki-Tierney (Westport, CT: Bergin & Garvey, 1993), 61–73, esp. 71–73 on "The Meaning of Shouting."

51. Cited by Sanders, *Saints in Exile*, 13.

52. See Teresa L. Reed, *The Holy Profane: Religion in Black Popular Music* (Lexington: University of Kentucky Press, 2004); and Delton L. Alford, *Music in the Pentecostal Church* (Cleveland, TN: Pathway Press, 1967). On the connections between gospel music and Pentecostalism, see Stephen R. Tucker, "Pentecostalism and Popular Culture in the South: A Study of Four Musicians," *Journal of Popular Culture* 16 (Winter 1982): 68–80.

53. Hurston, "The Sanctified Church and the Jook," in *The Sanctified Church*, 105, 136.

54. Sanders, *Saints in Exile*, 81.

55. Ibid., 79.

56. Ibid., 80; for a brief but useful overview on the historical debates between sacred and secular music, see Saadi A. Simawe, "What Is in a Sound? The Metaphysics and Politics of Music in *The Amen Corner*," in *Re-Viewing James Baldwin: Things Not Seen*, ed. D. Quentin Miller (Philadelphia: Temple University Press, 2000), 12–32, esp. 25–29.

57. Sanders, *Saints in Exile*, 56; Washington, *Black Religion*, 120.

58. Michael Lynch, "*Just Above My Head*: James Baldwin's Quest for Belief," *Literature and Theology* 11, no. 3 (September 1997): 229.

59. Cited by Barbara Olson, "'Come-to-Jesus Stuff,' in James Baldwin's *Go Tell It on the Mountain* and *The Amen Corner*," *African American Review* 31, no. 2 (1997): 296.

60. Baldwin, "The Fire Next Time," in *Collected Essays*, 296.

61. Ibid., 299.

62. Ibid., 301.

63. Ibid., 304.

64. Ibid., 304.

65. Ibid., 304–5.

66. Ibid., 306.

67. William R. Jones, *Is God a White Racist?: A Preamble to Black Theology* (1973; reprint, Boston: Beacon Press, 1998), xxi.

68. Baldwin, "To Crush a Serpent," 66.

69. West, *Prophesy Deliverance*, 109; see also O'Neale, "Fathers, Gods, and Religion," who locates Baldwin in a tradition of African American reinterpreters of white Christianity, from mid-eighteenth-century Africans to Countee Cullen, 127–29.

70. Baldwin, "The Fire Next Time," in *Collected Essays*, 307; James Cone, *Black Theology and Black Power* (New York: Seabury Press, 1970), 72.

71. Baldwin, "The Fire Next Time," in *Collected Essays*, 313.

72. Ibid., 309.

73., See Hardy, *James Baldwin's God*, 17–36.

74. Cone, *Black Theology and Black Power*, 121.

75. James Baldwin, *Blues for Mister Charlie* [1965] (New York: Vintage Books, 1992), 120.

76. James Baldwin, *Another Country* [1962] (London: Penguin, 1990), 93; *Tell Me How Long the Train's Been Gone* [1968] (London: Penguin, 1994), 56; *Just Above My Head* [1979] (London: Penguin, 1994), 422.

77. For the seminal texts on black power and religion, see James Cone, *Black Theology and Black Power* and *A Black Theology of Liberation* (Philadelphia and New York: J. B. Lippincott Company, 1970).

78. "Black Power: Statement by National Committee of Negro Churchmen," *New York Times* (July 31, 1966): E5; cited by Hopkins, *Introducing a Black Theology of Liberation*, 38. For an acerbic satire on the church's political weakness, see B. Caldwell, "Prayer Meeting: Or, the First Militant Minister," in *The Black Aesthetic*, ed. Addison Gayle Jr. (New York: Doubleday and Company, 1971), 588–94.

79. James Baldwin, "How Can We Get Black People to Cool It?" *Esquire* 70, no. 1 (July 1968): 52.

80. Baldwin, "The Fire Next Time," in *Collected Essays*, 309.

81. Ibid., 307.

82. Baldwin, "To Crush a Serpent," 70.

83. Baldwin, "The Fire Next Time," in *Collected Essays*, 310.

84. James Baldwin, *The Evidence of Things Not Seen* (1985; reprint, with a foreword by Derrick Bell and Dewart Bell; New York: Henry Holt and Company, 1995), 122.

85. Baldwin and Mead, *A Rap on Race*, 85.

86. Ibid., 7.

87. Ibid., 85–86.

88. Jordan Elgrably and George Plimpton, "The Art of Fiction: James Baldwin 1984," in *Conversations with James Baldwin*, 234–35.

89. Campbell, *Talking at the Gates*, 281.

90. Baldwin, "The Fire Next Time," in *Collected Essays*, 306.

91. James Baldwin, "The Uses of the Blues," *Playboy* (January 1964): 241; reprinted in James Baldwin, *The Cross of Redemption: Uncollected Writings*, ed. and introd. Randall Kenan (New York: Pantheon Books, 2010), 57–66.

92. James Baldwin and Nikki Giovanni, *A Dialogue*, foreword by Ida Lewis, afterword by Orde Coombs (London: Michael Joseph, 1975), 80.

93. Albert Murray and James F. Callahan, eds., *Trading Twelves: The Selected Letters of Ralph Ellison and Albert Murray* (New York: Vintage, 2001), 193.

94. Baldwin, "Sonny's Blues," in *Going to Meet the Man*, 139.

95. James Baldwin, *Go Tell It on the Mountain* [1953] (London: Penguin, 1991), 212–13.

96. James Baldwin, *The Amen Corner* [1968] (London: Penguin, 1991), 88.

97. Zora Neale Hurston, "The Sanctified Church and the Jook," in *The Sanctified Church*, 136.

98. Baldwin, *The Amen Corner*, 70.

99. Ibid., 69.

100. Ibid.

101. Baldwin, "The Uses of the Blues," 131.

102. Baldwin, *Just Above*, 8.

103. Robert Genter, *Late Modernism: Art, Culture, and Politics in Cold War America* (Philadelphia and Oxford: University of Pennsylvania Press, 2010), 109.

104. John Hall, "James Baldwin Interviewed," in *Conversations with James Baldwin*, 105; see also "The Fire Next Time," in *Collected Essays*, where Baldwin distinguishes love from "the infantile American sense of being made happy" (341).

105. Cornel West, *Race Matters* (Boston: Beacon Press, 1993), 19; Martin Luther King Jr., "Love in Action," in *Strength to Love* [1963] (London: Fontana Books, 1969), 50.

106. James Mossman, "Race, Hate, Sex, and Colour: A Conversation with James Baldwin and Colin MacInnes," in *Conversations with James Baldwin*, 48.

107. Cited by bell hooks, *Salvation: Black People and Love* (New York: Perennial, 2001), 7; Baldwin, "In Search of a Majority," in *Collected Essays*, 220.

108. Shulman, *American Prophecy*, 94. Shulman contrasts the politicized love of Baldwin and King with Hannah Arendt, for whom "love in Christian and erotic forms is antipolitical because it collapses the space-between in which action and plurality live" (94); Genter, *Late Modernism*, 193.

109. Baldwin, *Tell Me How Long*, 267–68.

110. Ibid., 270.

111. Eckman, *Furious Passage*, 32.

112. Richard Goldstein, "Go the Way Your Blood Beats: An Interview with James Baldwin," *Village Voice* (June 26, 1984): 13. Baldwin, "No Name in the Street," in *Collected Essays*, 385.

113. Eckman, *Furious Passage*, 31.

114. Baldwin, "The Fire Next Time," in *Collected Essays*, 297.

115. Ibid., 312.

116. Baldwin, "To Crush a Serpent," 68.

117. Baldwin, "The Fire Next Time," in *Collected Essays* 301–2.

118. Ibid., 299, 297.

119. Leeming, *James Baldwin*, 23.

120. Baldwin, "To Crush a Serpent," 68.

121. Baldwin, "The Fire Next Time," in *Collected Essays*, 303.

122. Leeming, *James Baldwin*, 30.

123. John S. Lash, "James Baldwin Beside Himself: A Study in Modern Phallicism," *James Baldwin: A Critical Evaluation*, ed. Therman O'Daniel (1977; reprint, Washington, DC: Howard University Press, 1981), 54.

124. Baldwin, "The Fire Next Time," in *Collected Essays*, 311.

125. Robert Reid-Pharr, *Once You Go Black: Choice, Desire, and the Black American Intellectual* (New York: New York University Press, 2007), 105.

126. Baldwin, "Nothing Personal," in *Collected Essays*, 700.

127. Baldwin, "To Crush a Serpent," 70.

128. See Rosa Bobia, *The Critical Reception of James Baldwin in France* (New York: Peter Lang, 1997), where a French review of *Go Tell It* refers to the "troubling mixture of sensuality and of religion," 19.

129. Murray and Callahan, ed., *Trading Twelves*, 43.

130. Robert Bone, *The Negro Novel in America* (1958; rev. ed. New Haven, CT: Yale University Press, 1965), 239.

131. Ibid., 232, 234; Stanley Crouch, "The Rage of Race," in *Notes of a Hanging Judge: Essays and Reviews, 1979–1989* (New York: Oxford University Press, 1990), 235.

132. Bone, *The Negro Novel in America*, 238; Howard M. Harper, *Desperate Faith: A Study of Bellow, Salinger, Mailer, Baldwin, and Updike* (Chapel Hill: University of North Carolina Press, 1967), 157–58.

133. Baldwin, *Blues for Mister Charlie*, 105; see also Baldwin, *One Day When I Was Lost: A Scenario Based on the Life of Malcolm X* [1972] (New York: Dell, 1992). In a note, Baldwin states that people in this scene should show "the peace which follows an orgasm or a religious conversion," 142.

134. Michael Cobb, *God Hates Fags: The Rhetorics of Religious Violence* (New York: New York University Press, 2006), 63.

135. Leeming, *James Baldwin*, 89.

136. Baldwin, "The Discovery of What It Means to Be an American," in *Collected Essays*, 138.

137. See Jordan Elgrably and George Plimpton, "The Art of Fiction: James Baldwin 1984," in *Conversations with James Baldwin*, where Baldwin stated that *Go Tell It* was "about my relationship to my father and to the church, which is the same thing really. It was an attempt to exorcise something," 240.

138. Harold Norse, *Memoirs of a Bastard Angel*, preface by James Baldwin (New York: William Morrow & Co., 1989), 114.

139. Cited by W. J. Weatherby, *James Baldwin: Artist on Fire* (London: Michael Joseph, 1990), 96. The original manuscript is more sexually explicit; see James Baldwin, Typescript of *Go Tell It on the Mountain*. c. 1950 (The James Baldwin Collection. MG 278. The Schomburg Center for Research in Black Culture).

140. Cited by Norse, *Memoirs*, 114.

141. Bryan R. Washington, "Wrestling with 'The Love That Dare Not Speak Its Name': John, Elisha, and the 'Master,'" in *New Essays on* Go Tell It on the Mountain, 78; see also Vivian M. May, "Ambivalent Narratives, Fragmented Selves: Performative Identities and the Mutability of Roles in James Baldwin's *Go Tell It on the Mountain*," in *New Essays on* Go Tell It on the Mountain, 97–126; cited by Eckman, *Furious Passage*, 30.

142. Cobb, *God Hates Fags*, 53.

143. Ibid., 72.

144. Baldwin, *The Amen Corner*, 11.

145. Richard K. Barksdale, "Temple of the Fire Baptized," in *Critical Essays on James Baldwin*, 145.

146. See Margo Natalie Crawford, "The Reclamation of the Homoerotic as Spiritual in *Go Tell It on the Mountain*," *James Baldwin's* Go Tell It on the Mountain: *Historical and Critical Essays*, ed. Carol E. Henderson (New York: Peter Lang, 2006). Crawford argues that Baldwin "locates a homoerotic spirituality that emerges as a liberation theology," adding that "Baldwin's reclamation of the homoerotic as more spiritual than carnal is as revolutionary as any liberation theology," 76.

147. Baldwin, *Go Tell It*, 34.

148. Ibid., 18.

149. Ibid., 68.

150. Ibid., 39.

151. Ibid., 57.

152. Ibid., 57, 58.

153. Ibid., 17.

154. Ibid., 19.

155. Ibid., 16.

156. Baldwin, *Another Country*, 177–78.

157. Baldwin, *Go Tell It*, 17.

158. Ibid., 145.

159. Ibid., 41.

160. Ibid., 20.

161. Ibid., 20.

162. Ibid., 30.

163. Ibid., 14.

164. Ibid., 61.

165. James Baldwin, "The Outing," in *Going to Meet the Man* (London: Penguin, 1991), 39.

166. Ibid., 41.

167. Baldwin, *Go Tell It*, 224, 224, 225.

168. Baldwin, "Nothing Personal," in *Collected Essays*, 700.

169. Baldwin, "The Outing," in *Going to Meet the Man*, 47.

170. Ibid., 48.

171. Brown, "I, John Saw the Holy Number," 61.

172. Ibid., 65.

173. Baldwin, *Go Tell It*, 21.

174. Baldwin, "The Death of the Prophet," in *Commentary* 9 (March 1950): 260; reprinted as "The Death of a Prophet," in *The Cross of Redemption*, 293–300.

175. Baldwin, "The Death of the Prophet," 258, 261.

176. Baldwin, *Another Country*, 143.

177. Baldwin, *Tell Me How Long*, 390, 142.

178. Ibid., 229.

179. Baldwin, *Just Above*, 349.

180. Baldwin, *Tell Me How Long*, 328.

181. Trudier Harris, "The Eye as Weapon in *If Beale Street Could Talk*," in *Critical Essays on James Baldwin*, 215.

182. Ibid.

183. Baldwin, *If Beale Street*, 73.

184. Harris, "The Eye as Weapon in *If Beale Street Could Talk*," 213.

185. Baldwin, *If Beale Street*, 169.

186. Baldwin, *Just Above*, 576. When Arthur dies, Baldwin describes Jimmy's revisiting of their old haunts as a pilgrimage, a trip to "the Stations of the Cross," 50.

187. Baldwin, *Just Above*, 18; *Tell Me How Long*, 64.

188. James Baldwin, *Giovanni's Room* [1956] (London: Penguin, 1990), 158–59.

189. Baldwin, *Just Above*, 589.

190. Baldwin, *If Beale Street*, 100.

191. Ibid., 210.

192. Baldwin, *Just Above*, 496.

193. Ibid., 326.

194. Baldwin, *Go Tell It*, 39, 120.

195. Baldwin, *Just Above*, 252.

196. Baldwin, *If Beale Street*, 55, 97.

197. Ibid., 95.

198. Baldwin, *Go Tell It*, 223, 224.

199. Baldwin, *If Beale Street*, 97, 170.

200. Baldwin, *Just Above*, 222.

201. Baldwin, "The Male Prison," in *Collected Essays*, 234; "Here Be Dragons," reprinted as "Freaks and the American Ideal of Manhood," in *Collected Essays*, 814, 827.

202. Baldwin, *Just Above*, 87.

203. Ibid., 326.

204. Ibid., 148.

205. Ibid., 12, 17.

206. Quincy Troupe, "The Last Interview," in *James Baldwin: The Legacy*, ed. Quincy Troupe (New York: Simon & Schuster, 1989), 207.

207. For a useful overview of the blend between sacred and secular in gospel music, see Sanders, *Saints in Exile*, 71–90.

208. Baldwin, *Just Above*, 24–25.

209. Ibid., 90.

210. Ibid.

211. Ibid., 113.

212. James Baldwin, "Sonny's Blues," in *Going to Meet the Man*, 141; see also Tish's revelation in *Beale Street*. As she listens to Ray Charles, she notes how "everything seemed connected," 54.

213. Baldwin, *Just Above*, 8.

214. Ibid., 512.

215. Baldwin, *If Beale Street*, 95. Cited by Harris, "The Eye as Weapon in *If Beale Street Could Talk*," 214.

216. Baldwin, *If Beale Street*, 97.

217. Reid-Pharr, *Once You Go Black*, 108.

218. Baldwin, *Just Above*, 206.

219. Ibid., 207.

220. Ibid., 575.

221. Ibid., 470–71.

222. Ibid., 177.

Chapter 4

1. James Baldwin, *Giovanni's Room* [1956] (London: Penguin, 1990), 11.

2. See Magdalena Zaborowska's illuminating chapter on *The Welcome Table* in *James Baldwin's Turkish Decade: Erotics of Exile* (Durham: Duke University Press, 2009), 249–64.

3. Ida Lewis, "Conversation: Ida Lewis and James Baldwin," in *Conversations with James Baldwin*, ed. Fred. L. Standley and Louis H. Pratt (Jackson: University Press of Mississippi, 1989), 83.

4. Cited by Rebecca M. Schreiber, *Cold War Exiles in Mexico: US Dissidents and the Culture of Critical Resistance* (Minneapolis: University of Minnesota Press, 2008), 139.

5. Cited by Zaborowska, *James Baldwin's Turkish Decade*, 18.

6. Ibid., 110. There is indeed scholarship on Baldwin and transnationalism or exile, but he is also frequently overlooked in this context. See, for example, Wendy Walters, ed., *At*

Home in Diaspora: Black International Writing (Minneapolis: University of Minnesota Press, 2005). There are chapters on Richard Wright, Chester Himes, and Simon Njami, but no focus on Baldwin. More recently, see Kim Fortuny, *American Writers in Istanbul: Melville, Twain, Hemingway, Dos Passos, Bowles, Algren, Baldwin, and Settle*, foreword by Roger Allen (Syracuse, NY: Syracuse University Press, 2009). Fortuny makes the point that "no efforts have been made to . . . locate Istanbul in the heart of North American literature or in the heart of its mid-twentieth century literature," 195. For an excellent account of Baldwin's direction of the Turkish production of Canadian playwright John Herbert's *Fortune and Men's Eyes* (which ran in Istanbul from 1969 to 1970), see Çiğdem Üsekes, "In Another Country: James Baldwin and the Turkish Theatre Scene," *New England Theatre Journal* 21 (2010): 99–116. Üsekes traces Turkish theater criticism of the production and notes that the "lavish critical praise Baldwin and his cast received was astounding," 104.

7. Zaborowska, *James Baldwin's Turkish Decade*, 17. See Baldwin, "Letters from a Journey," in *Soon, One Morning: New Writings by American Negroes, 1940–62*, ed. Herbert Hill (New York: Alfred A. Knopf, 1966), 46, where he notes that, while in Turkey, "the whole somber question of America's role in the world today stared at me in a new and inescapable way."

8. Baldwin, "Letters from a Journey," in *Soon, One Morning*, 46.

9. See ibid., 43, 44.

10. In *How Their Living Outside America Affected Five African American Authors: Toward a Theory of Expatriate Literature*, preface by Richard Yarborough (Lewiston, NY: Edwin Mellen Press, 2010), Ewa Barbara Luczak claims that Baldwin and William Gardner Smith "exposed the inner contradictions at the heart of the French colonial world and saw beyond the surface of appearance," 30–31, but this stretches Baldwin's contributions to the portrayal of Algeria in France. Gardner Smith's *The Stone Face* (1964) is rightly acclaimed as a major critique of French colonialism, but Baldwin was less forthcoming at the time. There is discussion of North Africa in "This Morning, This Evening, So Soon" (first published in 1960), but no sustained discussion of Algeria until *No Name in the Street* 1972.

11. James Campbell, *Talking at the Gates: A Life of James Baldwin* (London and Boston: Faber and Faber, 1991), 107. See Rayford M. Logan, "The American Negro's View of Africa," in *Africa Seen by American Negroes: Africa from the Point of View of Negro Scholars*, ed. and introd. John A. Davis, preface by Alioune Diop (Paris: Présence Africaine, 1958), 217–27. Logan makes the astute point that "the American Negro's affection for France has led him to take a rosy view of French policy in Africa," 222. See, in particular, 222–24, for his reasons, which include language barriers and religious differences.

12. James Baldwin, "No Name in the Street," in *Collected Essays*, ed. Toni Morrison (New York: The Library of America, 1998), 473.

13. Baldwin, "Letters from a Journey," in *Soon, One Morning*, 44, 45.

14. Cheryl A. Wall, "Stranger at Home: James Baldwin on What It Means to Be an American," *James Baldwin: America and Beyond*, ed. Cora Kaplan and Bill Schwarz (Ann Arbor: University of Michigan Press, 2011), 37; Baldwin, "The Discovery of What It Means to Be an American," in *Collected Essays*, 137, 141.

15. James Baldwin, "No Name in the Street," in *Collected Essays*, 383.

16. Ibid. An earlier version of this section was published in *Paris, Capital of the Black Atlantic*, ed. Jeremy Braddock and Jonathan P. Eburne (Baltimore, MD: Johns Hopkins University Press, 2013), 175–99.

17. See Kevin Gaines, "Exile and the Private Life: James Baldwin, George Lamming, and the First World Congress of Negro Writers and Artists," in *James Baldwin: American and Beyond*, 173–74, who reads this confusion of dates as an expression of solidarity with those in the South and as an apology for self-exile.

18. Baldwin, "Princes and Powers," in *Collected Essays*, 143.

19. Baldwin, "Nobody Knows My Name," in *Collected Essays*, 198.

20. Baldwin, "No Name in the Street," in *Collected Essays*, 383, 435.

21. Ibid., 376.

22. Paul Gilroy, *The Black Atlantic: Modernity and Double Consciousness* (Cambridge, MA: Harvard University Press, 1993), 15.

23. Eve Auchincloss and Nancy Lynch, "Disturber of the Peace: James Baldwin—An Interview," *Conversations with James Baldwin*, 80.

24. Brent Hayes Edwards, *The Practice of Diaspora: Literature, Translation and the Rise of Black Internationalism* (Cambridge, MA: Harvard University Press, 2003), 7.

25. Walton Muyumba, *The Shadow and Act: Black Intellectual Practice, Jazz Improvisation, and Philosophical Pragmatism* (Chicago: University of Chicago Press, 2009), 5.

26. Baldwin, "Stranger in the Village," in *Collected Essays*, 129.

27. See Lawrence P. Jackson in *The Indignant Generation: A Narrative History of African American Writers and Critics, 1934–1960* (Princeton, NJ: Princeton University Press, 2010), who claims *Giovanni's Room* "offered a clear-sighted focus on the subject at hand, which perhaps had not quite been attempted by black writers before: the thoroughgoing perfidy of liberal whites," 411.

28. Leslie Conger, "Jimmy on East 15th Street," *African American Review* 29, no. 4 (1995): 557.

29. Baldwin, "Notes of a Native Son," in *Collected Essays*, 70–72.

30. Lewis, "Conversation: Ida Lewis and James Baldwin," in *Conversations with James Baldwin*, 84.

31. James A. Dievler, "Sexual Exiles: James Baldwin and *Another Country*," in *James Baldwin Now*, ed. Dwight A. McBride (New York: New York University Press, 1999), 169.

32. Baldwin, "Freaks and the American Ideal of Manhood" ["Here Be Dragons"], in *Collected Essays*, 821.

33. Ibid., 823.

34. Ibid.

35. W. J. Weatherby, *James Baldwin: Artist on Fire* (London: Penguin, 1990), 62.

36. James Campbell, *Exiled in Paris: Richard Wright, James Baldwin, Samuel Beckett, and Others on the Left Bank* (New York: Scribner, 1995), 33.

37. Baldwin, "Alas, Poor Richard," in *Collected Essays*, 249.

38. Ibid. Wright may have been referring to Rudolph Fisher's 1925 story, "The City of Refuge," in *The New Negro: Voices of the Harlem Renaissance*, ed. Alain Locke; introd. Arnold Rampersad (New York: Touchstone, 1997), where Harlem is, for King Solomon Gillis, "Land of plenty. City of refuge—city of refuge. If you live long enough," 7. It's possible that Baldwin did not pick up on Wright's ironic reference to the Fisher story but the older writer may have been reinforcing his views on the sanctity of Paris echoed in his unpublished 1951 essay, "I Choose Exile." For a useful overview of the "Paris Essays," see James Miller, "What Does It Mean to Be an American? The Dialectics of Self-Discovery in Baldwin's 'Paris Essays' (1950-1961)," *Journal of American Studies* 42, no. 2 (April 2008): 51–66.

39. Baldwin, "Equal in Paris," in *Collected Essays*, 103.

40. Gilroy, *The Black Atlantic*, 4.

41. Baldwin, "Encounter on the Seine: Black Meets Brown," in *Collected Essays*, 86.

42. See Baldwin's description of Wright's meeting of the Franco-American Fellowship Club in "Alas, Poor Richard," in *Collected Essays*, esp. 264–65.

43. Kevin Bell, "Assuming the Position: Fugitivity and Futurity in the Work of Chester Himes," *Paris, Capital of the Black Atlantic*, 150.

44. Edwards, *The Practice of Diaspora*, 5.

45. Ibid., 5.

46. Baldwin, "Encounter on the Seine," in *Collected Essays*, 85.

47. Ibid., 88.

48. Baldwin, "Equal in Paris," in *Collected Essays*, 106.

49. Baldwin, "The Discovery of What It Means to Be an American," in *Collected Essays*, 137.

50. Wall, "Stranger at Home," 39.

51. Baldwin, "Equal in Paris," in *Collected Essays*, 110.

52. See Jacques Howlett, "*Présence Africaine*, 1947–1958," *Journal of Negro History* 43, no. 2 (April 1958): 140–50.

53. Baldwin, "Encounter on the Seine: Black Meets Brown," in *Collected Essays*, 89.

54. Harold Isaacs, "Five Writers and Their Ancestors Part 2," *Phylon* 21, no. 4 (1960): 324.

55. Edwards, *The Practice of Diaspora*, 7.

56. Baldwin, "Princes and Powers," in *Collected Essays*, 152; Edwards, *The Practice of Diaspora*, 5.

57. Baldwin, "No Name in the Street," in *Collected Essays*, 383.

58. See David Macey, *Frantz Fanon: A Biography* (New York: Picador, 2000), 279, for key details about the conference that Baldwin omits. As Macey notes, sixty-three delegates from twenty-four countries were invited, with the majority coming "from the Francophone Africa and the Caribbean." Lawrence P. Jackson in *The Indignant Generation* also points out that Baldwin does not mention the final talk of the conference: Frantz Fanon's "Racism and Culture," 450.

59. Baldwin, "Princes and Powers," in *Collected Essays*, 148. See Akin Adesokan, "Baldwin, Paris, and the 'Conundrum' of Africa," *Textual Practice* 23, no. 1 (2009): 73–97, for a useful reading of the gaps in Baldwin's report of the conference.

60. Baldwin, "Stranger in the Village," in *Collected Essays*, 119.

61. Baldwin, "Princes and Powers," in *Collected Essays*, 147.

62. Ibid., 150.

63. Ibid., 154.

64. Ibid., 152.

65. Ibid., 153. In contrast to Baldwin's uncertain views on black transnationalism, see St. Clair Drake, "Hide My Face? On Pan-Africanism and Negritude," in *Soon, One Morning*, 78–105. St. Drake traces the complex network of arguments for and against négritude with consummate clarity, refuting notions of biology and psychology, but concluding that there might be "subtle African orientations" in African American culture, 94.

66. François Bondy, "James Baldwin, as Interviewed by François Bondy," *Transition* 0, no. 12 (January–February 1964): 16.

67. Baldwin, "Princes and Powers," in *Collected Essays*, 148. There are a number of parallels between US civil rights and colonialism. See Luczak, *How Their Living Outside America Affected Five African American Authors*, 11. Luczak points to Harold Cruse's "Revolutionary Nationalism and the African American," published in *Black Fire* (1968), where he writes: "from the beginning, the American Negro has existed as a colonial being [whose] enslavement coincided with the colonial expansion of European powers and was nothing more or less than a condition of domestic colonialism." As she notes, J. H. O'Dell made a similar point in *Freedomways*, arguing that American racism was "a special variety of colonialism," 11.

68. See Penny M. Von Eschen, *Race Against Empire: Black Americans and Anticolonialism, 1937–1957* (Ithaca: Cornell University Press, 1997), 175. Von Eschen notes that Baldwin's defense of the United States as "open and free" in "Princes and Powers" "profoundly underscores the hegemony of this particular framing of Cold War anticolonialism." I would recast this as an example of Baldwin's misguided strategic exceptionalism in his attempts to distinguish between the experiences of African Americans to the Africans he discusses.

69. Rosa Bobia, *The Critical Reception of James Baldwin in France* (New York and Washington: Peter Lang, 1997), 13.

70. Cited by Bobia, *The Critical Reception of James Baldwin in France*, 16.

71. Ibid., 25.

72. In Baldwin's unpublished play, *The Welcome Table*, there is an assembled cast from different countries. See David Leeming, *James Baldwin: A Biography* (New York: Alfred A. Knopf, 1994), who reads the play as a work about "exile and alienation," 373–74. For a useful reading of this short story in relation to migration, see Magdalena Zaborowska, "'In the Same Boat': James Baldwin and the Other Atlantic," in *A Historical Guide to James Baldwin*, ed. Douglas Field (New York: Oxford University Press, 2009), 177–211.

73. Baldwin, *Giovanni's Room*, 11.

74. Edward Said, "Intellectual Exile: Expatriates and Marginals" (1993), in *The Edward Said Reader*, ed. Mustafa Bayoumi and Andrew Rubin (New York: Vintage, 2000), 369.

75. James Baldwin, *Tell Me How Long the Train's Been Gone* [1968] (London: Penguin, 1994), 282.

76. Ibid.

77. Baldwin, *Tell Me How Long*, 294.

78. "The Black Scholar Interviews James Baldwin," in *Conversations with James Baldwin*, 154.

79. Baldwin, *Another Country*, 184.

80. Ibid., 245.

81. Cyraina Johnson-Roullier, "(An)Other Modernism: James Baldwin, *Giovanni's Room*, and the Rhetoric of Flight," *Modern Fiction Studies* 45, no. 4 (Winter 1999): 938.

82. Baldwin, *Giovanni's Room*, 34, 87.

83. Donald Martin Carter, *Navigating the African Diaspora: The Anthropology of Invisibility* (Minneapolis: University of Minnesota Press, 2010), 13.

84. Baldwin, "Encounter on the Seine," in *Collected Essays*, 90.

85. Ibid., 89.

86. Baldwin, "Many Thousands Gone," in *Collected Essays*, 19–20.

87. Leeming, *James Baldwin*, 10.

88. Edwards, *The Practice of Diaspora*, 5.

89. There are, however, moments where McKay's novel converges with Baldwin's musings on nationalism and exile. See Claude McKay, *Banjo* (London: Black Classics, 2000), where the narrator encounters an American who observes that "Europe had taught him to be patriotic; it had taught him that he was American," 117. Banjo, however, considers himself "a child of deracinated ancestry," 118.

90. Baldwin, *Giovanni's Room*, 9. See Miko Tuhkanen, "James Baldwin on the American Express and the Queer Underground," *English Language Notes* 45, no. 2 (Fall/Winter 2007): 123–31. Tuhkanen focuses on the railroad in relation to Baldwin's second novel, pointing out that "railwaydom is a recurrent chronotype in Baldwin's work and the African American tradition in general," 123. He also makes reference to water and drowning, noting how "David's fall into homosexual spaces . . . is described as submersion and drowning," 135.

91. Zaborowska, "In the Same Boat," 178.

92. Gilroy, *The Black Atlantic*, 12.

93. Gilroy, *The Black Atlantic*, 15; Baldwin, "This Morning, This Evening, So Soon," in *Going to Meet the Man* (London: Penguin, 1991), 163.

94. Baldwin, *Giovanni's Room*, 11.

95. Ibid., 46.

96. Ibid., 77.

97. Ibid., 31, 82.

98. Ibid., 80–81.

99. Ibid., 25.

100. Ibid., 62.

101. Ibid.

102. Ibid., 9, 11.

103. Ibid., 47; Judith Butler, *Precarious Life: The Powers of Mourning and Violence* (New York: Verso, 2004), 33–34.

104. Gilroy, *The Black Atlantic*, 13; Graham Robb, *Strangers: Homosexual Love in the Nineteenth Century* (London: Picador, 2003), 110.

105. Allen Ginsberg, "Howl," in *Howl and Other Poems* (San Francisco: City Lights Books, 1956; 1996), 13.

106. Baldwin, *Giovanni's Room*, 88.

107. Ibid.

108. Ibid.

109. Ibid.

110. James Weldon Johnson, *The Autobiography of an Ex-Colored Man* [1912] (New York: Dover Publications, 1995), 94.

111. Baldwin, *Giovanni's Room*, 156.

112. Gilroy, *The Black Atlantic*, 12.

113. See Robert Reid-Pharr, *Black Gay Man* (New York: New York University Press, 2001), 127, who is attuned to the economic situation of Giovanni, noting how the eponymous protagonist's "nominally white, southern Italian body is bought and sold in the course of the novel."

114. Gilroy, *The Black Atlantic*, 19.

115. Baldwin, "No Name in the Street," in *Collected Essays*, 364. See also later in the essay when Baldwin writes "[o]ne can wonder to whom the 'we' here refers," 452.

116. Baldwin, "No Name in the Street," in *Collected Essays*, 364.

117. Baldwin, "Stranger in the Village," in *Collected Essays*, 121.

118. Baldwin, "No Name in the Street," in *Collected Essays*, 382.

119. Baldwin, "The Discovery of What It Means to Be an American," in *Collected Essays*, 137.

120. Bill Lyne, "God's Black Revolutionary Mouth: James Baldwin's Black Radicalism," *Science and Society* 74, no. 1 (January 2010): 29.

121. Besenia Rodriguez, "'Long Live Third World Unity! Long Live Internationalism': Huey P. Newton's Revolutionary Intercommunalism," in *Transnational Blackness: Navigating the Global Color Line*, ed. Manning Marable and Vanessa Agard-Jones (New York: Palgrave Macmillan, 2008), 152.

122. Ibid., 151.

123. Baldwin, "No Name in the Street," in *Collected Essays*, 376–77.

124. Gilroy, *The Black Atlantic*, 133.

125. Baldwin, "No Name in the Street," *Collected Essays*, 366.

126. Ibid., 405.

127. Ibid., 368.

128. Ibid., 377.

129. Ibid., 394.

130. Ibid., 430.

131. Ibid., 395.

132. Ibid., 397.

133. Ibid., 402.

134. Ibid., 387.

135. Isaacs, "Five Writers and Their Ancestors, 327.

136. Baldwin, "Notes of a Native Son," in *Collected Essays*, 64.

137. Baldwin, "Autobiographical Notes," in *Collected Essays*, 7.

138. Isaacs, "Five Writers and Their Ancestors," 328.

139. Baldwin, *Go Tell It*, 125.

140. Baldwin, "Notes of a Native Son," in *Collected Essays*, 65.

141. Campbell, *Talking at the Gates*, 109.

142. See Ezenwa-Ohaeto, "Notions and Nuances: Africa in the Works of James Baldwin," in *Of Dreams Deferred, Dead or Alive: African Perspectives on African-American Writers*, ed. Femi Ojo-Ade (Westport, CT: Greenwood Press, 1996), 110, who writes how "real Africa [in Baldwin's writing] is clearly the sub-Saharan zone" and I'm mindful of not replicating this view. It is beyond the scope of this chapter, however, to discuss Baldwin's writings on Algeria: see in particular "This Morning, This Evening, So Soon" and *No Name in the Street*.

143. Fern Marja Eckman, *The Furious Passage of James Baldwin* (New York: M. Evans & Co, 1966), 24; Ernest Champion, *Mr. Baldwin, I Presume: James Baldwin-Chinua Achebe: A Meeting of Minds*, foreword by David Leeming (New York: University Press of America, Inc., 1995), 47–48.

144. Isaacs, "Five Writers and Their Ancestors," 324.

145. Ezenwa-Ohaeto, "Notions and Nuances," 108.

146. James Baldwin, letter to Sol Stein, November 9, 1956, *James Baldwin and Sol Stein: Native Sons*, ed. Sol Stein (New York: One World Books, 2004), 82; Baldwin, "No Name in the Street," in *Collected Essays*, 472–73.

147. Jackson, *Indignant Generation*, 480.

148. Femi Ojo-Ade, "Introduction," in *Of Dreams Deferred, Dead or Alive*, 1.

149. Countee Cullen, "Heritage," in *Color* (New York: Harper and Brothers Publishers, 1925), 36.

150. Isaacs, "Five Writers and Their Ancestors," 319.

151. Chimalum Nwankwo, "Richard Wright: A Dubious Legacy," in *Of Dreams Deferred, Dead or Alive*, 58.

152. Luczak, *How Their Living Outside America Affected Five African American Authors*, 14.

153. Ibid., 15.

154. Rayford W. Logan, "The American Negro's View of Africa," in *Africa Seen by American Negroes: Africa from the Point of View of Negro Scholars*, ed. and introd. John A. Davis, preface by Alioune Diop (Paris: Présence Africaine, 1958), 218.

155. St. Clair Drake, "An Approach to the Evaluation of African Societies," in *Africa Seen by American Negroes*, 11.

156. See Jackson, *The Indignant Generation*, 452. Jackson also claims that Baldwin was a member of AMSAC from 1958, 480. Jackson also notes that in 1959 "the organizers desperately wanted him there," 480, and how he was scheduled to speak at the June AMSAC conference but did not appear, 481.

157. Jackson, *The Indignant Generation*, 477.

158. Baldwin, quoted in Isaacs, "Five Writers and Their Ancestors," 328.

159. Baldwin, "Notes of a Native Son," in *Collected Essays*, 80.

160. See my article, "Pentecostalism and All That Jazz: Tracing James Baldwin's Religion," in *Literature and Theology* 22, no. 4 (December 2008): 436–57.

161. See, for example, Miriam Sivan, "Out of and Back to Africa: James Baldwin's *Go Tell It on the Mountain*," *Christianity and Literature* 51, no. 1 (Autumn 2001): 29–41.

162. Champion, *Mr. Baldwin, I Presume*, xviii; Babacar M'Baye, "African Retentions in *Go Tell It on the Mountain*," in *James Baldwin's* Go Tell It on the Mountain: *Historical and Critical Essays*, ed. Carol E. Henderson (New York: Peter Lang, 2006), 43.

163. M'Baye, "African Retentions," in *James Baldwin's* Go Tell It on the Mountain, 47–48.

164. Ibid., 44.

165. Carolyn L. Holmes, "Reassessing African American Literature through an Afrocentric Paradigm: Zora N. Hurston and James Baldwin," in *Language and Literature in the African American Imagination*, ed. Carol Aisha Blackshire-Belay (Westport, CT: Greenwood Press, 1992), 49.

166. Ibid., 49, 41.

167. Baldwin, "The Outing," in *Going to Meet the Man*, 44.

168. Ibid., 41, 45.

169. Hurston, *The Sanctified Church*, 103; Kalamu ya Salaam, "James Baldwin: Looking Towards the Eighties," in *Conversations with James Baldwin*, 182. See also Baldwin, "Introduction," in *The Price of the Ticket*, where he compares black and white churches: "We do not . . . share the same hope or speak the same language," xix.

170. Zora Hurston, *Jonah's Gourd Vine*; reprint, with afterword by Holly Eley [1934] (London: Virago, 1993), 59, 62.

171. Ibid., 145–46, 221.

172. Joseph A. Brown, "'I, John Saw the Holy Number': Apocalyptic Visions in *Go Tell It on the Mountain* and *Native Son*," *Religion and Literature* 27 (1995): 55.

173. This is also explored in detail in my article "Pentecostalism and All That Jazz."

174. Amitai F. Avi-Ram, "The Unreadable Black Body: 'Conventional' Poetic Form in the Harlem Renaissance," *Genders* 7 (Spring 1980): 37.

175. See Michael Eric Dyson, "When You Divide Body and Soul, Problems Multiply: The Black Church and Sex," in *Race Rules: Navigating the Color Line* (Reading, MA: Addison-Wesley Publishing, 1996). Dyson focuses on the physicality of black worship, calling for a "theology of eroticism."

176. Avi-Ram, "The Unreadable Black Body," 36; quoted in Dyson, *Race Rules*, 92.

177. See David Bergman, *Gaiety Transfigured: Gay Self-Representation in American Literature* (Madison: University of Wisconsin Press, 1991), 172–83. However, see also Molefi Kete Asante, *Afrocentricity: The Theory of Social Change* (Buffalo, NY: Amulefi, 1980), who sees homosexuality as "un-African," writing that it is "a deviation from Afrocentric thought," 64–65.

178. Baldwin, "Letters from a Journey," in *Soon, One Morning*, 39, 42.

179. Campbell, *Talking at the Gates*, 152.

180. Lewis, "Conversation," in *Conversations with James Baldwin*, 85.

181. Leeming, *James Baldwin*, 207; Baldwin, "Letters from a Journey," in *Soon, One Morning*, 40.

182. Campbell, *Talking at the Gates*, 152.

183. Eckman, *The Furious Passage*, 169; Leeming, *James Baldwin*, 207.

184. Baldwin, "Letters from a Journey," in *Soon, One Morning*, 46.

185. Leeming, *James Baldwin*, 210.

186. Nat Hentoff, "'It's Terrifying,' James Baldwin: The Price of Fame," in *Conversations with James Baldwin*, 34–35.

187. Ezenwa-Ohaeto, "Notions and Nuances: Africa in the Works of James Baldwin," 111.

188. *Nationalism, Colonialism and the United States: One Minute to Twelve*, a Forum sponsored by the Liberation Committee for Africa on its First Anniversary Celebration, June 2, 1961 (New York: Photo-Offset Press, 1961), 25; reprinted in James Baldwin, *The Cross of Redemption: Uncollected Writings*, ed. and introd. Randall Kenan (New York: Pantheon Books, 2010), 9–15.

189. Eldridge Cleaver, *Soul on Ice*, introd. Maxwell Geismar (New York: Ramparts, 1968), 99.

190. Ibid., 99, 100, 103.

191. Eve Auchincloss and Nancy Lynch, "Disturber of the Peace: James Baldwin—An Interview," in *Conversations with James Baldwin*, 71.

192. Champion, *Mr. Baldwin, I Presume*, 47–48.

193. Barbara Judson and Andrew Shin, "Beneath the Black Aesthetic: James Baldwin's Primer of Black American Masculinity," *African American Review* 32, no. 2 (Summer 1998): 257.

194. Baldwin, *Just Above*, 561, 564.

195. Judson and Shin, "Beneath the Black Aesthetic," 257.

196. Baldwin, *Just Above*, 564.

197. Edwards, *The Practice of Diaspora*, 5.

198. Champion, *Mr. Baldwin, I Presume*, 86.

199. Eleanor Traylor, "James Baldwin and Chinua Achebe: Transgressing Official Vocabularies," in *James Baldwin: American and Beyond*, ed. Cora Kaplan and Bill Schwarz (Ann Arbor: University of Michigan Press, 2011), 232.

200. Yvonne Neverson, "The Artist Has Always Been a Disturber of the Peace," in *Conversations with James Baldwin*, 168.

201. Studs Terkel, "An Interview with James Baldwin," in *Conversations with James Baldwin*, 17.

202. Neverson, "The Artist," in *Conversations with James Baldwin*, 168.

203. Jordan Elgrably and George Plimpton, "The Art of Fiction 1984: James Baldwin," in *Conversations with James Baldwin*, 246.

204. Baldwin, "Stranger in the Village," in *Collected Essays*, 121.

205. Baldwin, "No Name in the Street," in *Collected Essays*, 381.

206. Jordan Elgrably and George Plimpton, "The Art of Fiction," in *Conversations with James Baldwin*, 246.

207. Neverson, "The Artist," in *Conversations with James Baldwin*, 169.

208. James Baldwin, Romare Bearden, et al., *Perspectives: Angles on African Art*, interviewed by Michael John Weber, introd. by Susan Vogel (New York: Center for African Art, 1987), 115.

209. Baldwin et al., *Perspectives*, 119.

210. Traylor, "James Baldwin and Chinua Achebe," 235.

211. Baldwin, *Just Above*, 565.

212. Baldwin et al., *Perspectives*, 116, 122, 119.

213. Traylor, "James Baldwin and Chinua Achebe," 238.

214. Baldwin et al., *Perspectives*, 127.

Afterword

1. Consuela Francis, *The Critical Reception of James Baldwin, 1963–2010* (Rochester, NY: Camden House, 2014), 1.

2. Lawrie Balfour, *The Evidence of Things Not Said: James Baldwin and the Promise of American Democracy* (Ithaca: Cornell University Press, 2001), 23.

3. James Baldwin and Margaret Mead, *A Rap on Race* (New York: Dell, 1971), 105.

4. Conferences devoted to Baldwin include those held at Howard University (2000), Queen Mary, University of London (2007), Suffolk University, Boston (2009), New York University (2011), and Montpellier, France (2014).

5. Colm Tóibín, "James Baldwin and Barack Obama," *New York Review of Books* (October 23, 2008). http://www.nybooks.com/articles/21930.

6. James Baldwin and Nikki Giovanni, *A Dialogue*, foreword by Ida Lewis, afterword by Orde Coombs (London: Michael Joseph, 1975), 34.

7. Cheryl A. Wall, "Stranger at Home: James Baldwin on What It Means to be an American," in *James Baldwin: America and Beyond*, ed. Cora Kaplan and Bill Schwarz (Ann Arbor: University of Michigan Press, 2011), 40.

8. James Baldwin, "No Name in the Street," in *Collected Essays*, ed. Toni Morrison (New York: Library of America, 1998), 472, 473.

9. Baldwin, "Nothing Personal," in *Collected Essays*, 702.

10. James Baldwin, "As Much Truth as One Can Bear," *New York Times Book Review* (January 14, 1962), 38; reprinted in James Baldwin, *The Cross of Redemption: Uncollected Writings*, ed. and introd. Randall Kenan (New York: Pantheon Books, 2010), 28–34.

{ BIBLIOGRAPHY }

Aanerud, Rebecca. "Now More Than Ever: James Baldwin and the Critique of White Liberalism." In *James Baldwin Now*, edited by Dwight A. McBride, 56–74. New York: New York University Press, 1999.

Abelove, Henry, Michèle Aina Barale, and David M. Halperin, eds. *The Lesbian and Gay Studies Reader*. New York: Routledge, 1993.

Abrams, Nathan. *Commentary Magazine, 1945–59*. Foreword by Edward N. Luttwak. London and Portland: Valentine Mitchell, 2007.

Adams, Maurianne, and John Bracey, eds. *Strangers and Neighbors: Relations between Blacks and Jews in the United States*. Amherst: University of Massachusetts Press, 2000.

Adesokan, Akin. "Baldwin, Paris, and the 'Conundrum' of Africa." *Textual Practice* 23, no. 1 (2009): 73–97.

Alford, Delton L. *Music in the Pentecostal Church*. Cleveland, TN: Pathway Press, 1967.

Algren, Nelson. Review of *Giovanni's Room*, by James Baldwin. *Booklist* 53 (December 1, 1956): 174.

———. "Sashaying Around." Review of *Tell Me How Long the Train's Been Gone*, by James Baldwin. *The Critic* (October–November 1968): 86–87.

Amey, Lawrence, Timothy L. Hall, et al. *Censorship*. Vol. 1. Pasadena, CA, and Englewood Cliffs, NJ: Salem Press, 1997.

Anderson, Robert M. *Vision of the Disinherited: The Making of American Pentecostalism*. 1979. Reprint with a new preface by Robert Anderson. Peabody, MA: Hendrickson Publishers, Inc., 1992.

Asante, Molefi Kete. *Afrocentricity: The Theory of Social Change*. Buffalo, NY: Amulefi, 1980.

Avi-Ram, Amitai F. "The Unreadable Black Body: 'Conventional' Poetic Form in the Harlem Renaissance." *Genders* 7 (Spring 1980): 32–46.

Baker, Houston A. Jr. *Blues, Ideology, and Afro-American Literature: A Vernacular Theory*. Chicago: University of Chicago Press, 1984.

———. *Modernism and the Harlem Renaissance*. Chicago: University of Chicago Press, 1987.

Baldwin, James. *The Amen Corner* [1968]. London: Penguin, 1991.

———. *Another Country* [1962]. London: Penguin, 1963.

———. "As Much Truth as One Can Bear." *New York Times Book Review* (January 14, 1962): 1, 38. Reprinted in *The Cross of Redemption*, 28–34.

———. "Battle Hymn." Review of *Mother*, by Maxim Gorki. the *New Leader* 30, no. 29 (November 29, 1947): 10. Reprinted in *The Cross of Redemption*, 242–44.

———. *Blues for Mister Charlie* [1965]. New York: Vintage Books, 1992.

———. "Bright Word Darkened." Review of *Novels and Stories*, by Robert Louis Stevenson and *Robert Louis Stevenson* by David Daiches. the *New Leader* 30 (January 24, 1948): 11. Reprinted in *The Cross of Redemption*, 253–56.

Baldwin, James. "Change within a Channel." Review of *Flood Crest*, by Hodding Carter. the *New Leader* 31 (April 24, 1948): 11. Reprinted in *The Cross of Redemption*, 257–58.

———. *Collected Essays*, edited by Toni Morrison. New York: The Library of America, 1998.

———. *The Cross of Redemption: Uncollected Writings*, edited and introd. Randall Kenan. New York: Pantheon, 2010.

———. "Dead Hand of Caldwell." Review of *The Sure Hand of God*, by Erskine Caldwell. the *New Leader* 30 (December 6, 1947): 10. Reprinted in *The Cross of Redemption*, 248–49.

———. "The Death of the Prophet." *Commentary* 9 (March 1950): 257–61. Reprinted in *The Cross of Redemption*, 293–300.

———. "Everybody's Protest Novel." *Zero* 1 (Spring 1949): 54–58, and *Partisan Review* 16 (June 1949): 578–85. Reprinted in *The Price of the Ticket*, 27–33 and *Collected Essays*, 11–18.

———. *The Evidence of Things Not Seen*. 1985. Reprint, with a foreword by Derrick Bell and Dewart Bell. New York: Henry Holt and Company, 1995.

———. *The Fire Next Time* [1963]. London, Penguin, 1964.

———. "From Dreams of Love to Dreams of Terror." *Natural Enemies? Youth and the Clash of Generations*, edited by Alexander Klein, 274–79. Philadelphia: Lippincott, 1969.

———. *Giovanni's Room* [1956]. London: Penguin, 1990.

———. *Go Tell It on the Mountain* [1953]. London: Penguin, 1991.

———. "The Harlem Ghetto." *Commentary* 4 (February 1948): 165–70. Reprinted in *The Price of the Ticket*, 1–11.

———. "History as Nightmare." Review of *Lonely Crusade*, by Chester Himes. the *New Leader* 30, no. 25 (October 25, 1947): 11, 15. Reprinted in *Collected Essays*, 579–81.

———. *How Can We Get Black People to Cool It?* An Interview with James Baldwin. *Esquire* 50, no. 1 (July 1968): 49–53, 116–17.

———. *If Beale Street Could Talk*. London: Penguin, 1974.

———. "The Image of the Negro." Review of *Albert Sears*, by Millen Brand; *Kingsblood Royal* by Sinclair Lewis; *The Path of Thunder* by Peter Abrahams; *God Is for White Folks* by Will Thomas; *Quality* by Cid Ricketts Sumner. *Commentary* 5, no. 4 (April 1948): 378–80. Reprinted in *Collected Essays*, 582–87.

———. *Jimmy's Blues: Selected Poems*. London: Michael Joseph, 1983.

———. *Just Above My Head* [1979]. London: Penguin, 1994.

———. "Literary Grab-bag." Review of *The Portable Russian Reader*, ed., trans., and introd. Bernard Gullber Guerney. the *New Leader* 31 (February 28, 1948): 11. Reprinted in *The Cross of Redemption*, 261–63.

———. "Lockridge: 'The American Myth.'" Review of *Raintree County*, by Ross Lockridge Jr. the *New Leader* 31 (April 10, 1948): 10, 14. Reprinted in *The Price of the Ticket*, 13–18 and *Collected Essays*, 588–93.

———. "Maxim Gorki as Artist." Review of *Best Short Stories*, by Maxim Gorki. the *Nation* 164 (April 12, 1947): 427–28. Reprinted in *The Cross of Redemption*, 239–41.

———. "Modern Rover Boys." Review of *The Moth*, by James M. Cain. the *New Leader* 31 (August 14, 1948): 12. Reprinted in *The Cross of Redemption*, 259–60.

———. *Nobody Knows My Name: More Notes of a Native Son* [1961]. London: Penguin, 1991.

———. *Notes of a Native Son* [1955]. London: Penguin, 1991.

———. *One Day When I Was Lost: A Scenario Based on the Life of Malcolm X* [1972]. New York: Dell, 1992.

———. "An Open Letter to My Sister, Miss Angela Davis." *New York Review of Books* (January 7, 1971). http://www.nybooks.com/articles/10695. Reprinted in *The Cross of Redemption*, 206–11.

———. "Present and Future." Review of *The Person and the Common Good*, by Jacques Maritain. the *New Leader* 31 (March 13, 1948): 11. Reprinted in *The Cross of Redemption*, 264–66.

———. "Preservation of Innocence." *Zero* 2 (Summer 1949): 14–22. Reprinted in *Collected Essays*, 594–600.

———. *The Price of the Ticket: Collected Nonfiction, 1948–1985*. New York: St. Martin's/ Marek, 1985.

———. "Smaller Than Life." Review of *There Once Was a Slave: The Heroic Story of Frederick Douglass*, by Shirley Graham. the *Nation* 165, no. 3 (July 19, 1947): 78–79. Reprinted in *Collected Essays*, 577–78.

———. *Tell Me How Long the Train's Been Gone* [1968]. London: Penguin, 1994.

———. "To Crush a Serpent." *Playboy* 34 (June 1987): 66–70. Reprinted in *The Cross of Redemption*, 158–65.

———. "Too Late, Too Late." Review of *The Negro Newspaper*, by Vishnu V. Oak; *Jim Crow America* by Earl Conrad; *The High Cost of Prejudice* by Bucklin Moon; *The Protestant Church and the Negro* by Frank S. Loescher; *Color and Conscience* by Buell G. Gallagher; *From Slavery to Freedom* by John Hope Franklin; *The Negro in America* by Arnold Rose. *Commentary* 7 (January 1949): 96–99. Reprinted in *The Cross of Redemption*, 267–72.

———. "The Uses of the Blues." *Playboy*, no. 11 (January 1964): 131–32, 240–41. Reprinted in *The Cross of Redemption*, 57–66.

———. "When the War Hit Brownsville." Review of *The Amboy Dukes*, by Irving Shulman. the *New Leader* 30 (May 17, 1947): 12. Reprinted in *The Cross of Redemption*, 245–47.

———. "Without Grisly Gaiety." Review of *The Sling and the Arrow*, by Stuart Engstrand. the *New Leader* 30, no. 20 (September 1947): 12. Reprinted in *The Cross of Redemption*, 250–52.

———, Romare Bearden, et al. *Perspectives: Angles on African Art*. Interviewed by Michael John Weber. Introduction by Susan Vogel. New York: Center for African Art, 1987.

———, and Nikki Giovanni. *A Dialogue*. Foreword by Ida Lewis. Afterword by Orde Coombs. London: Michael Joseph, 1975.

———, and Shlomo Katz. "Of Angela Davis and 'The Jewish Housewife Headed for Dachau': An Exchange." *Midstream* 17, no. 6 (June/July 1971): 3–10.

———. and Audre Lorde, "Revolutionary Hope: A Conversation between James Baldwin and Audre Lorde." *Essence* 15 (December 1984): 72–74, 129–33.

———, and Margaret Mead. *A Rap on Race*. New York: Dell, 1971.

Balfour, Lawrie. *The Evidence of Things Not Said: James Baldwin and the Promise of American Democracy*. Ithaca: Cornell University Press, 2001.

Baraka, Amiri [LeRoi Jones]. *Eulogies*. New York: Marsilio Publishers, 1996.

———. *Home: Social Essays*. 1966. Reprint, with a preface by LeRoi Jones. Hopewell, NJ: Ecco Press, 1998.

Barksdale, Richard K. "Temple of the Fire Baptized." In *Critical Essays on James Baldwin*, edited by Fred L. Standley and Nancy V. Burt, 145–46. Boston: G. K. Hall, 1988.

Barry, Joseph A. "Americans in Paris." *New York Times* (March 27, 1949): BR5.

Bartley, Numan V. *The Rise of Massive Resistance: Race and Politics in the South during the 1950s.* Baton Rouge: Louisiana State University Press, 1969.

Bassard, Katherine Clay. *Spiritual Interrogations: Culture, Gender, and Community in Early African American Women's Writing.* Princeton, NJ: Princeton University Press, 1999.

Beam, Joseph. "James Baldwin: Not a Bad Legacy, Brother." In *Brother to Brother: New Writings by Black Gay Men*, edited by Essex Hemphill, 184–86. Boston: Alyson Publications, Inc., 1991.

Beam, Joseph, ed. *In the Life: A Gay Black Anthology.* Boston: Alyson Publications, 1986.

Bell, Kevin. "Assuming the Position: Fugitivity and Futurity in the Work of Chester Himes." In *Paris, Capital of the Black Atlantic: Literature, Modernity, and Diaspora*, edited by Jeremy Braddock and Jonathan P. Eburne, 149–74. Baltimore, MD: Johns Hopkins University Press, 2013.

Benshoff, Harry M. *Monsters in the Closet: Homosexuality and the Horror Film.* New York and Manchester: Manchester University Press, 1997.

Bergman, David. *Gaiety Transfigured: Gay Self-Representation in American Literature.* Madison: University of Wisconsin Press, 1991.

"Black Power: Statement by National Committee of Negro Churchmen." *New York Times* (July 31 1966): E5.

Blackstock, Nelson. *COINTELPRO: The FBI's Secret War on Political Freedom.* Introd. Noam Chomsky. 1975. Reprint, New York: Pathfinder, 1988.

Bloom, Alexander. *Prodigal Sons: The New York Intellectuals and Their World.* New York and Oxford: Oxford University Press, 1986.

Bloom, Harold, ed. *James Baldwin: Modern Critical Views.* New York and Philadelphia: Chelsea House Publishers, 1986.

Bobia, Rosa. *The Critical Reception of James Baldwin in France.* New York and Washington: Peter Lang, 1997.

Bondy, François. "James Baldwin, as Interviewed by François Bondy." *Transition* 0, no. 12 (January–February 1964): 12–19.

Bone, Robert. *The Negro Novel in America.* 1958. Reprint and rev. ed., New Haven, CT: Yale University Press, 1965.

Borstelmann, Thomas. *The Cold War and the Color Line: American Race Relations in the Global Arena.* Cambridge, MA: Harvard University Press, 2001.

Boyd, Herb. *Baldwin's Harlem: A Biography of James Baldwin.* New York: Atria Books, 2008.

Brooks, Joanna. *American Lazarus: Religion and the Rise of African-American and Native American Literatures.* New York and Oxford: Oxford University Press, 2003.

———. "From Edwards to Baldwin: Heterodoxy, Discontinuity, and New Narratives of American Religious-Literary History." *American Literary History* 22, no. 2 (2010): 439–53.

Brown, Joseph A. "'I, John Saw the Holy Number': Apocalyptic Visions in *Go Tell It on the Mountain* and *Native Son.*" *Religion and Literature* 27 (1995): 53–74.

Brown, Sterling A., Arthur P. Davis, and Ulysses Lee, eds. *The Negro Caravan: Writings by American Negroes.* Introd. Julius Lester [1941]. New York: Arno Press and the *New York Times*, 1970.

Broyard, Anatole. "A Portrait of the Hipster." *Partisan Review* 15 (June 1948): 721–27.

Butler, Judith. *Precarious Life: The Powers of Mourning and Violence*. New York: Verso, 2004.

Caldwell, Ben "Prayer Meeting: Or, the First Militant Minister." In *The Black Aesthetic*, edited by Addison Gayle Jr., 588–94. New York: Doubleday and Company, 1971.

Campbell, James. *Exiled in Paris: Richard Wright, James Baldwin, Samuel Beckett, and Others on the Left Bank*. New York: Scribner, 1995.

———. *Syncopations: Beats, New Yorkers, and Writers in the Dark*. Berkeley: University of California Press, 2008.

———. *Talking at the Gates: A Life of James Baldwin*. London and Boston: Faber and Faber, 1991.

Cantor, Milton. *Challenge! YPSL*. Vols. 1–4, 1943–46. Introd. to the Greenwood reprint. Westport, CT: Greenwood Press, 1970.

Carter, Donald Martin. *Navigating the African Diaspora: The Anthropology of Invisibility*. Minneapolis: University of Minnesota Press, 2010.

Cassidy, T. E. "The Long Struggle." *Commonweal* 58 (May 22, 1953): 186.

Cederstrom, Lorelei, "Love, Race and Sex in the Novels of James Baldwin." *Mosaic* 17, no. 2 (Spring 1984): 175–88.

Champion, Ernest A. *Mr. Baldwin, I Presume: James Baldwin-Chinua Achebe: A Meeting of Minds*. Foreword by David Leeming. New York: University Press of America, 1995.

Chapman, Rowena, and Jonathan Rutherford, eds. *Male Order: Unwrapping Masculinity*. 1988. Reprint, London: Lawrence & Wishart, 1996.

Chauncey, George. *Gay New York: The Making of the Gay Underworld, 1890–1940*. London: Flamingo, 1995.

Churchill, Ward, and Jim Vander Wall. *The COINTELPRO Papers: Documents from the FBI's Secret Wars against Dissent in the United States*. 1990. Reprint, Cambridge, MA: South End Press, 2002.

Clark, Kenneth B. "Candor about Negro-Jewish Relations: A Social Scientist Charts a Complex Social Problem." *Commentary* 1, no. 4 (1946): 8–14.

Clarke, Cheryl. "The Failure to Transform: Homophobia in the Black Community." In *Home Girls: A Black Feminist Anthology*, edited by Barbara Smith, 190–201. 1983. Reprint, New Brunswick, NJ: Rutgers University Press, 2000.

Cleaver, Eldridge. *Post-Prison Writings and Speeches*, edited by Robert Scheer. London: Panther Books, 1971.

———. *Soul on Ice*. Introd. Maxwell Geismar. New York and Toronto: Ramparts, 1968.

Cobb, Michael. *God Hates Fags: The Rhetorics of Religious Violence*. New York: New York University Press, 2006.

Cohen, William A. "Liberalism, Libido, Liberation: Baldwin's *Another Country*." In *The Queer Sixties*, edited by Patricia Juliana Smith, 201–22. New York: Routledge, 1999.

Coleman, James. *Faithful Vision: Treatments of the Sacred, Spiritual, and Supernatural in Twentieth-Century African American Fiction*. Baton Rouge: Louisiana State University Press, 2009.

Cone, James. *Black Theology and Black Power*. New York: Seabury Press, 1970.

———. *A Black Theology of Liberation*. Philadelphia and New York: J. B. Lippincott Company, 1970.

Conger, Leslie. "Jimmy on East 15th Street." *African American Review* 29, no. 4 (1995): 557–66.

Cooper, Anthony, ed. *The Black Experience, 1865–1978*. Dartford: Greenwich University Press, 1995.

Corber, Robert. "Everybody Knew His Name: Reassessing James Baldwin." *College Literature* 42, no. 1 (2001): 166–75.

———. *Homosexuality in Cold War America: Resistance and the Crisis of Masculinity.* Durham: Duke University Press, 1997.

———. *In the Name of National Security: Hitchcock, Homophobia, and the Political Construction of Gender in Postwar America*. Durham: Duke University Press, 1993.

Corey, Donald Webster. *The Homosexual in America: A Subjective Approach*. New York: Greenberg, 1951.

Crawford, Margo Natalie. "The Reclamation of the Homoerotic as Spiritual in *Go Tell It on the Mountain*." In *James Baldwin's* Go Tell It on the Mountain: *Historical and Critical Essays*, edited by Carol E. Henderson, 75–86. New York: Peter Lang, 2006.

Crouch, Stanley. *Notes of a Hanging Judge: Essays and Reviews, 1979–1989*. New York and Oxford: Oxford University Press, 1990.

Cruse, Harold. *The Crisis of the Negro Intellectual: A Historical Analysis of the Failure of Black Leadership*. 1967. Reprint, with a foreword by Bazel E. Allen and Ernest J. Wilson III. New York: Quill, 1984.

Cullen, Countee. *The Black Christ and Other Poems*. New York: Harper and Brothers, 1929.

———. *Color*. New York: Harper and Brothers, 1925.

Davenport, Guy. "If These Wings Should Fail Me Lord." Review of *Tell Me How Long the Train's Been Gone*, by James Baldwin. *National Review* 20 (July 16 1968): 701–2.

Davis, Angela. *An Autobiography*. 1974. Reprint, with a new introd. Angela Davis. London: The Women's Press, 1988.

Davis, James F. *Who Is Black? One Nation's Definition*. University Park: Pennsylvania State University Press, 1991.

Davis, John A., ed. *Africa Seen by American Negroes: Africa from the Point of View of Negro Scholars*. Preface by Alioune Diop. Paris: Présence Africaine, 1958.

DeGout, Yasmin. "'Masculinity' and (Im)maturity: 'The Man Child' and Other Stories in Baldwin's Gender Studies Enterprise." In *Re-Viewing James Baldwin: Things Not Seen*, edited by D. Quentin Miller. Foreword by David Leeming, 128–53. Philadelphia: Temple University Press, 2000.

Delany, Samuel R., and Joseph Beam. "Samuel Delany: The Possibility of Possibilities." In *In the Life: A Gay Black Anthology*, edited by Joseph Beam, 185–208. Boston: Alyson Publications, 1986.

de Romanet, Jerome. "Revisiting *Madeleine* and 'The Outing': James Baldwin's Revision of Gide's Sexual Politics." *Melus* 22, no. 1 (Spring 1997): 3–14.

D'Emilio, John. *Sexual Politics, Sexual Communities: The Making of a Homosexual Minority in the United States, 1940–1970*. Chicago: University of Chicago Press, 1983.

D'Emilio, John, and Estelle B. Freedman. *Intimate Matters: A History of Sexuality in America*. New York and Cambridge: Harper & Row, 1988.

Dickstein, Morris. *Gates of Eden: American Culture in the Sixties*. New York: Basic Books, 1977.

———, ed. *Critical Insights: James Baldwin*. Pasadena and Hackensack: Salem Press, 2011.

Dixon, Morris. *Ride Out of the Wilderness: Geography and Identity in Afro-American Literature*. Urbana and Chicago: University of Illinois Press, 1987.

Dollimore, Jonathan. *Sex, Literature and Censorship.* Cambridge: Polity, 2001.

———. *Sexual Dissidence: Augustine to Wilde, Freud to Foucault.* Oxford: Clarendon Press, 1991.

Doss, Erika. "Imaging the Panthers: Representing Black Power and Masculinity, 1960s–1990s." *Prospects* 23 (1998): 483–516.

Drake, St. Clair. "Hide My Face? On Pan-Africanism and Negritude." In *Soon, One Morning: New Writings by American Negroes, 1940–62,* edited by Herbert Hill, 78–105. New York: Alfred A. Knopf, 1966.

Dudziak, Mary. *Cold War and Civil Rights: Race and the Image of American Democracy.* Princeton: Princeton University Press, 2000.

Dunning, Stephanie K. *Queer in Black and White: Interraciality, Same Sex Desire, and Contemporary African American Culture.* Bloomington: Indiana University Press, 2009.

Dyson, Michael Eric. *Race Rules: Navigating the Color Line.* Reading, MA: Addison-Wesley, 1996.

Eckman, Fern Marja. *The Furious Passage of James Baldwin.* New York: M. Evans & Co, 1966.

Edelman, Lee. *Homographies: Essays in Gay Literary and Cultural Theory.* New York: Routledge, 1994.

Edwards, Brent Hayes. *The Practice of Diaspora: Literature, Translation, and the Rise of Black Internationalism.* Cambridge, MA: Harvard University Press, 2003.

Engelhardt, Tom. *The End of Victory Culture: Cold War America and the Disillusioning of a Generation.* Amherst: University of Massachusetts Press, 1995.

Epstein, William H. "Counter-Intelligence: Cold War Criticism and Eighteenth-Century Studies." *English Literary History* 57, no. 1 (1990): 63–99.

Eschen, Penny M. Von. *Race Against Empire: Black Americans and Anticolonialism, 1937–1957.* Ithaca: Cornell University Press, 1997.

Ezenwa-Ohaeto. "Notions and Nuances: Africa in the Works of James Baldwin." In *Of Dreams Deferred, Dead or Alive: African Perspectives on African-American Writers,* edited by Femi Ojo-Ade, 107–14. Westport, CT: Greenwood Press, 1996.

Fanon, Frantz. *Black Skins, White Masks.* Trans. Charles Lam Markmann (1952). Foreword by Homi K. Bhabha. London: Pluto Press, 1986.

Ferguson, Roderick A. *Aberrations in Black: Toward a Queer of Color Critique.* London and Minneapolis: University of Minnesota Press, 2004.

———. "The Parvenu Baldwin and the Other Side of Redemption: Modernity, Race, Sexuality, and the Cold War." In *James Baldwin Now,* edited by Dwight M. McBride, 233–61. New York: New York University Press, 1999.

Fichte, Hubert. "Hubert Fichte Interviews Jean Genet." In *Gay Sunshine Interviews.* Vol. 1, edited by Winston Leyland, 67–94. San Francisco: Gay Sunshine Press, 1978.

Fiedler, Leslie. *The Collected Essays of Leslie Fiedler.* Vol. 1. New York: Stein and Day, 1971.

———. "A Homosexual Dilemma." the *New Leader* 39, no. 10 (1956): 17.

———. *The Return of the Vanishing American.* London: Jonathan Cape, 1968.

Field, Douglas. "Pentecostalism and All That Jazz: Tracing James Baldwin's Religion." *Literature and Theology* 22, no. 4 (December 2008): 436–57.

———, ed. *A Historical Guide to James Baldwin.* New York and Oxford: Oxford University Press, 2009.

Firebaugh, Joseph J. "The Vocabulary of 'Time' Magazine." *American Speech* 15, no. 3 (October 1940): 232–42.

Fortuny, Kim. *American Writers in Istanbul: Melville, Twain, Hemingway, Dos Passos, Bowles, Algren, Baldwin, and Settle.* Foreword by Roger Allen. Syracuse, NY: Syracuse University Press, 2009.

Foster, Guy Mark. "African American Literature and Queer Studies: The Conundrum of James Baldwin." In *Companion to African American Literature*, edited by Gene A. Jarett, 393–408. Hoboken, NJ: Wiley-Blackwell, 2010.

Francis, Consuela. *The Critical Reception of James Baldwin, 1963–2010.* Rochester, NY: Camden House, 2014.

Frazier, E. Franklin. *The Negro Church in America.* Liverpool: Liverpool University Press, 1964.

Fremont-Smith, Eliot. "Another Track." Review of *Tell Me How Long the Train's Been Gone*, by James Baldwin. *New York Times* (May 31, 1968): 27.

Frese, Pamela R., ed. *Celebrations of Identity: Multiple Voices in American Ritual Performance.* Foreword by Emiko Ohnuki-Tierney. Westport, CT: Bergin & Garvey, 1993.

Freud, Sigmund. *On Metapsychology.* Vol. 11. Trans. James Strachey (1915). London: Penguin, 1984.

Friedman, Murray. *What Went Wrong? The Creation and Collapse of the Black-Jewish Alliance.* New York: Free Press, 1995.

Gaines, Kevin. "Exile and the Private Life: James Baldwin, George Lamming, and the First World Congress of Negro Writers and Artists." In *James Baldwin: American and Beyond*, edited by Cora Kaplan and Bill Schwarz, 173–87. Ann Arbor: University of Michigan Press, 2011.

Gallen, David, ed. *Malcolm X: The FBI File.* Introd. Spike Lee with commentary by Claybourne Carson. New York: Carrol & Graf, 1992.

Garrow, David J. *Bearing the Cross: Martin Luther King, Jr., and the Southern Christian Leadership Conference.* New York: Harper Perennial Modern Classics, 2004.

Gates, Henry Louis Jr. "The Black Man's Burden." In *Fear of a Queer Planet: Queer Politics and Social Theory*, edited by Michael Warner, 230–38. London and Minneapolis: University of Minnesota Press, 1993.

———. "Essay: Cabin Fever." *New York Times* (October 22, 2006). http://www.nytimes.com/2006/10/22/books/review/Gates.t.html.

———. *Thirteen Ways of Looking at a Black Man.* New York: Random House, 1997.

———. "The Welcome Table." *Lure and Loathing: Essays on Race, Identity and the Ambivalence of Assimilation*, edited by and introd. Gerald Early, 144–62. London and New York: Allen Lane, 1993.

Gayle, Addison Jr., ed. *The Black Aesthetic.* New York: Doubleday and Company, 1971.

———. *The Way of the New World: The Black Novel in America.* New York: Anchor Press/Doubleday, 1975.

Genet, Jean. *Here and Now for Bobby Seale.* New York: Committee to Defend the Panthers, 1970.

———. *May Day Speech.* Introd. Allen Ginsberg. San Francisco: City Lights Books, 1970.

———. *Prisoner of Love.* Trans. Barbara Bray. Introd. Edmund White. London: Picador, 1989.

Genette, Gérard. *Palimpsests: Literature in the Second Degree.* Trans. Channa Newman and Claude Doubinsky. Foreword by Gerald Prince. Lincoln: University of Nebraska Press, 1997.

Genter, Robert. *Late Modernism: Art, Culture, and Politics in Cold War America*. Philadelphia: University of Pennsylvania Press, 2010.

Gerstner, David A. *Queer Pollen: White Seduction, Black Male Homosexuality and the Cinematic*. Urbana and Springfield: University of Illinois Press, 2011.

Gibson, Donald. "James Baldwin: The Political Anatomy of Space." In *James Baldwin: A Critical Evaluation*, edited by Therman B. O'Daniel, 3–19. Washington, DC: Howard University Press, 1977.

Giles, James. "Religious Alienation and 'Homosexual Consciousness' in *The City of Night* and *Go Tell It on the Mountain*." *College English* 36 (1974): 369–80.

Gilroy, Paul. *The Black Atlantic: Modernity and Double Consciousness*. Cambridge, MA: Harvard University Press, 1993.

Ginsberg, Allen. *Howl and Other Poems*. 1956. Reprint, San Francisco: City Lights Books, 1996.

Ginsberg, Elaine K., ed. *Passing and the Fictions of Identity*. Durham: Duke University Press, 1996.

Goldstein, Richard. "Go the Way Your Blood Beats: An Interview with James Baldwin." *Village Voice* 26 (June 1984): 13, 14, 16.

Goodman, Paul. "Not Enough of a World to Grow In." Review of *Another Country*, by James Baldwin. *New York Times Book Review* (June 24, 1962): 5.

Gounard, François. *The Racial Problem in the Works of Richard Wright and James Baldwin*. Trans. Joseph L. Rogers. Foreword by Jean F. Béranger. Westport, CT: Greenwood Press, 1992.

Gordon, Brandon. "Physical Sympathy: Hip and Sentimentalism in James Baldwin's *Another Country*." *Modern Fiction Studies* 57, no. 1 (Spring 2011): 75–95.

Greenberg, Clement. "Avant-garde and Kitsch." *Partisan Review* 6, no. 6 (Fall 1939): 34–49.

Hakutani, Yoshinobu, and Toru Kiuchi. "The Critical Reception of James Baldwin in Japan: An Annotated Bibliography." *Black American Literature Forum* 24, no. 4 (Winter 1991): 753–79.

Hall, Stuart. "You a Fat Cow Now." Review of *Tell Me How Long the Train's Been Gone*, by James Baldwin. *New Statesman* (June 28, 1968): 871.

Hardy, Clarence E. *James Baldwin's God: Sex, Hope, and Crisis in Black Holiness Culture*. Knoxville: University of Tennessee Press, 2003.

Harper, Howard M. *Desperate Faith: A Study of Bellow, Salinger, Mailer, Baldwin, and Updike*. Chapel Hill: University of North Carolina Press, 1967.

Harper, Phillip Brian. "Eloquence and Epitaph: Black Nationalism and the Homophobic Impulse in Responses to the Death of Max Robinson." In *The Lesbian and Gay Studies Reader*, edited by Henry Abelove, Michèle Aina Barale, and David M. Halperin, 159–75. New York: Routledge, 1993.

Harris, Trudier. *Black Women in the Fiction of James Baldwin*. Knoxville: University of Tennessee Press, 1985.

———. "The Eye as Weapon in *If Beale Street Could Talk*." In *Critical Essays on James Baldwin*, edited by Fred L. Standley and Nancy V. Burt, 204–16. Boston: G. K. Hall, 1988.

———, ed. *New Essays on* Go Tell It on the Mountain. Cambridge and New York: Cambridge University Press, 1996.

Hempton, David. *Evangelical Disenchantment: Nine Portraits of Faith and Doubt*. New Haven, CT: Yale University Press, 2008.

Hentoff, Nat, ed., *Black Anti-Semitism and Jewish Racism*. New York: Richard W. Baron, 1969.

Hernton, Calvin. "Dynamite Growing Out of Their Skulls." *In Black Fire: An Anthology of Afro-American Writing*, edited by LeRoi Jones and Larry Neal, 78–104. New York: William Morrow & Co., 1968.

———. *White Papers for White Americans*. New York: Doubleday, 1966.

Hicks, Granville. "From Harlem with Hatred." Review of *Tell Me How Long the Train's Been Gone*, by James Baldwin. *Saturday Review* 51, no. 1 (June 1968): 23–24.

———. "Tormented Triangle." Review of *Giovanni's Room*, by James Baldwin. *New York Times Book Review* (October 14, 1956): 5.

Hill, Herbert, ed. *Soon, One Morning: New Writings by American Negroes, 1940–62*. New York: Alfred A. Knopf, 1966.

Holcomb, Gary Edward. *Code Name Sasha: Queer Black Marxism and the Harlem Renaissance*. Gainesville: University Press of Florida, 2007.

Holmes, Carolyn L. "Reassessing African American Literature through an Afrocentric Paradigm: Zora Neale. Hurston and James Baldwin." In *Language and Literature in the African American Imagination*, edited by Carol Aisha Blackshire-Belay, 37–51. Westport, CT: Greenwood Press, 1992.

hooks, bell. "Homophobia in Black Communities." In *The Greatest Taboo: Homosexuality in Black Communities*, edited by Delory Constantine-Simms, 67–73. Los Angeles and New York: Alyson Books, 2001.

———. *Salvation: Black People and Love*. New York: Perennial, 2001.

———. *Yearning: Race, Gender and Cultural Politics*. Boston: South End Press, 1990.

Hopkins, Dwight N. *Introducing a Black Theology of Liberation*. New York: Orbis Books, 1999.

Howe, Irving. "From Harlem to Paris." Review of *Notes of a Native Son*, by James Baldwin. *New York Times* (February 26, 1956): 26.

———. "James Baldwin: At Ease in Apocalypse." *Harper's* 237 (September 1968): 95, 96, 100.

———. *Selected Writings, 1950–1990*. San Diego: Harcourt Brace Jovanovich Publishers, 1990.

Howlett, Jacques. "*Présence Africaine*, 1947–1958," *Journal of Negro History* 43, no. 2 (April 1958): 140–50.

Hughes, Langston. *Tambourines to Glory, Five Plays by Langston Hughes*, edited and introd. by Webster Smalley. Bloomington: Indiana University Press, 1968.

Hurston, Zora Neale. *Jonah's Gourd Vine*. 1934. Reprint, with afterword by Holly Eley. London: Virago, 1993.

———. *The Sanctified Church*. Foreword by Toni Cade Bambara. New York: Marlowe & Co., 1981.

Huyssen, Andreas. *After the Great Divide: Modernism, Mass Culture, Postmodernism*. Bloomington: Indiana University Press, 1986.

Hyman, Stanley Edgar. "No Country for Young Men." the *New Leader* 45 (June 25, 1962): 22–23.

Ikard, David. *Breaking the Silence: Toward a Black Male Feminist Criticism*. Baton Rouge: Louisiana State University Press, 2007.

Isaacs, Harold. "Five Writers and Their Ancestors Part 2." *Phylon* 21, no. 4 (1960): 317–36.

Jackson, George. *Soledad Brother: The Prison Letters of George Jackson*. Foreword by Jonathan Jackson Jr. Introd. Jean Genet. Chicago: Lawrence Hill Books, 1994.

Jackson, Lawrence P. *The Indignant Generation: A Narrative History of African American Writers and Critics, 1934–1960.* Princeton: Princeton University Press, 2010.

Jackson, Rosemary. *Fantasy: The Literature of Subversion.* London and New York: Routledge, 1995.

Johnson, E. Patrick, and Mae Henderson, eds. *Black Queer Studies: A Critical Anthology.* Durham: Duke University Press, 2005.

Johnson, James Weldon. *The Autobiography of an Ex-Colored Man* [1912]. New York: Dover Publications, 1995.

Johnson-Roullier, Cyraina. "(An)Other Modernism: James Baldwin, *Giovanni's Room,* and the Rhetoric of Flight." *Modern Fiction Studies* 45, no. 4 (Winter 1999): 932–56.

Jones William R. *Is God a White Racist?: A Preamble to Black Theology.* 1973. Reprint, Boston: Beacon Press, 1998.

Jongh, James de. *Vicious Modernism: Black Harlem and the Literary Imagination.* Cambridge: Cambridge University Press, 1990.

Judson, Barbara, and Andrew Shin. "Beneath the Black Aesthetic: James Baldwin's Primer of Black American Masculinity." *African American Review* 32, no. 2 (Summer 1998): 247–61.

Jules-Rosetta, Benetta. *Black Paris: The African Writers' Landscape.* Foreword by Simon Njami. Urbana and Chicago: University of Illinois Press, 1998.

Jumonville, Neil, ed. *The New York Intellectuals Reader.* New York: Routledge, 2007.

Kaiser, Ernest, ed. *A Freedomways Reader.* Introd. James Baldwin. New York: International Publishers, 1977.

Kaplan, Cora, and Bill Schwarz, eds. *James Baldwin: America and Beyond.* Ann Arbor: University of Michigan Press, 2011.

Kapp, Isa. "In Perspective and Anger." the *New Leader* 51, no. 12 (June 3, 1968): 18–20.

Katz, Shlomo. "An Open Letter to James Baldwin." *Midstream* 17, no. 4 (April 1971): 3–5.

Kenan, Randall. *The Fire This Time.* New York: Melville House Books, 2007.

King, Lovalerie, and Lynn Orilla Scott. *James Baldwin and Toni Morrison: Comparative Critical and Theoretical Essays.* New York: Palgrave Macmillan, 2006.

King, Martin Luther Jr. *Strength to Love.* 1963. Reprint, London: Fontana Books, 1969.

Kinnamon, Keneth, ed. *James Baldwin: A Collection of Critical Essays.* Englewood Cliffs, NJ: Prentice-Hall, 1974.

Kinsey, Alfred. *Sexual Behavior in the Human Male.* Philadelphia: W. B. Saunders Company, 1948.

Köllhofer, Jacob, ed. *James Baldwin: His Place in Literary History and His Reception in Europe.* Frankfurt am Main and Bern: Peter Lang, 1991.

Larsen, Nella. *Quicksand and Passing.* 1928. Reprint, London: Serpent's Tail, 1989.

Lash, John S. "James Baldwin Beside Himself: A Study in Modern Phallicism," *James Baldwin: A Critical Evaluation,* edited by Therman O'Daniel, 47–55. 1977. Reprint, Washington, DC: Howard University Press, 1981.

———. "On Negro Literature." *Phylon* 6, no. 3 (1945): 240–47.

———. "What Is 'Negro Literature?'" *College English* 1, no. 9 (1947): 37–42.

Lee, A. Robert, ed. *Black Fiction: New Studies in the Afro-American Novel since 1945.* New York: Barnes and Noble Books, 1980.

———. *Multicultural American Literature: Comparative Black, Latino/a and Asian American Fictions.* Edinburgh: Edinburgh University Press, 2003.

Leeming, David. *James Baldwin: A Biography.* New York: Alfred A. Knopf, 1994.

Leyland, Winston, ed. *Gay Sunshine Interviews*. Vol. 1. San Francisco: Gay Sunshine Press, 1978.

Lively, Adam. *Masks: Blackness, Race and the Imagination*. London: Vintage, 1999.

Llorens, David. "Books Noted." Review of *Tell Me How Long the Train's Been Gone*, by James Baldwin. *Negro Digest* (August 1968): 51–52.

Locke, Alain, ed. *The New Negro: Voices of the Harlem Renaissance*. Introd. Arnold Rampersad. New York: Touchstone, 1997.

Lockett, Reginald. "Die Black Pervert." In *Black Fire: An Anthology of Afro-American Writing*, edited by LeRoi Jones and Larry Neal, 364. New York: William Morrow & Co., 1968.

Logan, Rayford W. "The American Negro's View of Africa." In *Africa Seen by American Negroes: Africa from the Point of View of Negro Scholars*, edited and introd. by John A. Davis, preface by Alioune Diop, 217–27. Paris: Présence Africaine, 1958.

Lowenstein, Andrea. "James Baldwin and His Critics." *Gay Community News* (February 9, 1980): 10, 11, 17.

Luczak, Ewa Barbara. *How Their Living Outside America Affected Five African American Authors: Toward a Theory of Expatriate Literature*. Preface by Richard Yarborough. Lewiston: Edwin Mellen Press, 2010.

Lynch, Michael F. "Beyond Guilt and Innocence: Redemptive Suffering in Baldwin's *Another Country*." *Obsidian* 2, no. 1–2 (Spring–Summer 1992): 1–18.

———. "The Everlasting Father: Mythic Quest and Rebellion in Baldwin's *Go Tell It on the Mountain*." *CLA Journal* 37, no. 2 (December 1993): 156–75.

———. "A Glimpse of the Hidden God: Dialectical Visions in Baldwin's *Go Tell It on the Mountain*." In *New Essays on* Go Tell It on the Mountain, edited by Trudier Harris, 29–57. Cambridge and New York: Cambridge University Press, 1996.

———. "*Just Above My Head*: James Baldwin's Quest for Belief." *Literature and Theology* 11, no. 3 (September 1997): 284–98.

Lyne, Bill. "God's Black Revolutionary Mouth: James Baldwin's Black Radicalism." *Science and Society* 74 (2010): 12–36.

Macebuh, Stanley. *James Baldwin: A Critical Study*. New York: Third Press, 1973.

Macey, David. *Frantz Fanon: A Biography*. New York: Picador, 2000.

Marable, Manning. *Malcolm X: A Life of Reinvention*. New York: Allen Lane, 2011.

Marable, Manning, and Vanessa Agard-Jones, eds. *Transnational Blackness: Navigating the Global Color Line*. New York: Palgrave Macmillan, 2008.

Margolies, Edward. "The Negro Church: James Baldwin and the Christian Vision." In *James Baldwin*, edited by Harold Bloom, 59–76. New York: Chelsea House, 1986.

Maxwell, William B. "African-American Modernism and State Surveillance." In *A Companion to African American Literature*, edited by Gene Jarrett, 254–68. Oxford: Blackwell, 2010.

———. "Total Literary Awareness: Why Cold War Hooverism Pre-Read Afro-Modernity Writing." In *American Literature and Culture in an Age of Cold War: A Critical Reassessment*, edited by Steven Belletto and Daniel Grausam, 17–36. Iowa City: University of Iowa Press, 2012.

May, Elaine Tyler. *Homeward Bound: American Families in the Cold War Era*. New York: Basic Books, 1988.

May, Vivian M. "Ambivalent Narratives, Fragmented Selves: Performative Identities and the Mutability of Roles in James Baldwin's *Go Tell It on the Mountain*." In *New Essays on* Go Tell It on the Mountain, edited by Trudier Harris, 97–126. Cambridge and New York: Cambridge University Press, 1996.

M'Baye, Babacar. "African Retentions in *Go Tell It on the Mountain.*" In *James Baldwin's* Go Tell It on the Mountain: *Historical and Critical Essays*, edited by Carol E. Henderson, 41–54. New York: Peter Lang, 2006.

McBride, Dwight A. "Can the Queen Speak? Racial Essentialism, Sexuality and the Problem of Authority." *Callaloo* 21, no. 2 (Spring 1998): 363–79.

———, ed. *James Baldwin Now.* New York: New York University Press, 1999.

McCarthy, Mary. "Baldwin." In *James Baldwin: The Legacy*, edited by Quincy Troupe, 47–50. New York: Simon & Schuster, 1989.

Macdonald, Dwight. "The Soviet Cinema, 1930-1938." *Partisan Review* 5, no. 2 (July 1938): 37–50.

McKay, Claude. *Banjo.* 1930. Reprint, London: Black Classics, 2000.

Medovoi, Leerom. "Reading the Blackboard: Youth, Masculinity, and Racial Cross-Identification." In *Race and the Subject of Masculinities*, edited by Harry Stecopoulos and Michael Uebel, 138–69. Durham: Duke University Press, 1997.

Mengay, Donald H. "The Failed Copy: *Giovanni's Room* and the (Re)Contextualisation of Difference." *Genders* 17 (1993): 59–70.

Mercer, Kobena, and Isaac Julien. "Race, Sexual Politics and Black Masculinity: A Dossier." In *Male Order: Unwrapping Masculinity*, edited by Rowena Chapman and Jonathan Rutherford, 97–164. 1988. Reprint, London: Lawrence & Wishart, 1996.

Meyer, Michael, ed. *Literature and Homosexuality.* Amsterdam: Rodopi, 2000.

Miller, D. Quentin. *A Criminal Power: James Baldwin and the Law.* Columbus: Ohio State University Press, 2012.

Miller, James. "What Does It Mean to Be an American? The Dialectics of Self-Discovery in Baldwin's 'Paris Essays' (1950–1961)." *Journal of American Studies* 42, no. 2 (April 2008): 51–66.

Mitchell, Angelyn, ed. *Within the Circle: An Anthology of African American Literary Criticism from the Harlem Renaissance to the Present.* Durham: Duke University Press, 1994.

Morey, Ann-Janine. *Religion and Sexuality in American Literature.* Cambridge: Cambridge University Press, 1992.

Morgan, Bill, and Nancy J. Peters, eds. *Howl on Trial: The Battle for Free Expression.* San Francisco: City Lights Books, 2006.

Morrison, Toni, ed. *Race-ing Justice, En-gendering Power: Essays on Anita Hill, Clarence Thomas, and the Construction of Social Reality.* New York: Pantheon Books, 1992.

Moss, Carlton. "The Great White Hope." In *A Freedomways Reader*, edited by Ernest Kaiser, foreword by James Baldwin, 50–63. New York: International Publishers, 1977.

Murphy, Geraldine. "Subversive Anti-Stalinism: Race and Sexuality in the Early Essays of James Baldwin." *English Literary History* 63 (1996): 1021–46.

Murray, Albert. *The Omni-Americans: New Perspectives on Black Experience and American Culture.* New York: Outerbridge & Dienstfrey, 1970.

Murray, Albert, and James F. Callahan, eds. *Trading Twelves: The Selected Letters of Ralph Ellison and Albert Murray.* New York: Vintage, 2001.

Murray, Rolland. *Our Living Manhood: Literature, Black Power, and Masculine Ideology.* Philadelphia: University of Pennsylvania Press, 2007.

Muse, Benjamin. *Ten Years of Prelude: The Story of Integration since the Supreme Court's 1954 Decision.* Beaconsfield: Darwen Finlayson, 1964.

Muyumba, Walton. *The Shadow and Act: Black Intellectual Practice, Jazz Improvisation, and Philosophical Pragmatism.* Chicago: University of Chicago Press, 2009.

Myers, Robin. "Socialists Expose Sham Old Party Race Pranks." *Challenge* 2, no. 3 (October 1944): 1, 8.

Nagueyalti, Warren. "The Substance of Things Hoped For: Faith in *Go Tell It on the Mountain* and *Just Above My Head*." *Obsidian* 2, no. 1–2 (Spring–Summer 1992): 19–31.

Nationalism, Colonialism and the United States: One Minute to Twelve. A Forum sponsored by the Liberation Committee for Africa on its First Anniversary Celebration. June 2, 1961. New York: Photo-Offset Press, 1961.

Nelson, Emmanuel. "Critical Deviance: Homophobia and the Reception of James Baldwin's Fiction." *Journal of American Culture* 14 (1991): 91–96.

———. "James Baldwin's Vision of Otherness and Community." *Melus* 10 (Summer 1983): 27–31.

———. "John Rechy, James Baldwin and the American Double Minority Literature." *Journal of American Culture* 6, no. 2 (1983): 70–74.

———. "The Novels of James Baldwin: Struggles of Self-Acceptance." *Journal of American Culture* 8, no. 4 (1985): 11–16.

Noakes, John A. "Racializing Subversion: The FBI and the Depiction of Race in Early Cold War Movies." *Ethnic and Racial Studies* 26, no. 4 (July 2003): 728–49.

Norman, Brian. *The American Protest Essay and National Belonging: Addressing Division.* Albany: SUNY Press, 2007.

Norse, Harold. *Memoirs of a Bastard Angel: A Fifty-Year Literary and Erotic Odyssey.* Preface by James Baldwin. New York: William Morrow & Co., 1989.

Nwankwo, Chimalum. "Richard Wright: A Dubious Legacy." In *Of Dreams Deferred, Dead or Alive: African Perspectives on African-American Writers*, edited by Femi Ojo-Ade, 53–64. Westport, CT: Greenwood Press, 1996.

O'Daniel, Therman B. *James Baldwin: A Critical Evaluation.* Washington, DC: Howard University Press, 1977.

O'Neale, Sondra. "Fathers, Gods, and Religion: Perceptions of Christianity and Ethnic Faith in James Baldwin." In *Critical Essays on James Baldwin*, edited by Fred Standley and Nancy V. Burt, 125–44. Boston: G. K. Hall, 1988.

Ojo-Ade, Femi, ed. *Of Dreams Deferred, Dead or Alive: African Perspectives on African American Writers.* Westport, CT: Greenwood Press, 1996.

Olson, Barbara. "'Come-to-Jesus Stuff,' in James Baldwin's *Go Tell It on the Mountain* and *The Amen Corner*." *African American Review* 31, no. 2 (1997): 295–301.

O'Reilly, Kenneth. *Black Americans: The FBI Files*, edited by David Gallen. New York: Carroll & Graf Publishers, 1994.

———. "Racial Integration: The Battle General Eisenhower Chose Not to Fight." *Journal of Blacks in Higher Education* no. 18 (Winter 1997–98): 110–19.

———. *"Racial Matters": The FBI's Secret File on Black America, 1960–1972.* New York: Free Press, 1989.

Orlansky, Harold. "A Note on Anti-Semitism among Negroes." *Politics* 2 (August 1945): 250–52.

Ové, Horace, Dir. *Baldwin's Nigger.* 1969.

Parish, Richard. "How Jim Crow is Building a Tension That Will Explode in Race Riots." *Challenge* 1, no. 5 (October 1943): 2, 6.

Podhoretz, Norman. "In Defense of a Maltreated Best Seller." *Show* 2, no. 10 (October 1962): 91–92.

Pomerantz, Charlotte, ed. *A Quarter-Century of Un-Americana, 1938–1963: A Tragi-Comical Memorabilia of HUAC.* New York: Marzani & Munsell Publishers, 1963.

Porter, Horace A. *Stealing the Fire: The Art and Protest of James Baldwin.* Middletown, CT: Wesleyan University Press, 1989.

Posnock, Ross. *Color and Culture: Black Writers and the Making of the Modern Intellectual.* Cambridge, MA: Harvard University Press, 1998.

Potash, John. *The FBI War on Tupac Shakur and Black Leaders: US Intelligence's Murderous Targeting of Tupac, MLK, Malcolm, Panthers, Hendrix, Rappers & Linked Ethnic Leftists.* 5th ed. Foreword by Pam Africa with Mumia Abu-Jamal. Afterword by Fred Hampton, Jr. New York: Progressive Left Press, 2010.

Puzo, Mario. "His Cardboard Lovers." Review of *Tell Me How Long the Train's Been Gone,* by James Baldwin. *New York Times Book Review* (June 23, 1968): 5, 34.

Quinn, Laura. "'What Is Going on Here?' Baldwin's *Another Country.*" In *Gay and Lesbian Literature since the War: History and Memory,* edited by Sonya L. Jones, 51–66. London and New York: Harrington Press, 1998.

Rampersad, Arnold. *The Life of Langston Hughes.* Vol. 1. New York: Oxford University Press, 1988.

———. *Ralph Ellison: A Biography.* New York: Alfred A. Knopf, 2007.

Reed, Theresa L. *The Holy Profane: Religion in Black Popular Music.* Lexington: University Press of Kentucky, 2004.

Reid-Pharr, Robert. *Black Gay Man.* New York: New York University Press, 2001.

———. *Once You Go Black: Choice, Desire, and the Black American Intellectual.* New York: New York University Press, 2007.

———. "'Tearing the Goat's Flesh': Homosexuality, Abjection and the Production of a Late Twentieth Century Masculinity." *Studies in the Novel* 28, no. 3 (1996): 372–94.

Riggs, Marlon. "Black Macho Revisited: Reflections of a SNAP! Queen." In *Brother to Brother: New Writings by Black Gay Men,* edited by Essex Hemphill, 253–57. Boston: Alyson Publications, 1991.

Robb, Graham. *Strangers: Homosexual Love in the Nineteenth Century.* London: Picador, 2003.

Robins, Natalie. *Alien Ink: The FBI's War on the Freedom of Expression.* New Brunswick, NJ: Rutgers University Press, 1992.

Robinson, Layhmond. "Robert Kennedy Consults Negroes Here about North," *New York Times* (May 25, 1963): 1, 8.

Rodriguez, Besenia. "'Long Live Third World Unity! Long Live Internationalism': Huey P. Newton's Revolutionary Intercommunalism." In *Transnational Blackness: Navigating the Global Color Line,* edited by Manning Marable and Vanessa Agard-Jones, 149–74. New York: Palgrave Macmillan, 2008.

Rolo, Charles. Review of *Giovanni's Room,* by James Baldwin. *Atlantic Monthly* 198 (December 1956): 98.

Ross, Andrew. *No Respect: Intellectuals and Popular Culture.* New York: Routledge, 1989.

Ross, Marlon B. "Some Glances at the Black Fag: Race, Same-Sex Desire, and Cultural Belonging." In *The Black Studies Reader*, edited by Jacqueline Bobo, Cynthia Hudley, and Claudine Michel, 153–73. New York: Routledge, 2004.

———. "White Fantasies of Desire: Baldwin and the Racial Identities of Sexuality." In *James Baldwin Now*, edited by Dwight A. McBride, 13–55. New York: New York University Press, 1999.

Roth, Philip. "Blues for Mister Charlie." In *Modern Critical Views: James Baldwin*, edited by Harold Bloom, 37–44. New York: Chelsea House, 1986.

Rowden, Terry. "A Play of Abstractions: Race, Sexuality, and Community in James Baldwin's *Another Country*." *The Southern Review* 29 (1993): 41–50.

Said, Edward. "Intellectual Exile: Expatriates and Marginals" [1993]. In *The Edward Said Reader*, edited by Mustafa Bayoumi and Andrew Rubin, 368–81. New York: Vintage, 2000.

Sanders, Cheryl J. *Saints in Exile: The Holiness-Pentecostal Experience in African-American Religion and Culture*. New York and Oxford: Oxford University Press, 1996.

Sarna, Jonathan, ed. *Minority Faiths and the Protestant Mainstream*. Urbana: University of Illinois Press, 1998.

Saunders, Frances Stonor. *Who Paid the Piper? The CIA and the Cultural Cold War*. London: Granta, 2000.

Savran, David. *Communists, Cowboys and Queers: The Politics of Masculinity in the Work of Arthur Miller and Tennessee Williams*. London and Minneapolis: University of Minnesota Press, 1992.

Schlesinger, Arthur M. Jr. *Robert Kennedy and His Times*. New York: Ballantine Books, 1978.

Schreiber, Rebecca M. *Cold War Exiles in Mexico: US Dissidents and the Culture of Critical Resistance*. London and Minneapolis: University of Minnesota Press, 2008.

Scott, Lynn Orilla. *James Baldwin's Later Fiction: Witness to the Journey*. East Lansing: Michigan State University Press, 2002.

Scott, Milton C., ed. *African American Religious History: Documentary Witness*. Durham: Duke University Press, 1999.

Shachtman, Max. *Race and Revolution*, edited and introd. by Christopher Phelps. London and New York: Verso, 2003.

Sheehan, Jonathan. "Enlightenment, Religion, and the Enigma of Secularization: A Review Essay." *American Historical Review* 108, no. 4 (October 2003): 1061–80.

Shockley, Ann Allen. *Say Jesus and Come to Me*. 1982. Reprint, Tallahassee, FL: Naiad Press, 1987.

Shulman, George. *American Prophecy: Race and Redemption in American Political Culture*. Minneapolis: University of Minnesota Press, 2008.

Simawe, Saadi A. "What Is in a Sound? The Metaphysics and Politics of Music in *The Amen Corner*." In *Re-Viewing James Baldwin: Things Not Seen*, edited by D. Quentin Miller, 12–32. Philadelphia: Temple University Press, 2000.

Simmons, Ron. "Some Thoughts on the Challenges Facing Black Intellectuals." In *Brother to Brother: New Writings by Black Gay Men*, edited by Essex Hemphill, 211–28. Boston: Alyson Publications, 1991.

Sivan, Miriam. "Out of and Back to Africa: James Baldwin's *Go Tell It on the Mountain*." *Christianity and Literature* 51, no. 1 (Autumn 2001): 29–41.

Smith, Barbara. "We Must Always Bury Our Dead Twice: A Tribute to James Baldwin." In *The Truth That Never Hurts: Writings on Race, Gender, and Freedom*, 75–80. London and New Brunswick, NJ: Rutgers University Press, 1998.

Smith, Patricia Juliana, ed. *The Queer Sixties*. New York: Routledge, 1999.

Smythe, Mabel M., ed. *The Black American Reference Book*. Englewood Cliffs, NJ: Prentice-Hall, 1976.

Speeches from the Soledad Brothers Rally, Central Hall, Westminster. London: Friends of Soledad, 1974.

Spenser, Jon Michael. "The Ritual of Testifying in the Black Church." In *Celebrations of Identity: Multiple Voices in American Ritual Performance*, edited by Pamela R. Frese, foreword by Emiko Ohnuki-Tierney, 61–73. Westport, CT: Bergin & Garvey, 1993.

Standley, Fred L., and Nancy V. Burt, eds. *Critical Essays on James Baldwin*. Boston: G. K. Hall, 1988.

Standley, Fred L., and Louis H. Pratt, eds. *Conversations with James Baldwin*. Jackson: University of Mississippi Press, 1989.

Staples, Robert. *Black Masculinity: The Black Man's Role in American Society*. San Francisco: Black Scholar, 1982.

Stecopoulos, Harry, and Michael Uebel, eds. *Race and the Subject of Masculinities*. Durham: Duke University Press, 1997.

Stein, Sol, ed. *James Baldwin and Sol Stein: Native Sons*. New York: One World Books, 2004.

Stevens, Hugh. *Henry James and Sexuality*. Cambridge: Cambridge University Press, 1998.

Strong, Augusta. Review of *Another Country*, by James Baldwin. *Freedomways* (Fall 1962): 500–503.

Summers, Claude. *Gay Fictions: Wilde to Stonewall: Studies in a Male Homosexual Literary Tradition*. New York: Continuum, 1990.

Sundquist, Eric J. *Strangers in the Land: Blacks, Jews, Post-Holocaust America*. Cambridge, MA: Harvard University Press, 2005.

Sylvander, Carolyn. *James Baldwin*. New York: Frederick Ungar Publishing, Co., 1980.

Taylor, Douglas. "Three Lean Cats in a Hall of Mirrors: James Baldwin, Norman Mailer and Eldridge Cleaver on Race and Masculinity." *Texas Studies in Literature and Language* 52, no. 1 (Spring 2010): 70–101.

Taylor, Wayne. *Malcolm X: The FBI Files*, by Wayne Taylor (2004). http://wonderwheel.net/work/foia/.

Teres, Harvey. *Renewing the Left: Politics, Imagination and the New York Intellectuals*. New York and Oxford: Oxford University Press, 1996.

Thelwell, Mike. "*Another Country*: Baldwin's New York Novel." In *The Black American Writer*. Vol. 1: *Fiction*, edited by C. W. E. Bigsby, 181–98. Baltimore, MD: Penguin Books, 1969.

Tuhkanen, Miko. "James Baldwin on the American Express and the Queer Underground." *English Language Notes* 45, no. 2 (Fall/Winter 2007): 123–31.

Tinney, James S. "The Blackness of Pentecostalism." *Spirit* 3, no. 2 (1979): 27–36.

Tóibín, Colm. "James Baldwin and Barack Obama." *New York Review of Books* (October 23, 2008). http://www.nybooks.com/articles/21930.

———. "The Last Witness." *London Review of Books* 23, no. 18 (September 20, 2001): 15–20.

Traylor, Eleanor. "James Baldwin and Chinua Achebe: Transgressing Official Vocabularies." In *James Baldwin: American and Beyond*, edited by Cora Kaplan and Bill Schwarz, 229–40. Ann Arbor: University of Michigan Press, 2011.

Trotsky, Leon. *Literature and Revolution*, edited by William Keach. Trans. Rose Strunksy. Chicago: Haymarket Books, 2005.

Troupe, Quincy, ed. *James Baldwin: The Legacy*. New York: Simon & Schuster, 1989.

Tucker, Stephen R. "Pentecostalism and Popular Culture in the South: A Study of Four Musicians." *Journal of Popular Culture* 16 (Winter 1982): 68–80.

Üsekes, Çiğdem. "In Another Country: James Baldwin and the Turkish Theatre Scene." *New England Theatre Journal* 21 (2010): 99–116.

Vidal, Gore. *The City and the Pillar*. 1949. Reprint, with a new preface by Gore Vidal. London: Abacus, 1994.

Von Eschen, Penny M. *Race against Empire: Black Americans and Anticolonialism, 1937–1957*. Ithaca: Cornell University Press, 1997.

Wald, Alan M. *The New York Intellectuals: The Rise and Decline of the Anti-Stalinist Left from the 1930s to the 1980s*. Chapel Hill: University of North Carolina Press, 1987.

Wall, Cheryl A. "Stranger at Home: James Baldwin on What It Means to Be an American." In *James Baldwin: America and Beyond*, edited by Cora Kaplan and Bill Schwarz, 35–52. Ann Arbor: University of Michigan Press, 2011.

Wallace, Maurice. "'I'm Not Entirely What I Look Like': Richard Wright, James Baldwin, and the Hegemony of Vision; or, Jimmy's FBEye Blues." In *James Baldwin Now*, edited by Dwight A. McBride, 289–306. New York: New York University Press, 1999.

Wallace, Michele. *Black Macho and the Myth of the Superwoman*. 1978. Reprint, with introd. Michele Wallace. New York: Dial Press, 1990.

Walters, Wendy, ed. *At Home in Diaspora: Black International Writing*. Minneapolis: University of Minnesota Press, 2005.

Warren, Nagueyalti. "The Substance of Things Hoped For: Faith in *Go Tell It on the Mountain* and *Just Above My Head*." *Obsidian* 2, no. 1-2 (Spring-Summer 1992): 19–31.

Washington, Bryan R. "Wrestling with 'The Love That Dare Not Speak Its Name': John, Elisha, and the 'Master.'" In *New Essays on* Go Tell It on the Mountain, edited by Trudier Harris, 77–96. Cambridge and New York: Cambridge University Press, 1996.

Washington, Joseph R. *Black Religion: The Negro and Christianity in the United States*. Boston: Beacon Press, 1964.

———. *Black Sects and Cults*. New York: Doubleday, 1972.

Wasserstrom, William. "James Baldwin: Stepping Out of the Promise." In *Black Fiction: New Studies in the Afro-American Novel since 1945*, edited by A. Robert Lee, 74–96. New York: Barnes and Noble Books, 1980.

Weatherby, W. J. *James Baldwin: Artist on Fire*. London: Penguin, 1990.

Weir, Stan. "Meetings with James Baldwin." *Against the Current* 18 (January-February 1989): 35–41.

Werner, Craig. "The Economic Evolution of James Baldwin." In *Critical Essays on James Baldwin*, edited by Fred L. Standley and Nancy V. Burt, 78–93. Boston: G. K. Hall, 1988.

West, Cornel. *Prophesy Deliverance! An Afro-American Revolutionary Christianity*. Philadelphia: Westminster Press, 1982.

————. *Race Matters*. Boston: Beacon Press, 1993.

"What Do Negroes Expect of Jews?" *Amsterdam News* (February 27, 1960): 4.

White, Edmund. *Genet: A Biography*. New York: Alfred A. Knopf, 1993.

Whitfield, Stephen J. *The Culture of the Cold War*. 2nd ed. Baltimore, MD: Johns Hopkins University Press, 1996.

Wiegman, Robyn. "Fiedler and Sons." In *Race and the Subject of Masculinities*, edited by Harry Stecopoulos and Michael Uebel, 45–68. Durham: Duke University Press, 1997.

Williams, Kemp. "The Metaphorical Construction of Sexuality in *Giovanni's Room*." In *Literature and Homosexuality*, edited by Michael Meyer, 23–33. Amsterdam: Rodopi, 2000.

Wills, D. W. "Exodus Piety: African American Religion in an Age of Immigration." In *Minority Faiths and the Protestant Mainstream*, edited by Jonathan Sarna, 116–88. Urbana: University of Illinois Press, 1998.

Wisse, Ruth R. "The New York (Jewish) Intellectuals." *Commentary* 84, no. 5 (1987): 28–38.

Wright, Derek. "African American Tensions in Black Writing of the 1960s." *Journal of Black Studies* 19, no. 4 (June 1989): 442–58.

Wright, Richard. *White Man, Listen!* Westport, CT: Greenwood Press, 1957.

Zaborowska, Magdalena. *James Baldwin's Turkish Decade: Erotics of Exile*. Durham: Duke University Press, 2009.

{ INDEX }

Note: Locators followed by the letter 'n' refer to notes.

WITHDRAWN